After All

After All

MARY TYLER MOORE

G.P. PUTNAM'S SONS
NEW YORK

G. P. PUTNAM'S SONS
Publishers Since 1838
200 Madison Avenue
New York, NY 10016

ISBN 0-399-14091-3

Printed in the United States of America

This book is printed on acid-free paper. ∞

Book design by Julie Duquet

For Robert,
who turned on the light

My thanks to Laura Yorke, whose editorial
guidance gave shape to my words, and to
David Outerbridge for organizing the process.

And Terry Sims, that most noble keeper of
the tools.

Many writers added color to Mary Richards,
but the following people guarded her form:

Jim Brooks, Allan Burns, Treva Silverman,
Lorenzo Music, David Davis, Ed. Weinberger,
Stan Daniels, David Lloyd, and Bob Ellison.

Thanks for your memories:

Richard Blair, Larry Bloustein, Norton
Brown, Karen Brownlee, Allan Burns, Bill
Persky, and Beverly Sanders.

A final thanks to Amanda Urban for seeing the
possibilities, to begin with.

Prologue

❧

(INTERIOR ABSTRACT LIVING ROOM,
WITH BAR KITCHEN STAGE RIGHT)

(TWO WOMEN, STRIKINGLY SIMILAR, SIT COMFORTABLY
TOGETHER ON THE DOWNSTAGE CENTER COUCH.)

MTM

*Is it possible to separate us? I don't mean <u>separate</u> us, because you
know I'm very fond of you. You know that, don't you?*

MARY

(HESITANT—EXPECTING MORE) *Yeah. Well, sure.*

MTM

*I mean, I'm writing this autobiography in which I have to be
truthful about the way I look at things, where I've been, how I
feel—all the stuff that will finally show how unlike you I really
am.*

ix

❧

MARY

(TRYING TO UNDERSTAND) *So?* (SHE CROSSES TO THE
KITCHEN, PUTTING ON THE KETTLE AS MTM CONTINUES.)

MTM

*Look, they love you. People identify with your persona. You've
been their best friend, their best hope for something better . . .* (SHE
PAUSES NERVOUSLY) *. . . and now they're going to find out that
I'm not you, that all the time they were watching the show and
wishing they were you—so was I!* (SHE EXTENDS HER ARM FOR
EMPHASIS, LETTING IT SLAP AGAINST HER THIGH.)

MTM

(CONTINUES AS SHE PACES) *You've been so forthright, earnest,
always expecting one hundred percent from people and giving it in
return. God, you've even managed to show some character flaws,
nothing really rotten, just enough to make you human.*

MARY

(SETTING CUPS ON TRAY) *So what are you saying—you <u>are</u> rotten?*

MTM

(CROSSES TO MIRROR, PEERS INTO IT) *No! I don't know.
Sometimes I think I have been.* (SHE SHAKES HER HEAD IN
DISMAY AT WHAT SHE SEES.) (TURNS TO HER) *You just don't
change at all, do you? Depending on the rerun, thirty—thirty-
seven tops!* (THEN) *All right, here's the deal: I've loved working,
especially with you, but I put so much of myself into it, there
wasn't much left over for anyone else, including me! You know?*

*I don't remember the details of my marriages, for example. Of
course I remember this one to Robert. I mean, I'm in it now, so
there's not all that much to dig up. But Dick Meeker and Grant
Tinker, especially Grant—shouldn't I have a clear channel to all the
hours that went into those eighteen years? I'm not sure if I simply*

don't remember, or have blocked it from memory, or worse—was I so wrapped up in my chosen "salvation" that there was no room for a permanent imprint of anything else?

And as for Richie's childhood, I was so busy being Larry Mathews's mother on The Dick Van Dyke Show *that my own son might just as well have been Larry's stand-in for all the attention he got. Yes, I feel rotten about that—for him, and for me, too.* (MARY CROSSES TO HER WITH TEA, A LOOK OF CONCERN ON HER FACE.)

MTM

(LOOKS AT PLATE . . . THEN INCREDULOUSLY) *Oh my God, are these crumpets? Where did you ever find crumpets?*

MARY

I made them. (WITH EMBARRASSMENT) *It really wasn't that hard.*

MTM

There, you see! I'd never do that kind of thing for a guest. I'd probably never have a guest . . . for tea anyway. Drinks, oh yes, there was never a lack of drinks.

Wait 'til they find out I wasn't even remotely involved in the running of MTM! Why am I suddenly thinking of a cigarette?

MARY

You're being much too hard on yourself. Remember what Mom said about regrets?

MTM

Nanette Fabray—wasn't she just great as the mother?

MARY

No. Your mother, Marjorie.

MTM

(A SMILE PLAYING ACROSS HER LIPS) *Oh, yeah! "A shadow crosses the duck but once!" Is that the one?*

MARY

(LAUGHING AT HER) *No. "We all did the best we could at the time."*

So just write what comes to you, and be candid while you tell them who you are. If they don't like it—the hell with 'em!

MTM

You know what? You've got spunk! (AFTER A PAUSE) *All right, old friend, I'll do it.*

After All

1

With my first Emmy and first cultured pearls.

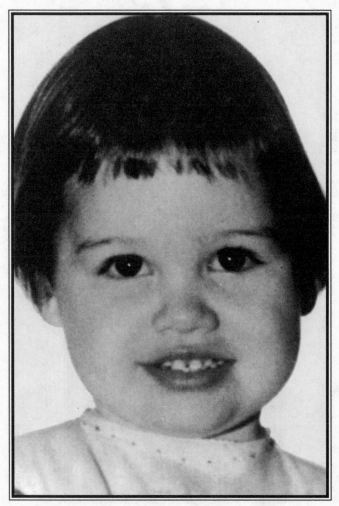

At age one. This photo won first prize in a
Kodak contest in the New York Times.

Myself, Then and Still Sometimes

ᔆ

$\mathcal{A}$ND THE EMMY GOES
to . . . Mary Tyler Moore!"

It is, if you can imagine, a pleasant punch in the stomach, a nice jolt that catapults you out of your seat, soaring above even the balcony. Then, in slow motion, the descent while you watch the audience become a court: queens and kings all applauding, welcoming you back to your rightful place among them. That's what I experienced in 1993, at the forty-fifth annual coronation celebration of its best by the Academy of Television Arts and Sciences. I turned to kiss my husband and reached for my father, who sat on the other side of him. Dad took my hand in both of his and kissed it.

I saw the moment as a happy-ending snapshot for the story of a child who failed as a youngster to win her father's approval and affection. Here I was urging him to get up off his knee and sit down. I felt that was a personal triumph. For Mary *the actress* it was a special Emmy, an award without the protective canopy of genius that surrounded me on the *Dick Van Dyke* and *Mary Tyler Moore* shows.

I'd won six of the statuettes for lead actress in those years. I couldn't help but look good standing in the midst of that talent. But

3

ᔆ

this Emmy for Outstanding Supporting Actress in a Miniseries was the first in fourteen years.

It was for *Stolen Babies,* a true story about the selling of children into adoption during the years 1936 through 1944. The character was Georgia Tann, director of the Tennessee Children's Home Society. I wanted to play her because she wasn't easily pigeonholed. She had started out a dedicated social worker struggling within the imperfections of the child-welfare system. Eventually she became a self-serving manipulator of young lives and of the parents who were forced to give up their children. Too often on television the good are good and the bad say things like, "I'll destroy you." I enjoyed bringing some humanity to her pinched face and wizened spirit. And I loved the improbable casting.

The Mary Tyler Moore Show went off the air in 1977, a decision that was made by the producers and writers, who felt that they had taken their characters down all the roads that held promise during the show's seven-year run.

It had been for us all personally enriching as well as satisfying professionally, and it had been a commercial hit. The show also garnered a total of twenty-nine Emmys, a record that stands to this day.

I didn't understand why "the guys" felt that we had exhausted the show's possibilities. The truth lay in the lure of fresh fields to plow, new series such as *Lou Grant, The Betty White Show, Taxi, Cosby.*

Was I fearful? Nah, nothing more than the terror a child feels being lost from her parents in a shopping mall. However, I marched out with that famous smile, looked the press straight in the face, and said, "Yes, this is a creatively healthy move we're making. Quit while you're still on top!"

After the announcement, as the countdown to the last episode moved on, I could feel the separation anxiety welling up daily. I had spent more of my waking hours with the people on this show than I did with my real family, including my then husband, Grant Tinker. The years that loomed ahead in my vision without the show seemed cold and gray and threatening. I would have to come to terms with what my abilities were. Did I have any talent? Or was I mostly a very determined kid who was also very lucky?

One might think that after so many years of success at least some of these questions would have been answered for me.

But if you look carefully while walking through the park, you will see that there are snakes in the trees. And those snakes are all-knowing—they see your core. As I write it, I don't know where this dark metaphor came from. Nor do I understand the insecurities and self-doubts that created it. Perhaps as I write down my story, I'll become enlightened.

I've two very distinct inner spirits who live my life for me, playing hide-and-seek at times. I don't mean this to sound like *The Three Faces of Eve* or a split personality. But there does seem to be one brooding, paranoid, and pessimistic Mary Tyler Moore. I think she's the one who supplies the comedy. The other Mary is a supremely confident champion. They do battle with each other, one emerging the ruler for a time depending on outside circumstance: Am I working? Has someone been unkind? Is someone angry—because of something I did (or *think* I did)? The possibility of the latter is the main reason I don't drive in New York City. How is it that as a successful woman I am intimidated by angry horns and yelling if I drive too slowly or make a mistake of some type?

I'm like a chameleon in that I take on the colors of success or failure, happy or sad, depending on what's going on, or how it *seems* to be going. They just gave me an Emmy so I must deserve it—for five minutes. If Sissy Spacek wins the Academy Award, as she did the year in which I was also nominated, it is because I am not good enough and never was. I can see with my intellect the ridiculous logic of this, but emotionally, I am, after all, the chameleon waiting to see what color I am meant to be.

My Father

❧

I WAS BORN DECEMBER 29, 1936, in Brooklyn Heights, New York, an area of Brooklyn that was distinctly superior to and separate from Flatbush (as I was to be reminded by my mother and her family). My birth occurred ten months after my parents married.

I was a demanding presence that neither of them was prepared for, financially or emotionally. My father, a cum laude graduate of Georgetown, cloaked his education and knowledge, cupping his arm around it and lowering his head, lest someone steal it from him. He chose to work as a clerk, first for Con Edison in New York, and then until his retirement in 1979, at the Southern California Gas Company. It was misuse of a superb intellect and social conscience.

In my earliest memories of him he's a grim-faced, handsome man who spent his time in the evenings and on weekends with books—Greek and Roman history—and listening to classical music. He was surrounded by what appeared to me to be a wall of newspapers and record albums.

My maternal grandmother lived in a house in Flushing, Long Island, with my mother's sister, Aunt Bertie. As it had an extra bed-

❧

room, shortly after I was born it was decided that the three of us would move in with them. Not only did this save rent for my parents, but it also allowed them freedom to go out with their friends and have some fun.

And so we became an extended family. Aunt Bertie, who worked at NBC Radio in New York City, fell naturally and happily into the mother role, giving me my morning and late-night bottles, bathing and dressing me before she took the subway to work. Grandma served as general homemaker for us all: cooking, mending, cleaning, shopping, and being my main bedtime storyteller. And thus it was that small cracks developed in the foundation of my relationships with my parents.

In our home, talking about other people, dissecting their behavior—especially other family members—was virtually a duty for the women who were raising me. It was, I am sure, an extension of their childhood competitiveness. As the lone male, my father became the recipient of their scalpel. He didn't stand a prayer of survival in that setup. It was twenty-four-hour surveillance.

Here was a Jesuit-educated Catholic who thought children should be born already eighteen, married, and living in a neighboring town; that they should be seen and not heard, be obedient, and spanked when not. Bertie and Grandma viewed him as Ivan the Terrible. And small ears hear well.

According to my father, I was "a rather uppity child." I'm sure he was right. I do remember feeling hostile sometimes. But which came first? An off-putting, sullen kid or a kid who was responding to a sullen, off-putting father—reaction being a facility for which I was to win awards in later life.

My father was, and is, an undemonstrative man. He could be expansive and witty when he chose, but normally was silent and contemplative. For as long as I can remember, Dad's dark side was singled out by the family as the probable cause of my mother's alcoholism. My mother, on the other hand, was thought of as an unfortunately weak-willed, yet adorable child—a woman who would someday see the error of her ways and become a responsible adult. How much sooner, the family thought, that would happen if she had married a Republican! A cordial, wealthy, Protestant one.

Looking back, I am sure that my mother, a good-hearted madcap who loved to laugh and be with friends, used my father's moods as a reason to make the good times seem longer and better by drinking even more, and more often. This, of course, only exacerbated my father's coldness.

$\mathcal{T}$he most consistent attention I received from my father were his reviews, as we walked home from church, of my behavior during Mass on Sundays. I was a "good girl" if my attention hadn't wandered, I had knelt when I should have, had stood when it was appropriate, and didn't slam my behind onto the bench when the longed-for sitting time came. So absorbed in this demeanor of good-girlness was I, that self-judgment consumed me.

Should I press the thumbs of my praying hands to my mouth for a truly fervent look, or would a rounded clasped pair of hands be right? Eyes closed, or open and looking heavenward? And not one thought of God.

As we walked together, sometimes, without saying a word my father would break into a Groucho Marx crouching walk that reduced me to stuttering shrieks of horror at how we must look to other people! He always had a good chuckle over this. Then he would resume the Olympian stride he had established.

So deftly tuned was his mercurial self-mastery that I never knew what to expect from him: the dark Gothic Catholicism and its dictates, or a devilish wit. He could tell a story or reprimand with the control and flourish of a Shakespearean actor, using his vocal range and strength to transfix his audience. Other people's children loved this about him and, because he couldn't care less for their affection, they seemed to be drawn to him. The difference being that they had fathers who held and kissed them and told them they were pretty. Mine never did, so I saw him a little differently.

Whenever we visited his parents, who lived in what could have been Tara, a Georgian mansion on one hundred and fifty acres in Winchester, Virginia, he often read to me from one of the Oz books by L. Frank Baum, a collection that rested on the shelves of the billiard room. I was transported by the adventures of Dorothy and her companions, the Tin Man, the Lion, the Scarecrow, and Toto, to that splendid state of mind—the Emerald City. I may not have had the affection I wanted from my father, but I had a most gifted actor to bring life to the characters who touched my heart and stirred my imagination. And as he read, I was the only audience he seemed to need. So that made me important.

Once, while climbing a tree at age seven, I heard him caution me with definite concern in his voice not to "fall and break your leg." He cares about me! "Because I can't afford the medical bills," he finished.

My Mother

❧

DURING THE YEARS
we all lived together in Flushing, the imprint being made on baby
Mary as she reached the age of two was that Aunt Bertie was
mother. She was the one most often there, even though she worked.
It was also a matter of sensing who took joy from my presence. I'm
sure that even then there was the feeling that my mother wanted
to be somewhere else.

I'm told that at the time my mother developed a fondness for
the pinball machines in the store around the corner. This growing addiction was kept hidden from my father. She spent so much
money on them that occasionally she had to borrow, in secret,
money from her mother to cover our share of the grocery and
household bills that my father assumed she was taking care of. He
never knew.

Recently, reminiscing about those days, my father said, "Did I
ever tell you about the six dollars you lost? Well, those were hard
times. One night when I came home from work your mother told

me that she had put her purse in the stroller with you. You must have opened it and thrown the money away when she wasn't looking. That was a lot of money to lose."

People used to tell me, "Your mother is the most caring and constant friend I have ever had." I have never seen elsewhere the depth of commitment my mother had for the friends she made. She would go the distance for them. I never felt that. I still remember her response to a friend of hers who said I was a pretty child: "Oh yes, but not nearly as pretty as yours." She didn't mean to hurt me, but her almost obsessive graciousness demanded that she give her friend the small triumph. Throughout my life she was always that way. She was devoted to strays, always inviting new people to dinner and even entire families when my father would permit it. (We didn't have a lot of money. In fact, were it not for the occasional gifts of cash from the rest of the family, we would've had to scrounge a bit.)

My mother came alive with friends in a way I never saw when she was with me. She loved to dance (it struck me as "show off") while singing songs like "Minnie the Moocher" at gatherings. I've never known anyone who had a better sense of humor than she did. And she always knocked 'em dead, especially the men. Everyone loved Marge and thought her very game to put up with my father, who would often announce shortly after dinner that he was going to bed and hoped that they'd have the decency to leave soon.

My mother was the youngest of six children and for most of their adult years was the only one to whom each of her brothers and sisters would speak. Bertie talked to Harold and Winnie, but not Cecil or Monty. Winnie tolerated Harold and loved Bertie. Cecil thought Bertie cheated him at backgammon once, thereby revealing her true character. Harold never forgave Monty for disapproving of his second marriage, which lasted for some thirty years. And Monty began the trip to paranoia after Harold was born, displacing him as number one in the family hierarchy.

In spite of my parents' differences in personality and temperament they did have common expectations of me, which among other things produced a child who was toilet trained at twelve months. I don't think psychologists had considered yet the impact of such control on a child's psyche, but everyone was mightily impressed with their parenting skills.

As remote as my mother and father seemed, Grandma and Aunt Bertie were warm and accessible. So it was a painful uprooting when my mother and father came to the inevitable conclusion that they needed their own apartment. By way of easing the pain of the move for me, my mother promoted our new dwelling, an apartment also in Flushing, as being "shiny and new, not like this dirty old house we live in now." From that time on it was referred to by all of us as "the dirty house." "Do you remember after we left the dirty house . . ." "How much rent did we pay for the dirty house? . . ." Poor old house.

After we moved, though, Bertie would take me every weekend to be with her and Grandma. A few years later, Bertie bought a log cabin in Northport, Long Island. She began a garden and she included me. She taught me to recognize weeds, and paid me a penny for every hundred I pulled. Even at that age I could tell I was being underpaid. So as I would remove a weed, I would turn away from her, split it in two, and place the evidence in the paper bag for counting at the end of the day. I made a nickel most days.

In our shiny new apartment I slept on a daybed just off the living room, unless my parents were having a party. Then I was sent to sleep in the apartment of their best friends, Lilly and Gordon Archer, who lived down the hall. They retrieved me and put me in my own bed when the party was over.

One night, Mr. Archer, apparently having downed a few too

many, left the party early and came home to go to bed. Which he did with me sleeping soundly beside him. I was awakened by his fingers between my legs, from behind me. They were inside my panties, touching and probing. I was paralyzed as I remembered where I was and who was making me feel this way. It had to be bad what he was doing, really bad. But it was Gordon Archer, my parents' good friend whom I'd been taught to respectfully call Mr. Archer. But he was now not only violating everything a six-year-old knows about trust, he was also tormenting me with confusion about the flickering of sexual arousal I also felt at his hand. I was ashamed and scared because I couldn't stop him. I don't think it was more than thirty seconds before his sour breath slowed and his hand went all limp, and I could slide away.

I told my mother, groping for words to describe what had happened. (The only word I knew for the entire genital area was "wee-wee," for God's sake.) My mother said, "No! That's not true." My mother said, "IT DIDN'T HAPPEN."

Strange it is how events that change a life inside and out take no more than a moment—"You got the *Van Dyke Show*." "Let's get married." "It didn't happen."

I never felt the same about her after that. My mother, by her denial, had abused me far more than her friend.

The next day, I marched down the hall to six-year-old David Archer's apartment, feeling a wild unvented anger, and told him exactly what his father had done to me. On his pale small face I saw the impact I'd hoped for from my mother, felt vindicated, and a little sick at what I had done to him, too.

2

The Moore family: Dad, Mom,
John, and me.

An early publicity "showgirl/gypsy" photo.

Legacies

❧

I'M A LITTLE TOO
retiring to do parades, but a few years ago when I was asked to be
Grand Marshall of the Winchester, Virginia, Apple Blossom Festi-
val and ride in an open car along a route lined with a quarter of a
million cheering onlookers, I said yes—provided my eighty-year-
old father, who had spent a good portion of his youth in and around
the Shenandoah Valley, be invited to join us. They were delighted
with the generational aspect his presence would lend, and arranged
for him to ride in the car with me. My father may not admit he car-
ries the detectable acting gene, but something in our lineage contributed to his comfort at being the object of the public's affection.
We were a big hit—my dad waving and smiling as though Mary
Tyler Moore may have been the Grand Marshall, but George Tyler
Moore was King. I took it to be further evidence of having been
accepted in the eyes of the man who had dismissed me early on.

Some of my happiest recollections come from the montage of
scenery and quiet events that once wove around my little girl's imagination—playing "catch me if you can"—at my grandparents' home

❧

in nearby Berryville, Virginia. The visits we made to my father's parents in the summertime always lifted his mood. And even though my mother (a non-Catholic) was as unacceptable to the Moores as my father was to the Hacketts, there seemed to be harmony between the two of them on these visits.

My grandfather Moore used to watch me prance about the porch of the great white fairy-tale house and shake his head in amazement at the time I could devote to dancing and singing. It is said that he remarked about me once, "This child will either grow up to be on the stage or in jail."

The family who now owns the house has done little to change it—my grandmother sold it with all its contents upon the death of Grandpa Moore. Still among the volumes on the billiard room bookshelves sits the collection of Oz books. The four-poster bed, my bed, with its familiar carvings that small fingers had traced before finally giving in to sleep, is there. The MARY that my grandfather carved into the concrete patch in the base of the old maple tree out front is there. Eerily, this house is still mine.

On one visit, my father was able to recover his grandfather's Civil War sword. Louis Tilghman Moore had been a lieutenant colonel in the Confederacy, a member of the search party that ultimately captured John Brown, the abolitionist, at Harper's Ferry. He was a friend of Thomas J. (Stonewall) Jackson. When Colonel Moore was wounded in the knee by a cannon-propelled minié ball, in the first Battle of Manassas (Bull Run), and had to be hospitalized for some time, he gave over his home to General Jackson to use as his headquarters. The house is now a museum—which for me is the next best thing to being a royal. A chilling portent of a father-son relationship to come (meaning my father and my brother John's) is the response of Colonel Moore's father (a Union man), who, upon learning his son's choice to fight for the South said, "May the first shot fired pierce your heart." They never spoke again.

The colonel's wife was a Shindler. Conrad Shindler was a German immigrant who settled in Pennsylvania and brought with him his craft, the making of copper kettles. I recently located one of Conrad Shindler, Jr.'s copper tea kettles, and brought it "home." To have created something, with such obvious care, that his great-great-great granddaughter could hold in her hands more than one hundred years later—this, for me, is the essence of "art." Art is for our children and our children's children to see and hear and touch and feel. It's our legacy, a reflection of our talent, patience, and values. I often lament that I am the last of the Moores, with no one after my brother John's daughter, Carole, to pass on my work. But then I remember the image of the giddy pre-teenage girl, waiting out in front of a theater to ask for my autograph, and the page from her scrapbook that featured a tattered picture of Laura Petrie alongside an homage to the then just departed grunge-rocker Kurt Cobain. I guess that's legacy enough for anyone.

Brooklyn—A Tree Grows

❧

𝕄 Y MOTHER'S OLDER
brother, Harold Hackett, tall, thin, and just as handsome as Ronald
Colman, was a dynamic influence on our lives. He was one of the
original team of agents at Music Corporation of America, representing such stars as Bob Hope, Abbott and Costello, Ronald
Reagan, and Jane Wyman. He was a great raconteur who loved
his work and the socializing that went with it. He would regale
us with stories about Hollywood deals, openings, infidelities (both
business and romantic), all the while singing the praises of that
town.

Growing up, Uncle Harold's daughter, Gail, and I were very
close. We were about the same age and both very happy to be "the
entertainment" for those occasions when the families celebrated a
birthday (which was as often as the calendar would allow if Mom
had her way). By the age of six or seven, Gail and I would sing and
dance, solo or as a pair, depending on how much rehearsal time we
had. She preferred the role of "pronouncer," as we called it, to that
of spellbinder. So most of the time it fell to me to wear the costumes she'd put together from our mothers' closets; and stepping
into the spotlight fashioned from a lamp with an acutely tilted shade,

❧

bring them to their knees—a reception they obligingly gave me to please Grandma, my biggest fan.

Judy Garland, Fred and Ginger, and Gene Kelly were my beckoning film idols. I watched them, not only for the escape they provided, but for anything I could use in my living-room act. Whatever song Betty Grable had sung in her latest movie was not soon to be forgotten by my family, because I relentlessly revived it at each show. Gail and I were especially fond of "On the Boardwalk in Atlantic City" sung with two black umbrellas a-twirl, just as Miss Grable and her sidekick did with pink parasols in *Mother Wore Tights*. I taught myself to tap-dance and did pretty well at it, too. (Of course, you had to imagine the rocket-fast footwork because I was doing it on carpet.)

I don't know what it's like to have one's parents' attention to the degree it is needed and craved, but the resultant feeling that came from those moments of living-room stardom were like finding the light switch in a dark room.

Nevertheless, even at the age of four or five I was aware that the affection given me by Bertie and Grandma was no substitute. I felt there was something wrong with me that caused this inability on my parents' part to show me love. But when I generated applause from my parents I could feel normal. And I made it happen! Never mind that I probably evidenced no talent at that point—I bought the lie and ran with the booty.

Whatever the flaws in my parents' nurturing, I didn't lack a sense of right and wrong. One incident I remember well. When I was four I palmed a Tootsie Roll in a candy store from one of those shelves that's just the right height for a child to attempt such pre-felon practice. It went off without a hitch, too, until we were almost home and my mother, noticing that her daughter's marsupial cheeks were fully engorged, asked me what I was eating and where it had come from. "Phuh ghengend doah," I replied, whereupon she took me by the hand and marched me, small feet only occasionally touching the sidewalk, right back to the store to return the un- as well as partially used portion to the lady at the counter and to confess my crime. The grotesque expression on the shopkeeper's face was, I'm sure, more a reaction to the formless, glistening brown spoils I spat out for her, than to the crime itself. But she was impressive, and I'll always remember the shame I felt.

*W*hen I was "too old not to have learned it by now!", my father, on discovery that I couldn't recite the Lord's Prayer, took on the task of teaching me to memorize it.

This shocking state was discovered at the end of dinner, one night. My father told me to get ready for bed, that he'd be right in. My mother usually "tucked me in" and said my prayers with me, settling for the non-denominational and brief "Now I lay me down to sleep. . . ." Tonight, it would be the prayer that is the foundation of all Christian communication with God.

My father knelt beside me, our elbows resting on the bed, both of us with hands pressed together, and began. He said, "Repeat after me. 'Our Father who art in Heaven,'" and I did, then he added, "Hallowed be thy name," so far, fine. Next came, "Thy kingdom come, thy will be done," which had to follow the first part without a slipup. As I remember it, I made several tries at just that much without success, and we were still at the beginning.

I don't remember how long it took me to say it all the way through without faltering, but it must have been some time because, not only was I unable to concentrate toward the end of this session, but I was getting increasingly drowsy, too. I pleaded with him to let me go to sleep, but he was determined that I come to know the joy of this prayer and reap its rewards that very night.

I bear a few psychic scars from the episode—in particular the sense of God as dictator (when I think of God at all). But I can memorize lines faster (and with longer retention) than most of my fellow actors.

My brother, John, was born seven years after I was, on June 13, 1943. His conception was planned less from the desire to have another child than as a hedge against the draft of World War II. One child could postpone a father being called up, but two made military service even less likely.

I don't remember ever being jealous of my baby brother, although at about the time of his arrival, I developed an urge to pinch or in some way make the occasional baby cry when I'd see one on the street.

My father seemed fond of John when he was a tot. Combing his very blond hair and putting a part in it, he'd take him for walks in the stroller crooning the *Ave Maria* or an aria from *The Barber of Seville*. Dad's affection was to wane as John grew older and began to present more problems than my father was prepared to deal with.

Living in Brooklyn, hardly a week went by that a squabble didn't become a punching and kicking fest, rolling on the sidewalk with one or more of my sworn tormentors. For the last two of my then eight years I was never without several cuts and bruises in various stages of healing. Sad to say, but prejudice on both sides lay at the core of these fights. We were the Catholic Moores living in what had become a devoutly orthodox Jewish neighborhood. It's hard enough for children to sort out fairness issues as they push the boundaries of friendship while defining themselves. Here it was complicated by a basic distrust of each other born of adult whisperings about differences in behavior on Friday nights and Sunday mornings. Underlying it all, was the inevitable Jesus problem, which was even more significant than Santa Claus. We were not a happy bunch.

But when the war ended, so did mine. The wagons were in line. We were moving west. Uncle Harold preceded us, settling in the Emerald City, Los Angeles. He encouraged us all to follow him. "There'll be jobs for everyone!" he promised. "Come to this grand place where you can live in sunshine all year long!"

While I was deciding which dolls to bring with us, I was also imagining the various ways in which I would be discovered in Hollywood. In the movie version of becoming a film star you didn't work toward a goal by studying, auditioning, and looking for an agent. You were found on the street, or sitting at a soda fountain. To this day, there is a part of me that pulls in my stomach and seeks a bit of backlight whenever possible. (You just never know when you're finally going to be found for the "big" role. It's a Pavlovian response, with a life of its own, I guess.)

Whenever I come across a scene in which a little girl (Margaret O'Brien, say) has to face the fear of moving to a new place and the sadness of leaving her playmates behind, I remember the relief I felt at realizing I'd never have to see any of those little shits again. Whether I'd earned it or not, I was the least popular kid on the block and I was mad. Since self-analysis was not yet within grasp, I naturally put myself in the role of martyr. I was a young Joan of Arc who did battle with the enemy.

The Trip
West

❧

HE ENTIRE FAMILY
was moving west in two cars. Not surprisingly, I went with Aunt
Bertie and Grandma. The used car that Bertie had purchased for our
trip seemed a good choice—a 1941 Chevrolet coupe previously
owned by the New York City Police Department. She would later
discover that it had been used in a few real-life car chases. That's
why whenever we stopped for gas, the oil had to be replenished at
the same rate. It was not a wonderful trip.

No matter the speed, Grandma was always clutching something
fiercely: the armrest, the dashboard, the window frame, or Bertie's
arm, causing her hands to turn purple and white. It was scary and
quite visible to me from my position on the seat back, elbows wide,
chin resting on my hands, which had turned into fists of terror, too.
She'd suck in her breath at the sight of an intersection with a car
anywhere in it, slam her foot on an imaginary brake pedal, and exclaim in a rapid-fire whisper, "Bertie, Bertie, Bertie, Bertie, Bertie,"
until the expected disaster had ceased to threaten us. Bertie was a
cautious driver and saintlike in her patience, but I began to think
of her as a lunatic behind the wheel as Grandma's contagious terror spread to the backseat. I was so fearful that when Bertie pointed

out a bridge in the distance once and announced that we'd soon be going over it, I was sure that she meant we'd be driving on the top of the arched frame that held the suspension cables. I sat, heart thwonking and stomach feeling like it contained live fish. I'd shut my eyes and curl up on the floor, the panic silently growing until we'd made it to safety on the other side. That's the way I crossed every bridge on the trip west.

We made our way shrieking and wincing through Pennsylvania, Ohio, and Indiana. Somewhere in Michigan or Wisconsin I began to scratch my head with a little more dedication than an average cooped-up kid would. So, Grandma had a look. COOTIES! I had lice in my hair! My God!

An agonizing half hour later, the car came to a rubber-burning stop in front of the next town's drugstore. As we entered, Bertie gave us the scenario for our little deception. We were there on behalf of someone else who lived far away from us. I gave an outstanding performance of innocence for the pharmacist as he described the steps to be taken by this other child who was not with us.

We called it a day immediately, checked in to the local motel at noon, and began the process of my redemption. I shampooed with a bar of green soap. Then while I knelt over the toilet bowl, Grandma removed the dead bodies with a fine-toothed comb. As I watched the rain of little black dots against the white porcelain, I experienced a phenomenon that I've not had since. When you cry upside down, your nose doesn't run.

We headed south through the Rocky Mountains, which brought Grandma's shrieks, intakes of breath, and "Bertie, Bertie, Berties" to a soaring level that matched the altitude. I was pretty scared myself, looking out the window at the impossibility of those roads and their alternative—certain death. And then we came to the Donner Pass.

The Donner
Pass

❧

*T*HE DONNER PASS WAS
the highlight of the trip for me. I remember the shock I felt at learning that in order to survive, some of those starving wretched souls
ate the flesh of their dead companions.

*A*lthough in my lifetime I've eaten my share of cheeseburgers,
veal, and lamb, I have come to feel that same revulsion I experienced at the Donner Pass at the thought of eating animals. My
proximity to the sheep, cattle, and geese who are now my neighbors in the country is what has finally turned me into a vegetarian. I talk to these animals when I walk. Sometimes I am lucky
enough to make physical contact with them, and as I look into
their eyes I see not only the innocence, but also the clear fact
that those eyes are no less complicated in their structure than my
own.

Don't we now have enough tasty things to eat from the garden
and all the delicious ways to prepare them?

❧

Whether it is a wild animal, or one bred to be eaten, death is never painless. I know there are many people who earn their livings hunting, ranching, raising, and slaughtering animals. I would say to them: "Find other work."

I also know how easy it is to assume something is right simply because that is the way it is and has always been. Most parents raise their children on a diet that includes meat. I grew up on that diet. To this day, when I smell roast beef or a hot dog, my mouth waters. I long for the taste and textures that were the source of such pleasure. But the scenes of what that satisfaction costs and the violence and trauma an animal suffers, snuffs that desire. And even if the desire is still there, it is something I cannot have. It's not that big a deal.

Recently, I attended a dinner party and the subject of the information-gathering abilities of animals came up. The discussion continued while some at that table were cutting into their juicy meat dish. Animals behave strangely before an earthquake. The communication skills of dolphins and whales are extraordinary; birds learn complex territorial rules, and some dogs have an ability to detect in advance the onset of an epileptic seizure by as much as a half hour. Scientists are teaching these dogs to bark so preventative medication can be taken.

About animals Voltaire wrote: "God has provided them with exactly the same organs of feelings as ours. So if they cannot feel, God has done a pointless job. God does nothing in vain."

Since I had become a firm convert to vegetarianism, it follows that I would eventually feel the same about wearing furs; what right do we have to take life painfully from an animal to eat something we don't need, or wear something we can do without? Unfortunately, I came to this enlightened belief just months after I'd bought a Russian sable coat. I'd worn it only a half dozen times when the violence that went into its creation made me ashamed to have it on.

I gave this extremely expensive disgrace to an organization called People for the Ethical Treatment of Animals (PETA), a well-intentioned but sometimes overly aggressive group. The coat now travels around the United States causing some, I am sure, to think I've lost my mind. But I believe it speaks to how deeply I regret what I had participated in, and what I would give to be able to undo it.

The Land of Sunshine

❧

*I*N SEPTEMBER OF 1945
we arrived in Hollywood in search of life's missing background
music. While my parents looked for an affordable house to buy, and
Grandma and Bertie did the same, we all stayed at Uncle Harold's
house. He had an enormous two-story mansion designed by the ar-
chitects Greene and Greene (the pacesetters for the southern
California sprawling clapboard "bungalow"). It nestled behind fif-
teen-foot flowering shrubbery on a couple of acres at the corner of
Fountain Avenue and Camino Palmero. Long since bulldozed, it
was the grandest house I had ever seen. And it was in a peopled setting. There were other large houses in the neighborhood, though
none as beautiful. There were sidewalks and cars on the streets, but
it wasn't a city. Movie stars lived close by, too. I was in heaven.

I shared Gail's bedroom, which was bigger than our own living
room in Brooklyn. There were maids and cooks who washed our
food and cooked our clothes. We didn't even have to make our own
bed. We could get away with things in that house, too. No one
could tell if we were still awake and giggling after bedtime. We
could snack on potato chip and chocolate-sauce sandwiches, because
the grown-ups were hardly ever around, and the maids and cooks

were scared to say "No." I pretended this was my life, not Gail's. In truth, I was an easily forgotten supporting player. I vowed that when I grew up my house would be like this one. It was, and as a grown-up I was hardly ever around, too.

My parents bought a house with help from Grandpa and Grandma Moore. It had two bedrooms, one bath; a postage-stamp version of Gail's. I was very much aware of the differences between us, as I unpacked my possessions in the tiny room I shared with my two-year-old brother.

Things got off to a bad start in that house. Uncle Harold had arranged for my father to be hired as an associate producer on "The Abbott and Costello Radio Show." The salary was $125 a week, a big increase over his New York job with Con-Ed. However, in a fit of self-righteousness after a week of trying to understand show business, he declared that his new position was a sham—a made-up job for a lackey—and that he couldn't live with the fraud. So after resigning from a job, which, like so many in Hollywood, could've been used as a stepping-stone to a dream, he folded whatever goals he'd had at Georgetown, and went to work for the Southern California Gas Company. The problem for him had been the necessary smiling and charm that were expected of him, a personality trait that he had when he wanted, but not on demand. Interestingly, he went to work in the complaint department at the gas company.

I think my father was without a job for maybe a week, and was just about to start work for the gas company when my teacher, Sister Veronica Ann, took me to task for not measuring up to fourth-grade standards. Realizing I had an opportunity to save myself, I begged her not to tell my parents. I claimed that my father was out of work, and we were all very sad at my house, and that this news would damage their precarious grip on sanity. The nun melted, and drew me to her starched white wimple in a neck-crunching embrace of protection and understanding. How brave I must be, she intoned, to have shouldered such insecurity and still manage to do any schoolwork, at all!

As I walked the six blocks home from school that afternoon, I felt proud of myself for having used a semi-true situation to save the day. Recalling the real tears I cried in front of the nuns, I wondered about the ease with which I could feel desolation and control at the same time.

As I walked up the dark green cement stairs leading to the front door, it opened with such speed that I misstepped and fell, banging my knee. Books went flying, some of them landing at the feet of my mother and father, who stood there in a rare moment of unity. My father was glowering. My mother was swaying a bit, and looking more perplexed than anything else—a look that was to become sickeningly familiar to me in time.

"St. Ambrose School called today to say how sorry they were for our troubles," my father said in a measured, flat tone. "They said they had put out the word in the parish that I was looking for work, and in the meantime did we need food?" I knew immediately the indignation he must have felt, perceived by the parish as a man who couldn't support his family, meet his obligations, do what was expected of him.

I confessed my self-serving crime and, sobbing breath-halting tears, tried to think past the nausea for something to say that would make it all right. But despite the "I'm sorry"s, the magical combination of words acknowledging my lie and his humiliation never presented themselves. I'm not at all sure that my misdeed had a serious effect on his feelings for me, but I date from about that time a greater withdrawal into himself. We no longer walked to Mass together, or anywhere else for that matter.

The day-to-day relationship between my parents was faltering, too. I don't know who fueled whom, but they seemed to be behaving *at* each other, adapting incendiary stances, unleashing provocative taunts to get a rise out of one another. Their feelings of anger dominated and colored everything else. One drinking because of the cold, the other turning down the heat even more. And my father did—literally. The house was so cold I dressed for school standing in the hall over the one floor heater that was turned on for only a few minutes.

The transfer from St. Rose of Lima in Brooklyn to St. Ambrose in Los Angeles proved difficult and apparently insurmountable. After six weeks of struggling, I couldn't keep up.

And right there, for all the school to see, I was demoted to the third grade. This was a small school, first through seventh grade, and, as was the case in those days in parochial school, no more than twenty students per grade. I was now not only the new kid, I was the stupid new kid, and the others delighted in tormenting me (not much different from Brooklyn). Walking home became a nightmare of catcalls—"Hi, dummy," "Hey, Miss Stupid."

My mother began drinking in the afternoon, so that walking in the house became something I dreaded even more than the walk home. I never knew who was going to be there: my mother, or this other woman with slurred speech, perplexed look, and that funny dimple that only appeared when she had been drinking. Sometimes I'd find her asleep on the couch, unarousable. It was the immutable proof of her condition. Like all alcoholics, her denial was too solid for her to see what she was doing to herself and her family. She would take offense to our pleading, and try to discount it. "Oh no, that's not true." Then eventually she'd break down and say, "Okay, you're right. But it's not my fault. It's your father. If he were just a little kinder to me." Or, sometimes she'd just toss if off, "Oh, you just don't have any sense of fun." She would appease our complaints, individual or as a group (Bertie, Grandma, and me), with the promise to stop, or at least cut down. But she couldn't pull it off for more than a few months at a time, and she would degenerate into being drunk for days at a time.

Unfortunately for my young brother, John was growing up in a house devoid of consistency and short on affection. There was no one to give him the kind of security and relief I found on my stays with Bertie and Grandma. The atmosphere in that house had its effect on John, who began rebelling when he was quite young. A series of misdeeds, and the subsequent mishandling of him on the part of my parents, established patterns that would last for his lifetime. He was not himself doing his own dance. My parents were puppeteers manipulating his every move; my mother by her inconsistencies, my father with his glowering expression.

John got into the typical kind of trouble that boys will. He began early and with fireworks. He played with matches one day in a neighbor's garage, and it burned to the ground. Sometimes he refused to eat the eggs my father cooked in the morning, claiming they made him sick to his stomach, and he'd have to be slapped on the side of his head for this disobedience. Who can understand the ferocity of the demons standing guard of my father's indignation.

One day years later, shortly before he died, John and I were talking about our shared personal experiences with alcoholism. He told me that when he was five or six and Mom and Dad had friends in for parties, he'd watch everyone standing around laughing and talking until someone put a drink down on a table. Then, when they weren't watching, his small hand would snatch it and bring it to his hiding place. Sitting cross-legged on the floor behind his dad's favorite chair, he'd sip his drink quite happily until the glass was empty.

From time to time my mother stayed with friends all night, not returning until the next day. Sometimes she took John with her. I remember one return when John was three or four. As they walked up the path to those green steps, my father stopped them. "You're not wanted here," he shouted at them both. I think he was sick from worry. He must have been blind to John's presence, or somehow, in his fury, saw them as one source of pain, hand in hand as they were. His gust of dark words sent me to the corner of my own quiet rage. I was mad at my mother, too, and felt vindicated that she was being yelled at. She'd stabbed us all now—my little brother, too.

She scooped up John and ran with him, both crying, back to the car. I have never been able to let go of that picture, or the scatter-shot emotions that it evoked: I was hurt for my innocent three-year-old brother that he had to be subjected to the screaming rage of my father; I was upset that my father was screaming at my mother, whom I loved, but also glad that he was screaming at her because she deserved it; no one was paying any attention to me, and I was hurt. I was angry at her, him, and I was afraid for John. Dad never said anything to me. He just left for the bus that took him downtown to work.

After school, I took a new route home. I curled up in my grandmother's big comforting arms, and told her what had happened.

That night after Mom returned, a discussion was held among the adults. Everyone agreed that there was just too much for Mom to handle, and not enough money to bring some rewards into her life. So an attempt at easing the sameness of my mother's life was made. Mom went to work as a telephone operator for a department store, while John was sent to nursery school where "professionals" could watch after him. I was to stay with Bertie and Grandma.

It was a life preserver—one I knew from the past and I took it.

Bertie would wake us up in the morning, having already turned on the heat, and make breakfast for the three of us. She'd bring it on a tray to Grandma's bed, where we'd chatter away or fall into unthreatening silences sometimes. Bertie and I would secretly acknowledge to each other the occasional but familiar short bursts that emanated from beneath the blanket. It was a fine way to start the day—with a smile.

The Ward Sisters

❧

*A*FTER I'D BURROWED myself comfortably in this nest for a few months, a dancing school opened just a few blocks away—the Ward Sisters Studio of Dance Arts. These were two spinster ladies. One of them, Agnes, taught tap, ballet, and acrobatics. Her older sister, Ann, accompanied on piano. They had left Minneapolis to set up shop in Los Angeles, seeking fame and fortune as mentors to the stars. They were the second answer to my prayers—people who would take my talent and shape it.

I still was barely scraping by in school, and still without friends. I don't know if I couldn't or just wouldn't. There was little in my life which I did well. One evening Bertie, arriving home a few minutes late from work, found Grandma wringing her hands and pacing back and forth as she did whenever Bertie was more than eight minutes past her usual arrival time. I must tell you, I was by this time frantic, too, imagining all the disasters that Grandma suggested as possible causes of this tardiness, most of which included some form of bleeding from the head. Her terrors played a strong part in shaping my own.

Well, anyway, Bertie did get home and brought the news that

one of her colleagues knew these sisters Ward and had very nice things to say about them. Before she became a movie star, Arlene Dahl had been their student. I knew right then I was definitely going to be in the movies, and the Ward sisters were going to see to it! Despite the fact that Bertie could afford very little more than the movies and Friday-night dinners out at the local diner, she was prepared to pay for lessons.

The next day she brought me to their studio so they could take a look at my self-taught gyrations and give an opinion of my potential. It was a storefront duplex, mirrors covering one whole wall of the eighteen-by-thirty-foot room. A ballet barre spanned the opposite wall. Leaden, two-inch-thick mats were piled in the corner, promising a slightly more cushioned landing than the wooden floor for acrobatics. Agnes had Arlene Dahl—red hair, a tight little body, and a warm smile. Her perfume (something that none of the women in my family wore) spoke to me of chiffon, point shoes, and fairy dust. In the twenty years I was to know her, she never changed brands.

Her sister, Ann, the pianist, walked with a limp (the result of childhood polio) and hardly ever smiled. In addition to the music, she took care of the records and billings. Her hair was gray, only a few shades darker than the skin next to it. What a hotbed of resentment must have lain just below that contorted exterior. In shows yet to be performed it was she who would scream out to me from her seat at the piano, "Smile!" I wonder if it was that hobbled, frowning woman who was the impetus for the Mary Tyler Moore smile to come.

Agnes asked if I'd like to show her what I could do. Without a choreographic comma, I burst into a dance that was part twirling, some leaping, sometimes, impossibly, both at once, and many quick little baby steps all followed by a lunge forward, arms outstretched, and a verbal "ta-da."

My heart was thudding with expectation and fear. Everything depended on this woman's verdict. Agnes told me that I obviously didn't know anything about dancing, but, because I seemed to want it so much, she would be happy to have me as a student. As I flew out of the front office, suspending myself in mid-air long enough for it to register, I noted the autographed photo of Arlene Dahl. With a combination of awe and jealousy, I vowed that my picture would be on that wall someday, too.

And so I began my lessons, two a week, and also began to feel that at last I had something that made me special. And my schoolwork began to improve proportionately to my mastery of the pirouette. I no longer felt lonely, either. As I learned the dance steps and began to excel, in tap especially, the girls at school started paying attention to me. I spent Saturdays at the studio taking extra classes and helping to herd the three- and four-year-olds through Miss Ward's baby classes.

*A*fter little more than a year, we gave our first recital. I was in the chorus of two dances. One was a Hungarian tap. The other was a dance in which we were a line of chefs, with wooden bowls and spoons cleverly augmenting the taps our pitiful feet weren't yet able to master. Grandma made all my costumes, and they were standouts. If the pattern called for a row of ruffles made from two yards of fabric, she'd use four. The spats that fit over my shoes to give the look of boots for the Hungarian "parade" were made from lining so stiff that it made her fingers bleed as she stitched them by hand. The other girls' costumes, which had been bought from a catalogue, paled by comparison.

The best costume was a pink-and-green satin, hip-hugging, bare midriff señorita costume for my SOLO. I played the castanets and danced to "Malagueña."

I'll never forget the sickening stage fright I felt as I danced, blinded by the spotlight, sure that I'd end up facing the wrong way, or maybe not even get that far because I'd forget the steps. I remember thinking that my job was to take a group of people who really didn't like me, and show them that if I couldn't win them over at least I'd remain upright and smiling when the music ended. There was no pleasure in it—just the challenge. This is what I did as a kid at that first recital, and I've brought that trait with me throughout life.

There's a difference between stage fright and general insecurity. Stage fright is a finite condition. It has a beginning, middle, and end; and it can be dealt with. I know by the time I'm on stage I will be so absorbed in creating the attitude I want, there is no room in my makeup for fear. Whereas, insecurity is not as dramatically felt but is *always* there. Its presence undermines everything. Unfortunately, I've carried that trait with me as well.

I can't imagine why the community paper sent a critic to this local dance recital for kids, but they did. I had my very first review. "Miss Moore danced well, but her head work seemed stiff." It was as though the last four words were all capitals.

My reaction to a negative review hasn't changed much since that day, I'm afraid. When I'm praised—"They probably don't understand the work." But let someone point to a misstep and it's—"How perceptive they are." And that's what's engraved in my head.

Dancing became the center of my life. While others won holy cards at school for excellence in scholarship, I was adding another second or two of balance to my arabesque. Miss Ward's smile marked the achievement.

Using her more than willing students, Miss Ward put on little musical shows for the local Kiwanis, Elk Club, or Veterans Hospital. A show was comprised of an eight-person chorus line. We were ten- to fourteen-year-olds, looking as disparate as girls of that age do. Some had braces, at least two were overweight, one was small for her age. Each had developing breasts of various shapes, or none as of yet.

I truly envied one classmate, whose solo included baton-twirling and tap-dancing in white boots with tassels. However, Grandma pointed out the dismal career opportunities for twirlers in show business. "All that effort and for what, Mary?"

"You get to wear white boots with tassels, is what, Grandma!"

My own solo was a modern ballet. Stage fright would make me nauseous and light-headed for hours before a performance. You never knew how slippery the floor surface would be. How big an area? What kind of audience? Would they like me?

Besides having a solo, I was also chosen to be the Mistress of Ceremonies, an honor I treasured. I did something no one else did: I introduced everyone. "And now, ladies and gentlemen, Gail Mosher will delight you with her dazzling rendition of 'Limehouse Blues.' You may want to wear your sunglasses as she demonstrates the versatility of her flashing feet!"

Once we played to a group at a place called St. Anne's. There were no men in the audience, only women. Most of them seemed hardly older than we were, and they all had big bellies. As the show progressed it dawned on us that we were actually in a home for unwed mothers. We were alternately shocked and fascinated, only recently having been told, or figured out, the facts of life. The question we asked on the way home in the bus, "Can you have a baby and not be married?", found its way to our parents and the Ward sisters were summarily taken to task for poor judgment in exposing us to such immorality. For us, however, it had been even more fun than the psych ward at the Veterans Administration a few weeks before. What a lot of conjecture we had to chew on. "What exactly must have gone on while they were doing 'it'?"

Mostly, we performed for groups of retired people, or church clubs. The point of these performances was for us to gain experience. Those ridiculous words I was given to speak were my acting lessons. I pretended I wasn't afraid and that I knew how to be a good performer. Perhaps the biggest pretense of all was that I was having fun. As much as I loved what I was doing, the doing of it terrified me. I was excelling at something that fed my self-doubts rather than eased them.

Jack O'Brien

∾

*J*ACK O'BRIEN, A square-jawed, blond Adonis of a boy, joined our fifth grade late in the semester and aside from dance class became the other element in my life. He had a shy smile, one that didn't match his confident swagger. The sleeves of his tee shirt were always rolled up, revealing pretty mature biceps—something not seen in the fifth grade. He wore small heel-saving taps on his shoes (loafers—which no one else wore). His hair was laden with a rose-smelling pomade so you always knew where Jack was. He wasn't very tall, his stinging blue eyes leveling out at about my shoulder. But that would be okay once we sat down to do the serious kissing I so wanted to try, when I looked at him. All the other girls were just as taken with this diminutive god as I, although no one ever talked of such things. The boys liked him, too.

I was living with my mother and father again, and Mom was making a real effort to be a better parent. Uncharacteristically, she had joined the Mothers' Club (parochial version of the PTA), and had been asked to be a chaperone at the altar boys' picnic. Every boy over nine was expected to volunteer for duty at Mass once or twice a week, and the picnic was Father O'Toole's way of saying, "Thank you."

Mom, to my delight, felt it would be better to bring me along than send me to my grandmother's house for one day. I couldn't believe my good fortune as I put together the possibilities. Jack O'Brien and I had been experimenting with eye contact, but found no outlet for further expression. We were eleven years old. Well, I was. I think he was ten.

At the picnic, the mothers set tables while the boys climbed rocks. Then everyone was to sit down to eat cold chicken.

During the "boys climb rocks" part, Jack and I managed to separate ourselves from the group and consummate our affair. We kissed a full frontal lip-to-lip kiss. I was done for. Fireworks, heartbeats, streamers, and some kind of stringed instrument. I was to be forever changed in that moment.

I was as filled with pleasure and validation by that kiss as any that would follow in adulthood.

When you're eleven there's very little to support the assumption of a relationship—no one went out on dates; but I was certain Jack felt these strange feelings for me, too. After school, he and his gang of three or four boys (who followed him everywhere) would show up on the corner outside my house. He would lean against a tree, or be fixing a bicycle chain. It was all very casual, and surprise would register on his face when I approached, as though he kept forgetting I lived there.

One Saturday afternoon, as we made our way down the aisle of the local movie theater, two of my friends and I spotted Jack and his entourage already seated. The movie, *Gilda*, starred Rita Hayworth. It wasn't a new movie, so the place was pretty empty.

Subtlety of action isn't a big issue at that age, still I knew on some level there might be reason to question the choice I was making as I sat down next to him. Full coquettishness was not yet part of my arsenal.

So there we sat, Mary and Jack, flanked by our attendants, George Mitchell and Terry Sweeny for the groomlet, Valerie Yerke and Ann Powers for me. On the screen Rita Hayworth took off her gloves with the sensuality of someone removing a more personal item of clothing. And then, as she tossed her long black-and-white tresses and sang "Put the Blame on Mame" I was exquisitely aware of Jack's arm, which had magically made its way to the top of my seat back and was now actually in contact with the nape of my neck. But, alas, that was it. Maybe Rita Hayworth made him realize how unworthy I was. I don't know why, but the magic of eye contact would never again happen. He stopped coming by, and started hanging around Ann Connelly.

The inevitable pain of this pure little love, as it was carved into my heart upon ending, was an initiation against which all other heartbreaks would be measured. Jack O'Brien.

I confided in my mother, who obviously betrayed the confidence because every once in a while my father, staring out the front window, would say, "Here comes Jack O'Brien and he's on his knees. No, wait, he's standing up. He just looks like he's on his knees." He does it to this day.

Christmas

❧

DECORATING THE Christmas tree was an annual ritual. There were the shiny old glass objects, carefully wrapped in tissue, that we brought up from the basement, the impossible tangle that was the many sets of colored lights, and the tinsel—the dreaded tinsel.

My father had always decorated our tree himself. Oh, he'd occasionally allow one of us to place an ornament here and there. John's job was to set up the train under the tree and then back off. It was Dad's project, a part of the joyous festivities to be taken very seriously. He always began with the lights, making certain they were perfectly spaced and that not one color repeated itself too often. That was the foundation and therefore demanded precise attention to creating the random effect he wanted. Smaller balls belonged on top, graduating to larger sizes as the ladder was put aside and the lower branches were addressed. Color and mixture of plain and intricate baubles were an important part of this festive equation, too.

I remember how we'd all mourn the loss of one of the special ones—a Santa head, a small house with snow on its roof, as we'd carefully remove them from their boxes and assess the damage that some unseen and unreasonable Christmas devil had wreaked in the past eleven and a half months of dormancy.

And now, with angel in place at her post on the top of the tree, the final most crucial work began—the meticulous draping of the tinsel, so that not one strand touched the branch below it.

As an adult I carried on this tradition. Without the perspective of childhood or the dedication of fanaticism, however, it seemed always to cause more clenching than cheer. The tree and other festooneries became so important in my house, having it as right as I could make it, that Christmas became a grim affair. I even went so far in my attempts to match or outdo the master that once the tinsel was as symmetrical and perfect as physics would allow, I'd mix Ivory Flakes in a bowl with water, and when it was beaten to a frothy whipped cream–like consistency, I'd spoon dollops of it on the tops of the tinsel-strewn, ornament-laden tree, creating the look of fallen snow. It dried to an air-filled, thin crust, adding, I thought, an inspiration for the next generation to adopt. My father, after allowing me my triumph that first year, would from then on remark that it looked like a snowman had thrown up on the tree.

This focus on perfection—every piece of tinsel having to be perfectly placed—is with me still. But today I have the ability to look at myself and remember where it comes from. The ideal tree fits into my, until recently, absorption with things square. Everything had to be exactly as it was meant to be. Now, my happiest moments are creating things that are wild and random and without lines and definitions, like gardens. Horses that make a mess in the stall. So what?

School Days

 ⸙

 $\mathcal{B}$ ECAUSE OF MY mother's inability to stop her heavy drinking, I lived at home only about half the time during my school years. I find it interesting that I have just now referred to my parents' house as "home." Certainly, it was more comfortable being secure, and outwardly loved, with Grandma and Bertie. Yet no matter how they reassured me that my friends didn't suspect some mysterious problem with my parents, I remained self-conscious and guilty about my address.

It was all very embarrassing to me. When I was living with Bertie, why wasn't I living with my parents? When I was living at home, why was the house so unkempt, so tiny; why was my mother so often drunk?

The size of the house my parents bought was a reflection of their tight money situation, but I wondered at the time if they had counted on my not living there. It had two bedrooms and one bath. How were they planning to accommodate the needs of an adolescent girl and a toddling boy in the same room? As John grew older, modesty drove me to the living-room couch, where I slept in fear of being spied upon from the outside. The front door was made of panes of glass and was only three feet from my makeshift bed. I feared classmates peering in and seeing me asleep with my mouth open, drooling. I was afraid that one of my friends from school would appear on the front porch and discover that not only did I sometimes live elsewhere, I didn't even have a bedroom at home.

This stuff was very important to me. Everywhere I looked other families seemed normal. They didn't have a lot of money, but their mothers were reliable, their fathers smiled at them, and only sisters shared a room. Looking back on it, I am sure there were some real horror stories I never knew about, but at the time I felt that there was a lot I had to hide.

Apparently, my brother, John, had pushed the limits of his first-grade nun's patience. Christ! How bad could it have been? He was seven.

The punishment they meted out made less sense than a stockade. He was banned from his classroom for a month. He had to arrive on time with everyone else, but then was sent to the bottom step at the back of school, where he remained facing the play yard until the end of the school day. For one whole month he received no teaching, no friendship, and no protection from his parents, who were too cowed by the nuns' authority to step in on his behalf. I was living safely with Bertie and Grandma at the time, and I confess wanting to believe that those nuns knew what they were doing. So his big sister failed him, too. The following year, he was sent to a Catholic military school. Nice environment for an eight-year-old, eh?

I wonder what other tortures they devised for children who confounded them. Was their search for perfection so enormous that it obliterated compassion? Didn't they empathize with that little boy who sat, outcast on the steps, enduring the jibes and dismissal of his schoolmates day after day?

They were fearsome, those nuns, in God's name.

I'm aware of a strong emphasis on dogma in my memories of religion class and sermons at Mass. A person's goodness, it seems, was measured by how often Holy Communion was received, not by small acts of kindness.

The Catholic faith gives such hope and solace to its followers as they seek salvation through a litany of shalts and shalt nots, but compassion for our fellows is a quality that requires little knowledge and is, I think, the true redemption, after all.

When it came time to choose a high school, I wanted to go to the one many of my classmates had decided on, Immaculate Heart High School. It was prohibitively expensive. "Well," my mother said, "there's no money for Immaculate Heart. We simply can't afford it." Then, thinking aloud she said, "If Mrs. Moore were asked, she might do something. . . ."

Grandma Moore, having lost my grandfather to a stroke, sold their great old house in Virginia and was now living near us in Los Angeles, a member of St. Ambrose parish, as well.

Catholicism was the most important thing in her life. Upon being introduced to someone she would immediately ask, "Are you Catholic?" If the answer were no, she'd excuse herself politely and walk away, leaving her new acquaintance dumbstruck. I flagrantly appealed to her on the basis of her religious fervor. "I'll get the finest Catholic education at Immaculate Heart, Grandma."

Hoarding her money, of which there was plenty, was the second most important thing in her life. When my grandfather was alive and they went to a restaurant, he'd make a big show of calling the waiters over to personally tip them well, in cash. On the way out my grandmother would excuse herself, pleading a last stop in the ladies' room. As soon as he was out the door, she would go back to each one of the people he'd tipped, and demand the cash from them saying, "He doesn't know what he's doing."

She was a beautiful, tall woman, whose hair had turned white when she was in her late twenties and which she wore rolled into a halo around her head. Large brown eyes that truly twinkled, a full mouth, and gentle Southern charm gave the impression of warmth. Toward the end of her life, when she was in her eighties, she could still turn men's heads. I like to think that it is her posture gene that speaks for her in me. Not much else.

My grandmother agreed to Immaculate Heart, and for the next four years was willing to help when the extras were called for as well. And it was her money that paid for John's military boarding school, so she had the satisfaction of prevailing over my mother's Protestantism with both her grandchildren.

*M*y memories of IHHS are pleasant enough. I made some great pals but seldom saw them off-campus. I thought of school as something that had to be gotten through until I could step into the real world, the happy one as a *star.*

In those early days searching for stardom, I came to censor my words and say that I was an actress seeking interesting work and that stardom facilitated the broadest scope of choice. But at the time I really wanted to *be a star,* and it wasn't about self-expression. It was about being loved and applauded like the people I saw on the screen. And not only that, but to be happy all the time—offscreen as well as on, due to the fact that I was a star. It wasn't acting or dancing that satisfied my need. It was stardom.

But although it was what I wanted, at that time it was nearly impossible for me to imagine it happening because I wasn't "star pretty," and I wasn't "star talented."

After-school activity for me was class at the Ward sisters'. I wasn't even involved in the drama club at Immaculate Heart. In my arrogance, I felt it would have been an insult to the life I had chosen to indulge in *amateur* school plays. Today, I regret that I didn't reach out, grow in all directions. Had I gone to college, though, I might have ended up teaching English instead of entertaining, but I doubt it. As an actress, I simply would have more to draw upon. Exposure to history and the arts adds texture to the fabric we are given, any education does. On the other hand, I might never have had the wonderful experience I've had as a performer. But I was too involved in subconscious conflict between myself and those who would teach me to see the opportunities they offered. Furthermore, dancing removed the necessity to deal with my loneliness. I didn't have to make friends, because I was a *dancer*. It's a lone pursuit.

To this day I'll do anything to avoid revealing a lack of knowledge, especially that of poetry, classical music, or philosophy; knowledge I could have gained through a different approach to learning in those years. As it was, I barely got through high school—copying other people's assignments, faking book reports. My attention to studies was so poor that had it not been a private girls' school, one that had never not graduated one of its darlings (even though she might have ditched thirty days in her senior year), I'm sure the diploma I unrolled would have been blank.

By today's standards of teenage morality, I, like the rest of my friends, was pretty straight and narrow. Yes, I got drunk at a party once, was sneaking cigarettes regularly, and wore lipstick after school *in uniform,* but we didn't go all the way with boys. Wait. One girl did. She got pregnant and was missing from the graduation ceremony. Out of eighty girls, though, that's not bad.

And the Livin' Is Easy

❧

*I*N MY JUNIOR YEAR,
Bertie used some contacts to get me a dream summer job. Everyone
I knew who worked that summer was a salesgirl, dusted doughnuts
at her uncle's bakery, or ushered at a movie theater. But Bertie was
the assistant production manager at KNXT, the local CBS television
station, allocating studio space and assigning directors. Most important, to me, was the clout she had at KNX Radio where they produced live shows, everything from the fifteen-minute morning soaps
to Steve Allen and Bing Crosby specials. With a little nudge from
Bertie they realized that there was an opening in the mail room.

My job was to gather the outside and interoffice mail from the
mail room at specific hours, and deliver it to the offices that were
located throughout the building. I'd return to the mail room with
communiqués to be rerouted from the offices just visited. Since I
was already a master of the brisk walk that is so much a part of me
today, I found I often had time to poke my head into the empty
glass-walled clients' booths of studios that were being used for rehearsals. I watched Bing Crosby, Edgar Bergen, Gene Autry for as
long as time would permit, and then would resume my rounds. One
day it occurred to me that, even though I was given a time sched-

ule for pickup and delivery, nobody in the offices knew specifically
what those hours were. So I began gathering the mail and then hiding it in a darkened booth while I, enraptured, watched nearly a
whole show rehearse. When it was over, I'd return to the mail room
for a new batch, swing by the empty clients' booth to pick up my
stash, and resume operations.

Where I should have made eight runs a day, I allocated four. I
was able to pull this off most of that summer, until some work-ethic
fanatic blew the whistle on me. Apparently, an employee went into
the clients' booth and stumbled onto the evidence. I was taken to
task, and from that time on all mail-room workers had to punch a
time card every time they entered and left.

My Affair with
Marlon Brando

❧

*B*ACK AT IHHS WITH
no real boys to answer our pubescent yearnings, we spent our free
time indulging in fantasies about Marlon Brando. *On the Waterfront*
had propelled him to the number one position as leading man.
There wasn't a line of dialogue we didn't know by heart, or a moment unrecalled when he was on the screen. We took turns creating scenarios of how each of us might meet him when we became
women. In one of my scenes, as we entered his apartment I remember that he would turn and say to me, "Martini or Manhattan?" (Even then, a drink was a not unusual prop.)

One of us found out his address up on Mulholland Drive. We
talked for days about going there, not ringing the doorbell, but just
waiting, parked across the street in DeDe Sawaya's car. Maybe we
would see him go out or come in. Oh God, what if he had a date
with him when he came home? Hideous!

The following Friday night, after we'd been dropped off at DeDe's
by our unsuspecting guardians, seven of us piled into her Christmas
present, a '53 DeSoto, and tore up Laurel Canyon toward heaven.

We didn't have any trouble finding the house, even though it
was mostly screened by a wall and tall shrubbery. We pulled up out

❧

front, DeDe turned the engine off, and we waited. We were out-side his house. Our hearts were beating in syncopated rhythms. He could actually be standing there by the gate at any moment! But the magic was not to come that night, or the following Friday or Sat-urday.

I think it was on our fourth or fifth visit that an old man with a limp exited his house and joined another man who waited outside in a car. We were so grateful for any action it didn't matter who it was. Someone had been in his house and come out! Then it oc-curred to us—it was Brando! He was wearing a disguise. As his car pulled away DeDe did, too, leaving just the right distance between us (as noted in movies). We tailed him for about a quarter of a mile. Breathing was getting difficult, my heart was pumping furiously as we shrieked and "Oh my God"-ed along the darkening, twisting Mulholland Drive. We were scared for our lives, too, because DeDe was now crying.

When we got to the place where Coldwater Canyon intersects, his car slowed down and a hand motioned from the passenger win-dow for us to follow to a wide spot on the side of the road. (That spot is still there, a vacant half-lot that flower and vegetable ven-dors use.) We came to a halt about two car lengths behind, and watched, slack-jawed, as Marlon Brando opened the car door and made his way toward us. The limp was gone, so was the gray wig. He was looking straight at us with his head sort of down and his eyes kind of up. There was a smile on his Marlon Brando face, a smile that could have meant anything. He never broke eye contact with us. (I'm pretty sure he was looking at me, but then I bet everyone in the car thought the same for herself.) He walked to us in the slowest, sexiest walk I'd ever seen.

He bent over, both hands on his knees, scanned the passengers for a moment, and then looking down at his feet said, "Don't you girls have anything better to do on a Saturday night?" We giggled, cleared throats, and made attempts at responses, but none of us was able.

"You should be with some guys parked up here, having a good time, not following me around." He gave us a heartbreaking smile and said, "Go on, now," as though he were giving each of us an affectionate swat on the rear end. He backed away a couple of steps, pointed his finger at us, and said, "No more, now." Marlon Brando got back in the car. The driver had to wait for a few cars to pass by to pull out and then we were alone. Seven girls whose hearts held so much love and pain and happiness, we were like a collage—one big merged entity that was now purified, chosen, spoken to by our idol.

Several years ago I was introduced to Marlon Brando in the VIP lounge of LAX airport. He was reading a magazine and remained in his slouched position, grunting his acknowledgment at my presence. That alone was pretty disappointing, but when a half hour into the flight he came over to my seat and said, "Excuse me, I didn't realize who you were," I felt betrayed. How could he *possibly* have forgotten our meeting that night in DeDe's car on Mulholland Drive?

3

With my son, Richie,
and Larry Mathews (Ritchie on The Dick Van Dyke Show.*)*

With Dick Van Dyke. I'm wearing those ubiquitous Capri pants.

Dick Meeker

❧

*I*N JANUARY OF 1955,
the year I was to graduate from high school, I met Dick Meeker.
He was a good-looking bachelor who had moved into one of the
small apartments that had been carved out of the house next door
to my parents'. I was quite taken with his blue eyes and confident
swagger, so when he acknowledged me with a smile, I decided it
was time to return home to sleeping on the living-room couch, the
potential proximity to the boy next door being too enticing to ignore. Bertie and Grandma were truly upset to see me go this time.
I think they could see where the path would lead me.

I was eighteen and he was twenty-seven, a difference in age that
might have unnerved my parents had this older suitor not made his
lair in full view of the even older and dominant male, my father.
His car, always parked in a dead-end driveway between his apartment and my parents' view out those French doors, afforded some
sense of security to my suspicious father regarding my whereabouts.

Mom and Dad were being especially loving and patient with each
other. Mom had just converted to Catholicism, which made my father so happy. She was hopeful of salvation from bourbon and
water, and he had a soul mate for Christ.

The closest Dad had ever come to a father/daughter talk about sex and morality was the caution he gave me as I left on one of my first dates, at age fifteen. "Remember, familiarity breeds contempt," he said. His entire face was furrowed as he said it, but I hadn't the least notion of how it applied to that night's date.

I felt "in love": pumping adrenaline, long kisses that for the first time made me want to go "the whole way" with Dick. With prior boyfriends it had been titillating to think about this, and I was definitely interested, but my upbringing in Catholicism had made sex a non-issue until marriage.

Dick worked as a salesman for Ocean Spray cranberry products. His job was to sell as many cans and jars and bottles as possible to the various stores and market chains which carried the line. He was expected to boost the sales by establishing prominent shelf space and selling outlets on the idea of mounting special displays, which might include a color cardboard cutout at point of sale.

I was so thrilled that he showed an interest in me. Without calculating it, I felt he was my salvation for getting out of my house and legitimately being on my own, even though I was to be totally dependent on him.

Dick's edges were rough. He was a sportsman: a mountain climber, fisherman, he hunted rabbits, liked target practice. He played poker, and the boys would come over to the house for a game regularly.

Clearly, in my family there was a snobbism that said, "It's too bad she's getting married—not at such a young age—but to a man who shows so little promise." And the lack of promise was because of his limited education.

College hadn't been on his agenda—the Navy capturing his spirit of adventure instead. All of this ruggedness, of course, appealed to my teenage perception of manliness and maturity. Part of what I refused to see and hear was the absence of career goals and the desire for the education that would facilitate them once they were formulated. He was an outgoing, spirited, and responsible young man, though, and I was sure he would find his way. "It's not important," I said to Bertie whenever she brought his poor grammar to my attention. And I tried hard to believe that it was the heart that mattered. That's what eighteen-year-old Mary held on to when faced with the possibility of her own home, one that contained only sober, cheerful people, each of whom would be loved and loving. So, several months later when Dick proposed to me a month before graduation and with no plan for what would come next, I said, "Thank you, God."

Dick accompanied me home to seek the ritual permission of my parents. Dad, upon hearing of our intention, leapt from his chair in the living room and stormed into John's bedroom where I kept my clothes, beckoning Dick to follow. He pulled open drawer after drawer, revealing a jumble of sweaters, underwear, socks—both clean and dirty. Seizing a nylon stocking that was hopelessly tangled in a decorative hair comb, he held it up and said, "Is this what you want to marry?"

Oh, how I wished that instead he had smiled warmly at me and said, "She's too young, not ready for the responsibilities of marriage. Let her remain a child awhile longer."

Through a friend of Bertie's at an advertising agency, I was called to an audition for a series of commercials on *The Adventures of Ozzie and Harriet* television show. Hotpoint Appliances was their sponsor, and the agency was looking for someone who could sing and dance and bring to life their logo, an elf named Happy Hotpoint.

The audition was a breeze—a few cartwheels, a back walkover, and a pertly spoken, "Hi, Harriet, aren't you glad you use Hotpoint?" My approach to this task wasn't dissimilar to the Mistress of Ceremonies role I'd so often played in the Ward sisters' shows— lotta smile, a lot of desperately hoping to please. They asked me to sing something, which I did without hitting any clinkers, and I left walking on the air. I was sure it would continue to lift me.

I got the job. There would be one commercial for each episode of the series, and filming would commence that summer after graduation.

As the seniors prepared to leave Immaculate Heart and to enter college, thinking about their life's work, we were each called into Mother Eucharia's office for a counseling session. She was a woman of important dimensions and few words. She ruled that school as though it were her own Vatican. Perhaps it was because her jaw was always clenched that she said so little. Although no one had actually seen her lose her temper, the explosive nature of her anger was legendary.

When it came time for my session, I entered her office with fear, anticipating the reaction to my goal of being a dancer. She stared at me from across her desk after a glance at my record, allowing an exhalation of breath to communicate her great sorrow, and said, simply, "I understand dancers sometimes wear short skirts—tutus, I think they're called? Don't do that."

End of counseling.

Dick and I became engaged but it was agreed that I wouldn't wear a ring until after graduation at the end of June. My father, always suspicious that the mice would fornicate while he was away, had a hard and fast rule about dating. If he and Mom had to be out when it came time for a date to pick me up, I had to wait on the front porch to prevent any chance of necking indoors. He continued to enforce this humiliation even after the engagement, and no amount of pleading on my part would budge him on this issue. On one of those lock-out occasions my mom, having lived through a few embarrassing moments herself, empathized with my plight and, delivering a "Psst—Come 'ere, kid," pointed out a potential solution—an easily overlooked, unlatched screen on one of the windows that could also be unnoticeably opened just a crack. I became pretty good at hoisting myself through the preset window without snagging a stocking or ruining my dress. I was so nervous, though, about Dick's presence in that unchaperoned house that I'd anticipate his arrival, peeking through the front windows, and leap down the porch steps, slamming the door behind me before he ever set foot on the lawn.

One day after school, and before my father got home (I think because he was embarrassed that it had happened), my mother told me that she was pregnant, that I would have a little sister or brother to play with come next March. Well, conversion had wrought a miracle, indeed. It just wasn't the one we'd hoped for. She was so heartbreakingly apologetic about it, as I think back, and I seized the opportunity to reinforce her misplaced feelings of remorse by giving voice to my own self-centered sense of betrayal. "Oh Mother, how could you?" were the words I used. Even though I was grateful for the sobriety her pregnanacy would demand, I couldn't understand why she would be willing to stop drinking for this unborn child but never could for me.

Alcoholic behavior seems so black and white to those who live with it. The drinker appears to mete out punishment or refuse love in the form of drunkenness, at will. As a result, each episode is misinterpreted as a deliberate act rather than the inevitable course of the disease I believe it is.

I was to begin filming the first Hotpoint commercials the day after the graduation prom. I had a six a.m. makeup call, and so, like Cinderella, I had to flee the ball early. I didn't mind a bit. My life was starting the next morning.

We filmed several commercials over a three-day period and more were planned for late fall. I was costumed in a head-to-toe gray leotard. An eared cap revealed my face with a blond curl at the forehead. Since pixies and elves are, of course, of neuter gender, I was asked to wear a bandeau, a sort of bra without cups, to minimize my femaleness. It was a bit uncomfortable since I was moderately well endowed. I was superimposed skating on the ice-cube trays in Harriet's freezer. She's talking back to me—"Hi, Happy." And I'm singing, "Every day's a holiday with Hotpoint." And every day was a holiday.

$\mathcal{D}$ick and I were busy planning our wedding at St. Ambrose Church and the reception afterward in my parents' backyard, and looking at apartments. Dick, who wasn't Catholic, was good-naturedly attending a required course on Catholicism, and the signing of papers that stated any issue of the marriage would be baptized and raised in the faith. Having children wasn't going to be a reality for quite some time, however, since we had agreed to use birth control until we were ready to be parents.

Birth control, being a mortal sin, meant I would be unable to receive the Sacraments. However, since my mid-teens, when I discovered that the blissful sensation called French kissing was a mortal sin (punishable by an eternity in Hell) I had decided that the church and I had no future together. It's always fascinated me that the dogma of Mother Church punishes equally a murderer and a French kisser—no difference, both burn the same amount. You'd think the kisser would get a few million years less, wouldn't you?

I hadn't been to confession and communion for some time—not with French kissing being the foundation, cornerstone, and spine of my sex life with Dick. About a week before the wedding, my father faced me at the kitchen table and with eyes staring intently past me said, "I want you to go to confession, and to receive communion before you get married." He got up, without waiting for a response, and took his plate to the sink, rinsed it, and left the room.

Confession terrified me. In the second grade I had been taken out of the girls' line while waiting, because I was caught talking. My punishment was to have to wait for confession in the boys' line. It destroyed me. I've had a fear of this sacrament, worse than anyone's fear of the dentist, ever since that time. It was double trauma now to contemplate not being truthful in the confessional.

I could feel the toast I had eaten turning into little balls of cement. A silent scream. Help! I couldn't receive communion, planning to use birth control. And I couldn't disobey my father, either.

There was a young assistant priest whose schedule for hearing confessions I began to study, almost like a stalker. Then, at a very early weekday mass, I joined the long line outside his confessional. It was barbaric to have to stand in line in front of the whole congregation who, I imagined, were all looking at me while they guessed what my sins were.

I will be forever grateful to that kind priest who listened to what I had to say and then asked, "Is your father here?" "No," I whispered. "Then this would be the best time for you to have already received communion (at a Mass where your father isn't) should you ever tell your father a lie, which is, after all, only a venial sin. Have a good marriage, Mary."

$\mathcal{D}$espite all the best intentions I'd shared with that priest, I was lax about using my new diaphragm. And so just six weeks after its initiation, I was pregnant! I was scared at first, and sat in a very hot tub in an effort to undo what I'd done. But by the time my skin had returned to its normal shade, I was thrilled with the notion. I wonder, had abortion been as routinely available as it is today, would I have considered it? Certainly any question I might have had about whether this marriage was the bliss I had hoped for was scrambled by the pregnancy because I had to then concentrate on motherhood. I started wearing maternity clothes right away because, of course, it was important to the part I was playing in this game of "house."

Fitting into Happy's elf costume for the next block of commercials proved to be a challenge. I was now three months pregnant and my breasts reflected that fact. I remember the pain of that neutering bra to this day. I looked a bit egg shaped, but we got away with Happy's little secret for that group of ads. The elf bit the dust afterward, though. The sponsor couldn't stop showing that character for the duration of my pregnancy and then bring her—it—back again. So off she—it—went. TV history.

Working Moms

❧

Y SISTER, ELIZABETH, was born in April 1956, nineteen years younger than I, and the most beautiful baby I had ever seen. She had blue eyes, perfect little features, and the patience of an old woman. She would whimper just a little when she wanted to be fed, and then occupy herself quietly while arrangements were being made.

I doubt that many mothers have had the opportunity that I had to practice for their own motherhood on a live model. Elizabeth was born three and a half months before my son, and I thank my mother for her willingness to allow me to participate in the early routines and rituals of the motherhood that obviously gave her so much happiness.

My relationship with my mother, during that time, was as close to normal as it had ever been. She was the teacher, and I her admiring student.

On July 3rd I was awakened at midnight with some ridiculously painful cramps in my belly that came and went every five minutes or so. Dick called the doctor, who said we could take our time getting there, but we should probably head over to the hospital. Of course, we took that to mean "NOW!" and tore out of our one-bedroom apartment (with its little crib in the corner) as fast as a woman who has gained forty-five pounds can move. As soon as we registered at the hospital I was taken to an examination room. After some poking and thumping, the Obstetrics nurse said that I hadn't dilated very much. "You may as well go home," she declared with the tone of someone who had been unnecessarily taken away from her duties. "You've got a long way to go."

"How could that be?" I asked myself, as I endured an unbelievably long and painful twinge.

Back we got into the car. During a particularly brutal twinge I emitted a screamlike roar, which sent Dick out of his lane directly into the path of an enormous truck. The sound of that driver's horn actually helped the pain. Its deep bellow was exactly what I was trying to express with my inadequate lungs. No sooner had Dick brought us safely home, than my water broke. What a shocking experience that is: not painful, but so unarguable in its declaration. No amount of description is enough to prepare you for that phase of motherhood. Nor was the anticipation of a human life that was going to be part of me something I could fathom. I couldn't wait to hold that baby in my arms. It was something I very much wanted, without any idea of what was involved.

I took a shower, lamenting the fact that the maternity dress I'd chosen to wear for this scene was now a sodden mess. It strikes me now that during most of the seminal moments in my life, my mind has gravitated to my wardrobe. I think the physical act of covering myself has always served as a tangible means of covering—and often burying—my emotions.

By the time we got back on the freeway once more, Dick had a real sense of urgency, and I think was hoping for a police escort. I know I was. Unfortunately, there was no traffic and no patrol car as we raced unencumbered and unaided all the way there.

When we arrived this time, they were ready for me and they were serious, too. I was snatched away from Dick, who was told to go home and wait for a call. The husband's presence in the labor room was forbidden then, but I did want him at least in the building. However, I was too intimidated to argue. Thinking back on that time, I find it absurd that women had to go into labor on their own, cut off from their husbands. No one was practicing Lamaze. We were alone in rooms with unknown attendants who dabbed and patted at us.

They brought me by wheelchair to a small room on a higher floor. It had a window that overlooked the parking area. As I waited for the nurses to prepare the bed, I tried to imagine how much more intense the pains would get before the baby came. And I watched our black Volkswagen pull away.

My mother had told me to remember that almost everyone throughout time had arrived here the same way. Instead, what I remembered through the next several hours was the phrase "Elvis the Pelvis Presley." I'd just seen him on *The Ed Sullivan Show*. I repeated it over and over again. It helped take the focus away from the all-encompassing pain.

At 10:10 a.m. on Tuesday, July 3, 1956, my son was born. He weighed nine pounds and three and a half ounces. He was so fat that his cheeks began at the edge of what were tiny slits for eyes and met in the middle of his chin. I loved him immediately, probably the more so because he was so funny-looking. I reminded myself of the agreement I had made with God: I prayed only for a healthy baby, the rest didn't matter.

Within weeks Richard Carleton Meeker, Jr. became as classically beautiful as anyone could hope for. But at the time I was so convinced that his was going to be a lonely life of rejection that I refused the photo they took at the hospital, thinking he wouldn't want to know how early his homeliness had begun.

I was as meticulous in my mothering as I was at housekeeping, the latter being a reversal of my early teen habits. I wanted this home and baby to have the perfection I thought everyone else had obtained. To be like life in the movies, Ozzie and Harriet.

I brought little joy to the small amounts of time I spent with Richie. Duty was the blanket in which I wrapped us both. I talked to him, and cooed as I bathed him; but I was always glad to put him clean, and sweetly dressed, back into his crib with the mobile dangling above to entertain him while I wrote about him in the baby book.

As he grew to be a toddler, I took great pride in his accomplishments, both small and major, but I was always comparing the progress he and his aunt Elizabeth were making. I would worry if he trailed her in walking, speaking, or general play skills. I was fearful that any stutter-step from her pace might indicate future shortcomings and troubles.

I saw the present as preparation for the future. Looking back on Richie's first year, I realize today the biggest mistake I made as a mother. I saw him as an adult in the making, not who he was at the time—a child. Why was there so little sense of the moment when he was in my care?

The reason lies partially in the way I was raised: a cool aloofness, and the belief that children were young people in formation, not important in and of themselves. The early years were perceived as a training period to get *over* childhood, to get rid of all that kid's stuff as quickly as possible in order to become a responsible adult.

I wanted to be a perfect mother. I wanted to teach Richie the things I wasn't taught. It didn't occur to me then that the most important issue for my child was to learn, by my attention, that he mattered. I wanted to cultivate in him the desire to be educated. I thought more about that than cuddling. I was raising Richie as if it were a dress rehearsal for something to come. Everything was in preparation for his school, boyhood, manhood.

Would I be a better mother today? I think so. I treasure the look from an animal's eyes, so it certainly would be compelling from my own son's eyes. Pace—movement from one goal to another—is not so urgent. Have I learned, and is it realized that I am a more giving, loving person than at age nineteen? I think so.

In those days I was, like most working mothers, eager to join the movement and proclaim our right and our need to express ourselves, to be fulfilled and happy knowing that every ounce of our creativity was being used. And that it was possible also to raise children at the same time.

I no longer believe that. I think there is something in nature that says women should work if they can, but once they commit to bringing life into the world that should be the first priority. When a child is raised in a day-care center, it is not the same thing. Many mothers *have* to work and there is no choice. But it's not the best beginning for children. I am surprised to find myself writing this. In my own case, it wasn't just a matter of not enough hours in the day to work and also to be with my child, it was complicated by an inability to enjoy my child, to understand what a child wants and needs.

Dick Meeker was, by 1950s standards, an unusually attentive father. He and Richie were as close as an outgoing, doting father and cheerful little boy could be.

Because Dick could choose his own route of the stores he covered, my inability to drive was no barrier to getting to interviews or work. For the short time an audition took, he and Richie waited outside doing the kinds of things that people who wait do. It was a bond they had, and while I was grateful for its existence, I also envied the connection.

And so we lived. The routines were set, and uneventful time passed by. As he learned to walk and talk Richie was never afraid to venture forth to investigate something new, or to say hello to a new tall person or a large dog or another kid. I remember wishing he were more reliant on me. I actually envied other mothers in the park whose children were shy and clung to them. Surely, they were responsive mothers to elicit such declarations of warmth and need from their children. But since I wasn't initiating any more interaction with mine than was necessary, I don't know what I expected.

Jimmy Durante

My mother had become friendly with a young woman in her neighborhood, whose husband was an associate producer on the *Eddie Fisher Show*. It was a one-hour variety show that alternated every week with *The George Gobel Show*. They were hit shows.

This family, Bernie and Margie Rich, became good friends to both my mother and me. They had a toddler the same age as Richie and Elizabeth. Margie had been a dancer and was Debbie Reynolds's best friend. So, with a little sleeve tugging, she was able to arrange an audition for me to join the chorus of one of the hottest TV shows—*Eddie Fisher*. The late fifties were the heyday of musical variety shows, both as specials ("spectaculars" they were called) and as weekly hour shows. Most of them were on NBC, and the broadcast studio in Burbank became my second home as that first show led to another.

Soon I was appearing on *The George Gobel Show* in its opening commercial spot. George would enter center stage, music up, audience cheering, and take a Chesterfield (the show's sponsor) from his pocket and place it in his mouth. Enter me—dressed in a glitzy, beaded leotard, heels so high it's amazing I didn't topple over. I "showgirl stepped" (a kind of knees high prance) over to him, carrying a four-foot-high cigarette lighter which serviced his need of the moment. It didn't take much rehearsing, but they would call me in for three days' work just because they liked me. They liked all the dancers.

Before long I found myself being used by the choreographers of most of the shows—Bob Hope, Dean Martin and Jerry Lewis, and Jimmy Durante. I always kept a high profile, hopeful of being given something extra to do—standing next to the star as a part of the glamor group that surrounded him when he sang a song, perhaps being given a line of dialogue, or a solo spot in one of the dance numbers. The potential could lead anywhere, if movie lore was to be believed. Most of the other girls seemed happy with their lot and didn't leap up, as I did, when the director said, "Okay, girls, we need someone to . . ."

I suppose it was gutsy, looking back on it, and perhaps even surprising, considering my confidence level. On the other hand, that kind of initiative was always part of me, in other ways. I've always been gutsy when I felt I was being dictated to, or when I've seen something really wrong.

I remember one situation when I was nine years old, having just arrived in California, that would change me. If it didn't change me, it certainly revealed a fearlessness I didn't know I possessed.

Having settled into the routine of a mostly uneventful walk home from school, I saw a man in an alley one day who was beating a dog with a big stick. Despite the dog's surrendering retreat, the man kept advancing, swinging wildly at the animal and connecting more often than not. "Stop it!" I screamed, but the deliberate cruelty continued amid snarling and cursing.

A rage suddenly boiled in me, leaving no space for thought, and I charged the man, beating and kicking him, punching him hard in the belly until he stumbled back and away from me, with a combination of disbelief and fear on his face. He took off into the dark recesses of the open-ended passageway, while I stooped down to embrace the object of my heroism. The dog wanted none of that mushy stuff. He did glance at me over his shoulder while he peed, and off he trotted.

From that moment on, I left behind my childish expectations of people and their innate goodness.

Once on a Jimmy Durante show, in which I was a chorus dancer, I placed myself in a difficult situation when we were asked if any of us spoke French. Naturally, I torpedoed myself front and center, beaming that it was the language I had studied in school. I didn't mention that it was high school, or that for four years straight I had been given Ds. I was handed a page from the script in which one of the girls (now me) would prance her way to Mr. Durante and exclaim in French over the handsomeness of his new beret. It was required that I write a speech to be about ten seconds long, all about the hat, and, of course, in FRENCH.

Bertie and Mom, both of whom had studied the language in college, could come up with no lyrical words of praise for the hat in this scene that, I was sure, would catapult me to stardom. So, I called Immaculate Heart and asked for that most disappointed linguist, my French teacher, Sister Gemma. I explained as truthfully as possible that I was so regretful of the lost opportunities in her class, and begged her for twenty ways to comment on a hat. I will always appreciate the kindness she extended to the girl who nearly made her cry with frustration in class.

It worked. And while there was no standing ovation, it was another bit of experience, another credit that could be exaggerated when needed.

During one rehearsal, Jimmy Durante asked us (there were six dancers) if we would help him out and consider being driven by chauffeur to the home of Dr. Stroub, who owned the Santa Anita Racetrack. We were to perform our number that night at a big party. "You'll be taken good care of, goils," he promised. Well, it sounded so glamourous and Mr. Durante was so sweet to us, always, no one could refuse him. Besides, it sounded unorthodox and exciting. "Dress nice, goils. The limos will pick you up at nine."

Mina Vaughn (another dancer) and I decided to share a ride just for safety. It was the first time I had ever been in that sleek black vehicle of the rich, and it was thrilling. When we drove through the gates of the Stroub home in Pasadena, and I took in the number of limos just like ours parked around the home that resembled a palace, my palms got a little sweaty. The house was immense, all white with a Mediterranean, multilevel, tiled roof. Fabulously dressed people wandered about, as if it were all normal.

The unsolved Black Dahlia murder case and stories of pretty girls found in lakes filled my head. There we were without escorts, brought to a lavish party in the middle of the night to entertain.

Could it be that there was a broader definition to this "performance"?

The guests ate dinner under a lavishly decorated tent brimming with flowers, something I had never seen before. We dancers dined in the kitchen, a room large enough to contain the two-bedroom apartment Dick and Richie and I now lived in.

It was show time. We were wrangled to an enclosure just off the small stage area. Jimmy Durante was introduced, and he performed his monologue and several songs. Then we were introduced and high-stepped our way to our positions surrounding Durante. The audience, as always, adored him. They were quite taken with our presence, too. There aren't many performers who bring six backups along for just one song.

When we finished we were asked to follow Dr. Stroub into the library of the house. There, he removed six crisp one-hundred-dollar bills from a silver box, and handed one to each of us along with his thanks.

I had never seen a hundred-dollar bill, much less held one that belonged to me. My pay for a week's work was $160.

On the way home, Mina said that she felt like an innocent hooker. She suggested that we go to her neighborhood hangout to celebrate this extraordinary event and I agreed. Why not pretend to be for one minute? We got some looks, but no one approached us as we sipped our Cokes. When the check came, I asked her to pay. I didn't want to let go of my talisman.

Dick was relieved to see me unsullied by the experience, and stunned by the money I had earned.

*A*lthough I was dancing in the chorus a lot and it was helping to pay the bills, it was also an ego cruncher. The directors and actors would laugh and flirt with dancers, but when the latter got in the way, they were told to sit in the corner and be quiet. Dancers generally live hand-to-mouth, the work is hard and underpaid, and they are thought of as charming, gifted monkeys. I crumbled because I couldn't stand being treated as one of the babbling herd. I still have a problem with that. Making a career of it would have killed me spiritually before it did physically (which happens in ten or fifteen years, anyway). That, plus the attention and consideration given to the stars fed my insecurity. A yearning for respect, more than a need for artistic fulfillment, drove me to seek an acting agent. His advice was to stop dancing. The caste system was too firmly rooted to try for both. Dancers cannot act, actors cannot dance, and that was the natural order of things.

So with an expensive book of eight-by-ten glossies and a biography that included not only my few real credits but also references to some plays that I had performed in Chicago with an obscure theater company, I made the rounds of casting agents' offices, and sometimes read for a specific part.

It wasn't easy to say no when I was offered "Gypsy" work (showbiz slang for chorus dancing), but I knew if I went back to dancing, my stargazing days would come to an abrupt end.

AT HOME

Aunt Bertie had been working with Dick, teaching him what he needed to know about television sales, so that he might take a turn off the narrow path he was following.

I admired the self-possessed men I was exposed to at work—the funny, articulate, successful men who commanded the conversation. I'm ashamed to admit that I carried their impressions home with me and allowed their bold colors to drain the vibrancy from the man who, without knowing it, was being assessed and found wanting.

If he'd stayed the man he'd been and not attempted the sophistication he probably wasn't meant to have, there might have been a less glaring difference between us. He referred to himself as a "food broker" instead of a salesman, which bothered me because I thought it was pompous. While it grated on me, I think it reflected on his own feeling of inadequacy as to what he did for a living.

I told no one in my family of our problems. I was raised to believe that life is supposed to be a certain way. I thought there must be something wrong with me if my marriage wasn't happy. I also didn't want them to know they were right in their original assessment of Dick. Of course, I would have opened up if he had been at fault. If it turned out he had been a wife-beater, the family would have come rushing to my defense.

But he'd entered my arena now and was no more comfortable fitting in than I'd have been in a hunting lodge. I blame myself for the pain I caused.

Sam

❧

ONE OF THE TOUGHEST adjustments a young actress faces is accepting rejection. During an interview you're selling yourself. You are your own product. Most of the time there are twenty or thirty others reading for the same part, and losing the sale is often to be expected. However, this can easily lead to a sense of inadequacy as a person. With time, it gets a bit clearer that you do not possess all the qualities that all the people want even some of the time.

But those early days of taking my eight-by-ten photos from casting office to producer's office were tough. I would always arrive smiling, wearing the most figure-revealing dress that propriety would permit, and more often than not walk away in disappointment. In retrospect, the fact that I was disappointed so much of the time was probably a tribute to the amount of interviews my agent arranged rather than an indictment of my sales technique.

I could play a pretty wide swing within the definition of ingenue. I could be vixen, the girl next door, or all business, saying, with tons of hidden value, "The doctor will see you now."

The producers and directors would evaluate me by asking chitchat kinds of questions about the weather, a current film, and so forth. And I, the auditionee, would respond "in character." I enjoyed the fake conversations these interviews required. You went in, you were charming or cute or sexy or very sad, and then you left. What are they looking for? Is it possible I can pretend to have it? Those same conversations in their real-life counterparts I hated.

I must be the only actress in Hollywood never to have had a pass made at her (or maybe I just didn't recognize one for what it was). I think we communicate how we expect to be treated personally even if auditioning to play a whore. Thinking back on it, I never did play a loose babe. What does that tell us?

I did commercials—cars, cigarettes, razor blades, the latter playing a checkout cashier to Rock Hudson's movie star buying "Gillette only, thank you."

The closest I came to playing a woman of questionable virtue was the character of "Sam," the sultry answering-service voice in the *Richard Diamond* detective series. She turned on every male viewer, and it wasn't with her smile. In fact, you never saw more than her legs, or the close reflection of her mouth in a compact mirror as she applied a deep red lipstick. As written, she was a master of the double entendre. As played, her voice was so sensual, so low, that the soundman had the final say on every take. She was a gimmick created to get a lot of good press, and throbbing letters from male viewers wanting more. It worked.

When I was signed to do the role it was for "scale," which at that time was eighty dollars a show. Since there was minimal camera coverage of my role, we could complete my part of an entire show in less than an hour. Sometimes, when they were prepared with advance scripts, we would do two or three episodes in a day and I would go home with two or three times eighty dollars.

There was great studio-generated hype about what this incredibly sexy-sounding dame looked like. Who was playing her? Back in the late fifties, television was so young that this kind of publicity could make a difference in a show's ratings. I was asked to re-

main silent on the issue, and not so happily I obliged. I understood
the point of the "mystery woman" aspect. And there was no way I
believed I could measure up to anyone's fantasy. Still, it gnawed at
me that I was never going to be able to build on this small achievement.

Sensing that there was an inequity here that needed righting, I
asked the producer if we could have a meeting about the money I
was getting for this big success that they were enjoying and I was
not. Without so much as a question asking how much more money
I wanted, the request for a meeting was denied. My agent was told
that since I was never seen anyway, I was easily replaced. And they
were right. After my thirteen episodes, no one detected the difference as another "Sam" slithered her way into the dimly lit close-
up of her left tit and whispered, "Hi, Mr. D."

The termination of the "Sam" experience had a nice benefit,
however. I was able to tell every casting agent in TV that I was Sam.
In turn, they were able to take advantage of this by casting me in
small parts, and then releasing blurbs to the press that if anyone
wanted to see what "Sam" looked like they could see her tonight
in *77 Sunset Strip* in the role of Pamela. Or in *Bourbon Street Beat* as
Sue.

I was getting a lot of work and the parts grew in size. Still, when
I watched the new "Sam," my proprietary hackles rose and I sneered
at what I saw as her inadequacies.

*D*ick continued to deliver and pick me up, as needed, while my
mother tended to Richie at her house. Our apartment was just a
few blocks away so I'd either bum a ride from someone or take a
taxi from the studio to her house if Dick couldn't be there. It gave
my mother and me some time to talk about the children as they
played together. It also restored the mother-daughter relationship
to its more natural dynamic—my mother the teacher to parent-in-
training, Mary. Watching those two angels separated in birth by only

three and a half months, it was strange to remember that Elizabeth was Richie's aunt, especially when she'd haul off and smack him one on the head if he displeased her. They would reach adulthood as brother and sister more than the aunt and nephew they, in fact, were. There was no preschool then as we know it now. Kids were simply kept out of danger, a kind of mass baby-sitting while their mothers held down jobs that were, in some cases, far from what could be called careers.

One day I got a call to read for the part of Danny Thomas's daughter (grown-up and returned from boarding school). I read with Danny himself and I thought it went well. Sheldon Leonard, his producer, laughed at some of the lines I spoke, and the expressions on the faces of writers, agents, sponsors, etc., seemed to confirm my sense of having done well. Over the next few weeks I was brought back to read again and again, until the choice was finally narrowed down to two of us.

An actress named Penney Parker got the job along with a useless section of my heart. I had come so close. Every time I'd read for the part it had worked. My disappointment was profound. It was Danny himself who braved telling me of the decision. He put his arm around my shoulder and said, "Don't ever doubt your talent. Here's the reason you didn't get the part—with a nose like yours, no one would believe you're my daughter." However, once again, in losing a job, something good was to happen.

A year later, unknown to me, when Danny Thomas, Carl Reiner and Sheldon Leonard were looking, so far in vain, for a TV wife for Dick Van Dyke's new series, it was Danny who said, "Who was the kid we liked so much last year, the one with the three names and the funny nose?" Eileen Brennan had been tentatively chosen to do it, and they were going to film the pilot in ten days. But Carl still felt there was something missing.

I had had an interview for a small part at Warner Bros. that morning which wasn't far from a friend's house. So I decided to have a cup of coffee with her, and called my agent to let him know where I was in case Warner called.

It had been a rough week. Every part I had read for was a no-go. I was variously too old, too scrubbed, too offbeat (which meant not pretty enough), too not good enough!

The Big Break

❧

$\mathcal{D}$RINKING MY COFFEE, I was well into a blow-by-blow of the week's rejections and savoring the resultant instant empathy from my friend when my agent phoned. He had just received a call from Danny Thomas's office. "They're looking for someone to play Dick Van Dyke's wife on a series he's producing with Carl Reiner. They want you to read with Reiner as soon as you can get over to Desilu-Cahuenga."

I felt as if the breath I had just taken had gone into my head instead of my lungs, feeling a dizziness that I imagine is the sensation just before fainting. I had a brief moment of recognition: this was mine, and it had come for me. But what I heard myself saying was, "I just can't take another rejection, especially not this one." I hung up and went looking for my friend's sympathetic shoulder but was met instead with "Are you crazy? Call your agent and get in the car."

On the way to the studio, I tried to imagine how I was going to maintain any adult, wifely composure while reading the script with the author himself, Carl Reiner. On *Your Show of Shows* he may have been Sid Caesar's straight man, but to me he was the closest thing to a sex symbol since my crush on Jerry Lewis.

❧

The inside of this studio lot was not very different from any other. But on this day, I was starring in my own movie. People seemed oddly good-looking, colorfully clothed, happy, all of them, and all of them happiest of all to see me. Strangers were giving me the thumbs-up sign. I could even hear "There's No Business Like Show Business" being fed to the lot through large speakers that were, yes, coming from my own chest. I took this ability to stand outside of myself and see the inappropriateness of the situation as a good sign. I'd do just fine!

I brought myself back to the practical matter of making my way through the door that said Calvada Productions, and the necessity of announcing myself to the young woman who sat at a desk. Feet back to floor, fade the music, tell her your name.

I was hardly through the door when Carl Reiner himself appeared before me, all cheery and warm and not at all scary. I don't remember what we talked about or for how long, but I knew I was with someone who understood how intimidating his presence could be. He did everything he could to make it painless.

Before I knew it, I found myself sitting on a metal chair opposite him, knees to knees, eyes moving from script to each other's face for all the world like we really were Rob and Laura Petrie. There was nothing on my mind now but convincing Rob that their son, Ritchie, was too sick for us to go out that evening. I actually noticed that the name was misspelled in the script. Well, I'd worry about that later.

We skipped ahead to the next big scene. When we were about halfway through it, he abruptly stopped and reached out his hand to the top of my head. He let it rest there for a moment and then said, "Come with me." I think he left his hand there, using it as a kind of rudder as he directed me down the hall into producer Sheldon Leonard's office, where he and my benefactor, Mr. Thomas, were waiting. They looked at Carl, who was beaming. It was clear that he was a happy man. He asked if I would read the first scene with him again.

It was six-thirty by the time I picked up Richie and got home. I was certain I had the part, but no one had actually said the words. My agent had left the office for the day. There were no answering machines in those days, so I didn't know if they had called my agent before they'd closed up shop. Everyone had gone home where they would likely sleep through the night, content with the day's events. But what about me?

It was afternoon of the next day before all the people who needed to had spoken to each other. The role was mine! They wanted to see me with Dick Van Dyke that afternoon, a formality. One other thing: they would like to see me on film, but the part was mine.

BUT . . . what if Dick Van Dyke didn't like me? Worse, what if their camera didn't?

Dick Van Dyke was a revelation, a comedian who didn't mind silence. I had spent enough time around comics in my chorus days to know that by constantly throwing "material" out they were able to reel in a few good ones to be stashed away for the act. When they're together in a room it is impossible. They are always laughing. Comedic courtesy. One colleague stroking another.

Dick was more like an actor, but without a measurable amount of ego or aloofness. He was warm, approachable, and open with his appreciation of my work. I liked him immediately in spite of myself.

The big screen test amounted to my standing in the middle of the living-room set. I was placed in back of the couch so there was something to do with my hands (a place to put them), while Carl stood off-camera and asked me questions. "Where did you grow up?" "What's been your professional experience?" I don't think they were looking for funny answers, which is good, but simply some reassurance that some horrible facial defect didn't suddenly materialize on screen. Though I didn't have the guts to protest the couch as a prop to aid me, I resented its presence. How were they going to see they had not only a fine actress, but also someone who could find things for her arms to do?

Dick Van Dyke, Rose Marie, Morey Amsterdam, Carl Reiner! Joining this group of comedy black belts was going to be tough, but I clung to the knowledge that unlike the rest of the cast I had a dramatic background. It was reassuring to remember that, and ignore from whence that experience came—quite mediocre TV. What a pain I must have been, smugly pointing out that some line that had gotten a big laugh in the reading was in conflict with a previously established character trait, making it a false laugh. Today, Carl kindly insists that I kept him honest.

Carl's original vision had most of the show based in the writer's office, with home scenes kept to a secondary level. This was a big change for situation comedies. In the past you were never really sure about just what it was that Daddy did for a living. Domesticity was the mainstay of television comedy.

This look at the character's—Rob Petrie's—work was also distinguished by revealing a behind-the-scenes view of writing for a variety show. It was generally considered bad form to reveal any of the magic that was show business. But Carl used his experiences as a writer on *The Sid Caesar Show* as the drawing board for building Rob Petrie and humanizing the television industry.

Carl had written the original pilot and first six episodes of what is now *The Dick Van Dyke Show* for himself as Rob. I don't think there's any question that Carl could have carried it. He would have been a less vulnerable Rob, and maybe that's why CBS urged him to continue the project but not as its star. At that time it was also thought that being Jewish, and expecting the greater TV audience to identify with that family, was asking too much. In 1961, everyone at CBS was challenged enough just dealing with the unexpected exploration of Rob's office life, without having to deal with cultural experimentation as well.

Nine years later, the network was still anxious about just how Jewish Lou Grant and Rhoda Morgenstern were going to turn out to be.

What a careful and restrained version of the Petries' life Carl had to write. And yet he broke ground in every area. If there was one thing the critics pointed to, it was the freshness of this show's style. Rob was a wonderful husband—well, as good as he could be, sleeping in obligatory twin beds. When we did the flashback stories of Ritchie's birth, the word "pregnant" was not allowed to be used. Come to think of it, it's amazing that Laura got pregnant at all, given the circumstances of the bed setup.

I immediately caused a stir in my style of dress. I wore pants. TV wives didn't do that. They wore full-skirted, floral-print dresses with high heels, even while vacuuming! My comedic insecurities pushed me to take a stand on something, and this seemed a reasonable issue. I may not have known jokes, but I knew what young wives were wearing. I was a young wife, and I wore pants.

Everyone I talked to agreed that it was appropriate—that's what their wives wore. But here again, television hadn't quite caught up with the times. And so it was, at my own suggestion, that in a long line of situation-comedy wives, I would be the first to disdain the costume of old and opt for what were then called Capri pants and flats.

It may not seem like much of a contribution to the evolution of women on television, but it became a cause célèbre. The sponsors objected to what could be considered a brazen look to all those circumspect buyers of the sponsor's—Procter & Gamble—products. It was resolved that I would wear these objects of sexual controversy in one scene only per episode. But I began to sneak them in here and there with Carl's blessing, after he promised the sponsors that my trousers wouldn't "cup under." After making that concession, he asked me what "cupping under" meant. I wasn't sure, but we figured it must be a rear-end issue. So we were careful about fit and camera angles for the first season. But once we'd established ourselves as a hit, the rear-end issue was applauded as a "firm" contributing factor.

Despite Carl's intention of showcasing an innovative look at the antics of comedy writing, the focus of the show ultimately veered toward the home life of Rob and Laura. The reviewers were enamored of these two nearly, actually, sexual beings who inhabited the television screen.

Almost as much as Carl's surprise was my own when one week I took a crying scene that he had written and made it funnier. I maneuvered and controlled the words and to my absolute delight, produced laughter!

It was an early episode in which Laura bleaches her hair blond because she thinks that Rob isn't excited by her anymore. After the deed is done, her friend, Millie, agrees with Laura that she is a better brunette. Desperately, she tries unsuccessfully to dye it back before Rob gets home. The result is a sobbing Laura with hair half blond and half brunette, who greets her bemused husband at the door and tries to explain all the imagined slights that drove her to this desperate act. I was very funny as I attempted my sobbing explanation through a clenched throat, which produced mangled speech, with eyes rolled up, and gulping for air.

It's powerful helping someone else get a laugh, standing next to him or her, helping to fill the time as you wait for the laugh to almost, but not completely, subside before speaking again. And then, knowing the audience is with you, you construct the foundation for the next one.

But it's God's own pleasure to get a laugh on stage for yourself, especially when the job is to feed straight lines to the star. It's a thrill, a feeling of completion. No one expected the role of Laura Petrie to be more than a cute straight man for Dick Van Dyke's genius. She was written with wit and bite, and for that distinction I was grateful.

"Blond-Haired Brunette" changed my working life. The writers began to test me further. Every episode gave me a few more funny moments to play with. And through all this evolution, Dick Van Dyke stood by, cheering my progress, giving me time to work things out for myself, and encouraging me to find the core within myself that would make the words mine.

Laura, as written, was a classy lady who had some thoughts of her own. However, my feeling of control, which was the result of this new dimension, added to her impact. I was a member, new, but still a member of the inner circle of comedians.

𝓛ucille Ball was our landlady at the studio, and would pay occasional and startling surprise calls on us, her tenants. We would be rehearsing when we would hear a laugh from an unexpected source—the catwalk above. This network of wooden bridges stretched high above the set and was intended for use by the lighting department. We would look up and there she'd be, as surprised that a laugh had escaped her as we were to hear it. There was no way of knowing how long she might have been watching before she betrayed her presence.

The first time she visited us we reacted like little kids who had been secretly monitored by the school principal. As she made her descent and walked to our quaking little mass, she smiled her unmistakable smile and extended her hand to us all, putting everyone at ease. She was effusive in her praise of the show, which had been on the air several weeks. She was surprisingly young-looking. She wore no makeup and had her hair covered with a scarf which added to her down-to-earth persona. The others laughed and chatted, but I was still speechless in her presence. She apologized for interrupting us, and moved toward the door, waving us back to our original rehearsal places. Then she stopped me briefly, not a full head-on stop, but enough to make the point, and said, "You're very good." Those words had a profound effect on me for their directness and simplicity. It made me feel that if important people were watching me, I had better be very, very good.

It was subconscious, but I can see now that I began adding just the hint of an impression of another idol, Katharine Hepburn, to my role. Looking at the show's first year, there is just a glimmer of Miss Hepburn, as I go about the business of interacting with Rob. I picked up her timing (which was good) and her refusal to pronounce the letter "r" (which was not). Darling, for me that year, was a brisk "dahling." Theater—"theatah," and so on. It is not obvious, but it is there if you look for it.

(My father never attended a Tracy-Hepburn movie after their first because of the whisperings of their alleged affair. That was enough for him! I wonder if my choosing her as an idol had anything to do with perversely taking a stand against Dad . . . Actually, I don't.)

As the show began to swing more and more to the home for its main stories and away from the writer's office, in equal proportion to my excitement was Rose Marie's disappointment. She was to have been the leading lady, if nothing else, by virtue of her billing. As a result, there developed between us a kind of trucelike work ethic. We were polite to each other, even if we didn't laugh at each other's work. I was very insecure with my newfound opportunity, and convinced that it might be taken away at any time were I not always on my toes. There was an ever-present wariness: two cats drawing a wide arc around each other. Today, Rosie and I can laugh about what then seemed to be life-threatening.

Laughter was a constant companion during the show's days of rehearsals. Whether it was the writing, or each other's contribution to that humor, or just life, we were constantly getting in trouble for having ruined a take on *Gomer Pyle*. Their soundstage was next door. Several times a week, their assistant director would come stomping onto our set to ask if we could please "hold down the laughter."

"Forever More,"
No More

❧

$\mathcal{D}$URING THE FIRST year of the show, as thrilled and bursting with the excitement over my work as I was, I was equally without emotion at home. What had begun sometime earlier as disinterest in sex had ripened into an absolute inability to engage in the physical part of my marriage. It may have been my mind's way of forcing an end to a marriage that was far from nurturing on my part. He was a good, kind, nice-looking, lovable man, a caring and involved father to Richie, and consistently supportive of me. But the fulfillment of an ultimatum never makes two people happy and seldom even one.

I felt so threatened by the heavy cloud that hung over us that I willfully denied its presence and bought a new house with the money and promise *The Dick Van Dyke Show* brought us.

One evening, after a very nasty argument, he stormed out of the house. But I think he believed I would cool down after a few days, and we'd be back together. From my point of view, it was over. It had played itself out.

Our son was devastated by his father's absence. He was now five years old. Already upset at having to leave the familiar environment

❧

of my mother and Elizabeth's surroundings, a new school added to his sense of disorder and fear.

One night about a week after Dick had moved out, Richie broke down as I tucked him in. He wept as he hadn't since he was a baby, saying, "I want my daddy home." His pain was so real, so huge, I found myself reacting to him as a fiercely protective mother. I drew his racked little body into my arms and said, "I'll get him. He's coming home now."

As soon as he quieted down, I went to the phone and called Dick at a friend's house where he was staying and said, "Dick, please come home. I want to try again."

But his voice could barely conceal the satisfaction he felt as he denied my earnest plea, saying, "If you like, maybe we can have dinner sometime, but I don't think I should come home." Whoever had counseled him on this tactic of negotiating a separation or reconciliation inadvertently gave me the necessary time to think it through before bringing Richie's father home to an unwilling wife.

Dick made a reservation for us to have dinner at the Bel-Air Hotel, a restaurant we could ill afford. He ordered the most expensive items on the menu for us both. A special bouquet at the center of the table had been prearranged, and wine was served, something we never drank. He was making a lot of eye contact, with lowered lids, but I could anticipate the reaction I would have, had I returned the gaze and gone the distance.

It was over for me. The eighteen-year-old I'd been when we were married was fading from view. If I didn't make him see that change, the process of my evolution would have been just that much harder for us all later on.

Our house was next door to Bertie and Grandma's on a tree-lined street in Studio City, California. Bertie had lent us the money for the down payment. Could she have known how tenuous our marriage was? Did she have some prescience of things to come, that led to the location of our house being where I needed us to be in order to survive? Their proximity was a godsend. Grandma was there to pick up Richie at school around the corner when I didn't make it home from rehearsals in time. And if a fuse blew or there was some other minor equipment malfunction, Bertie was there to fix it.

Richie began to do badly in school at about the time of the marital breakup. Why did that surprise me? Was I so unable to grasp the effect the loss would have on him? His report card described a lack of attention to work, and a need to be the class clown. Today, I realize his behavior was only natural. I am a comedian, and I have had great sadness in my life: a withholding father, a mother bouncing off doorjambs, early deaths. Comedians bring themselves out of sadness through humor. There is also a bid for attention from the comedian: love me, love me, laugh, show me you love me. A laugh is tangible.

Not believing in himself, not trusting other people because he couldn't even trust his mother to be there for him, how could Richie trust a teacher to lead him? There is no question about it— by the time Richie was five, I had already let him down. But back then it never occurred to me to get some counseling for him, or for myself. Counseling I saw as a last resort measure for the self-indulgent or the very ill. All that was needed here, I thought, were some serious talks about the importance of college and the necessity of preparing for it in the first grade.

At a period when he needed me the most, I was busier and even more self-concerned than I had been when he was an impressionable infant. I took Richie's school trouble personally. I felt that he was, for some reason, punishing me and that he could change if he really loved and respected me.

*L*ooking back on that marriage, I'm amazed at how little I can recall today of those six years. They are not even a blur, really. Of what we did on weekends, for example, I have no memory, except once we went rock-climbing at Point Dune, and I fell and cut the side of my head.

I'm sure that what we ate is blanked out because it was so boring. For dinner I would dish up hamburgers or maybe a steak, a frozen vegetable, and a baked potato (after I had learned to prick holes in them to prevent their exploding). Dessert would be something from Pepperidge Farm, which I would heat up. Our home became just another dwelling, that's all—a place to live. And Dick was a very kind and loving hotel manager.

God, what else did we do?

There should have been a period of mourning, a time to feel the absence that exists when three become two. Aside from the fact that Dick's departure was causing Richie pain, and *his* suffering caused my pain, I didn't miss Dick Meeker in my daily life. I was never aware of the vacancy his absence created. My life was so filled with *The Dick Van Dyke Show,* filled with brilliant people, satisfying creative work, I was validating myself. It filled up all the space so that there was none left for considering the loss.

Lancelot

❧

I WISH I HAD GONE
beyond the loneliness I sometimes felt and taken a look at myself before grasping the very good-looking hand that Grant A. Tinker extended. It pulled me to him with violins playing in the background,
which was a good trick because the earth was trembling, too.

He was handsome and charming, witty and educated. At the
time, 1961, Grant was an account executive with Benton & Bowles,
the advertising agency that represented Procter & Gamble. So he
was in a power seat, too. What could have been more irresistible
to an insecure, career-obsessed daddy-seeker? Being eleven years my
senior was almost too good to be true in fulfilling the latter hunger.
He filled all those empty places that were my father's legacy—his
reserve and wit. At last, someone to tell me what to do about—anything!

I am told that we first met during the filming of the *Van Dyke*
pilot, but I was so focused on the show, and the high it produced,
I don't remember meeting anyone. He made brief appearances on
the set from time to time, but as soon as it was noted in a newspaper column that my marriage had ended, he reintroduced himself.
He said he was sorry to learn of the breakup of my marriage, and

asked if I would care to go out to dinner with him. I demurred, saying that I thought some time should elapse before I "saw" anyone. He said he understood and wished me well. He almost made it to the door, when, without missing a step (a kind of slow turn), he came back and said, "I've been given a friend's house in Palm Springs for the weekend. Do you want to go?"

I didn't. I didn't go. I did want to, and thought wistfully about how that weekend might have played.

A few days later, I was asked by the publicist on *The Dick Van Dyke Show* if I could swing through New York during our next hiatus from filming to talk with some of the TV editors. It had been suggested, it turned out, by Mr. Tinker.

Mr. Tinker called, delighted to hear that I would soon be coming to New York, and to suggest that we have dinner and see the new Broadway hit *How to Succeed in Business Without Really Trying*.

We fell in love that night, and committed ourselves to each other. We talked about how soon we could settle our separate lives so that we could get married. Just as I was in a potentially compromising situation, so was he. His marriage to the mother of his four children was over. He had moved to a small apartment and was trying to handle the divorce and separation from his children with as little turmoil as possible.

Grant had just been offered a job in programming at NBC, and he was thrilled. He'd dreamed of being in programming someday. However, it involved his living on the East Coast, so we had some geographic obstacles to overcome. Visions of a Noel Coward marriage danced in my head. He, a successful programmer for television; me, a rising star in the medium that seemed to be embracing me. I truly had a premonition that evening of what we were eventually perceived to be. I even said to him at the time, "I bet we're going to be television's golden couple."

What I didn't see then was how empty the relationship would eventually become.

During the next six months, we worked out some of the difficulties our professional lives seemed to impose on our love. Amazingly, we did it long-distance.

Grant was happy to have Richie in his life. I think it eased his guilt about not being an active father to his own four in Connecticut. Richie was open to Grant, too, as best he could be. Grant had the same expectations of his children that he had for himself, leaving little room for failure. Richie was almost always falling short. Still he loved Grant, and saw him as a fair and kind person who loved him back. Somehow Richie was able to accept change without fear.

Their first meeting was a real test. Grant came to the house to take us for a drive to the beach. And as this game five-year-old was getting into the car, Grant accidentally slammed the door on his small fingers. This from the man Richie was pretty sure would make it impossible for his dad to return. My son always got high marks for his faith in people.

Over the seventeen years we were to be together, Grant's children were a sometimes long-distance part of my life, but often visited. When their father left and moved from New York to Los Angeles to marry Dick Van Dyke's television wife, Mark was ten, Michael almost nine, his daughter, Jodie, eight, and John, little more than a babe at four. It's a tribute to their mother that they remained trusting of their father and willing to believe that the toes of my shoes didn't curl up into points at night.

The five kids were seldom together all at once, but in packets of twos and threes they came to know Richie. As long as nobody touched anybody else's stuff, resentments were minimal. They grew to be fond of each other and it wasn't long before they were comfortable enough to fondly refer to me as "the wicked stepmother."

Mark and John lived with us and went to school in Los Angeles for a couple of years. Every time one of them left us to return to his mother, Richie would feel the loss of a newfound brother.

Both Mark and John still keep in touch with me, and though I don't see Michael and Jodie, I manage to keep tabs on how they are and what they're doing.

. . .

$\mathcal{B}$efore Grant and I wed, Richie and I had dinner with Bertie and Grandma most nights. As a result, there was in my kitchen the stuff of which breakfast is made and that was about all. After one evening out, early in our courtship, Grant opened my refrigerator door looking for a Coke, which he found along with a half a quart of milk and three eggs. "Geez, that's great!" he said. "What is?" I asked. "It's empty. I really like that."

The rest of my family was thrilled with Grant. Finally, a sophisticated, successful, well-educated man. My father was not too pleased with the idea of a second marriage. In referring to the impending mortal sin, and the subsequent eternal condemnation, he said only, "Rather you than me, kid."

Something Old,
Something Fur

❧

THERE WAS NO QUES-
tion in my mind that our love was meant to be, and that it would
be forever. And so, on June 1, 1962, we were married. Because of
some questions as to whether or not the state of California would
recognize our divorces, his in Alabama, mine in a small village in
Mexico, we had to swallow our pride and take our vows in Las
Vegas, Nevada. We further degraded the event by allowing a well-
meaning friend to talk us into borrowing the living room of a posh
suite owned by a local furrier at the now imploded Dunes Hotel.
Said furrier used it only occasionally and at that, only the bedroom.
Since privacy was a priority and it simply hadn't occurred to us to
arrange for our own suite, we gratefully accepted the offer.

While Grant waited in the living room with our attendants (old
friends of his who had flown in with us), I ducked into the bedroom to change into my wedding costume, a dark blue silk. The
room contained, instead of furniture, racks of furs—mink, sable,
possibly a wolverine or two.

Suddenly, the door from the hall to the bedroom flew open, and
the fiftyish, balding, very tan owner of the suite entered. He ap-

peared to be gripped by the first stage of a heart attack at seeing me. I leapt for cover behind my furry headless companions and shouted my name, lest he pull a gun.

"Ah, yes, of course, I remember. Well, *mazel tov* to you. I'll just be a moment—not to get in your way—some papers I'm looking for. Please, go on." He then began going through drawers, looking in and under boxes, paying no attention to me but reminiscing about Morey Amsterdam and creating havoc in his search. Since the rack of lynx provided adequate coverage for maintaining modesty, I continued my attempts at a wedding-day metamorphosis. "The judge is here, Missy," came Grant's voice through the door. There was no mirror in the room so I made a guess about the placement of my little white hat and veil and left my still chattering, still searching host and shut the door.

As I stepped to Grant's side, I realized I'd left my small bouquet behind, and excused myself to the judge, who was checking his watch. Back in the bedroom, the host abandoned his own search to try to help me find my flowers, which were nowhere in view. Thanking him for everything, I gave it up and reentered the nuptial interruptus. Fortunately, they had waited for me. So, damn the bouquet, let the wedding begin!

The words the judge spoke were moving and appropriate for two people engaged in the pressure-filled world of show business. He talked of supporting each other, whether or not a fickle public continued to add glamor to our blessed life together. He referred to the one path we would travel hand in hand.

A knock from the bedroom door alerted us to the crouched, furtive entrance of the furrier. He darted to where we were standing, mumbled an apology, and pushed the elusive bouquet into my hands. He then retreated as quickly as he'd appeared, and we continued with our little ceremony. After a few more words, the judge pronounced us "done." We kissed and left to get the next plane back to Los Angeles.

Several weeks later, recalling with fondness and pride the words of the man who married us, Grant wrote and asked if he would send us a copy of his very special words. He responded immediately saying he was so pleased that we liked the ceremony. "I wrote those lines for Nancy Sinatra and Hugh Lambert just a few weeks earlier for *their* wedding."

That Old Gang
of Mine

❧

*F*ROM THE WARM RE-
ception they gave to the announcement of my new name, Mary Tyler
Moore Meeker Tinker, the collective wives who hovered on the
outskirts of the *Dick Van Dyke* stage seemed to breathe a collective sigh
of relief—my six months of freedom having suggested a potential
threat, I guess. Marge Van Dyke was particularly touching, as she shared
with me her fear of my running off with her husband. She said she
felt threatened by those Capri pants or, rather, by the way they were
being worn. Nothing could have surprised me more. She was a whole-
some beauty with green eyes, the mother of their three children. They
had been childhood sweethearts. I thought true love endured.

Throughout *Van Dyke, The Mary Tyler Moore Show,* and beyond,
I've always enjoyed a comfortable relationship with women. Many
identified with me and have been influenced dramatically by my
roles. I am often told, "My husband is in love with you, but it's
okay." Of course, the person they are talking to is no longer living
in the same time frame as was the object of their husband's affection. But even back in real time, when the show and my life were
in sync, I never posed much of a threat. Except for the Capri pants,
I never calculated how to be sexy.

❧

$\mathcal{I}$t's hard to get close to Dick Van Dyke. He will give you his opinions and articulate them with candor and charm, but only a few people have been able to penetrate the facade. His personal assistant of fourteen years, Frank Adamo, the man who kept his appointment book for him, and drove his children to school, etc., never saw his boss lose his temper or say something unkind in all that time. In spite of having been exposed to his generosity and brilliance under pretty intimate circumstances throughout the thirty years we have known each other, I don't know the man much better than I did that first year.

Dick and I had side-by-side canvas dressing rooms on the stage, which we'd go to after makeup to dress and relax before filming began. Family, agents, writers with last-minute notes, would stop by for a few minutes to chat. I could hear every word spoken in his little cloth cell. This was to happen often, but the first time I was aware of it I was surprised: several people had stopped by briefly, each one of whom was greeted by Dick with the same words and in the same tone of voice, "Hi! How are ya?", slight lilting on the word "are." The last in the series of four turned out to be his wife, Marge. I wonder how difficult it was to live with a man who smiled back at you through a protective coating.

The seemingly uncomplicated all-around good guy that is Dick Van Dyke is also a genius. Despite his lack of ego and paranoia, the usual requirements for cultivating genius, he produced, with no obvious effort, the most ingenious array of amusements.

His pantomimes of a man walking a multidirectionally determined dog; the half man/half woman; or the drunken husband unable to stand or speak until his disapproving wife appears and then, suddenly, from sheer force of will, is able to carry on in perfect control until she turns her back again (the sequence occurring more and more rapidly until ultimately, she leaves the room and he passes out); and so many other sketches all came from his own invention. He never had a dancing lesson but danced, and he could do remarkable sleight-of-hand tricks. Being a self-taught pianist, to boot, he played Bach fugues.

My favorite Dick Van Dyke invention is very short: he sits on a chair and announces quite properly, "A Medley of Socially Offensive Noises," then at a pace he emits the following sounds—a cough, sneeze, hiccup, belch, and then, ever so slightly he raises one hip.

Occasionally, Dick would opt for a nap on one of those twin beds instead of lunch. An empty cavernous soundstage can be a remarkably cozy place. Soundless but for the reassuring puttering in the prop room, which recalls the familiar presence of Mother or Grandma in the kitchen, it restored body and mind.

Lunch hour over, the rest of us would gather outside the stage, forming a twenty- or thirty-person posse, and tiptoe to the set, where we'd silently surround his sleeping form. And there we would wait, staring at him until sometimes five or ten minutes later when he would open his eyes and bolt upward with shock, his heart racing with fear and confusion at the sight of us. We loved that.

*W*e had lunch most days in the so-called commissary on the lot. What a joke it was. The food was of the lard and white-bread variety and about as hygienically prepared as you might imagine a dinner in Tijuana! It was a hole-in-the-wall kind of a place that catered to the people who worked on that lot, but also advertised the fact with a large sign on the street—DINE WITH THE STARS it screamed at all who passed by.

Most people decided the health risk was too great, even for the chance to interrupt Danny Thomas, with a mouthful of cheeseburger, for an autograph. We were a little like zoo animals, tolerating the constant scrutiny of the public when they *did* join us. I pretended great impatience with these interruptions for autographs, as did my seniors, but secretly I loved it. What the hell, success is fun.

When there are six or seven regular cast members in a weekly show, not only is it necessary to create original scripts that make the viewers laugh, cry, or argue the stance, but each member of the cast must be featured from time to time. Not only does the audience want to see the underbelly of a particular character, but the actor's ego demands it. It keeps peace on the set, too.

I was eagerly awaiting the script that Carl had been alluding to without detail for weeks. I would be not only the focal point in that episode, but the fulfillment of several of the writers' fantasies as well, I was told. It was something so special that he wouldn't elaborate. I could hardly wait!

When, three weeks later, we sat around the table to read through the long-awaited script, my great expectations were dashed. It called for Laura (me) to be off-camera for much of the show, with my toe stuck in the faucet of a bathtub. While Rob Petrie (Dick) alternately tried to calm me and break down the locked door, I remained *off-camera*. It might just as well have been radio as far as I was concerned.

I was in the throes of nicotine withdrawal. I had stopped my two-pack-a-day habit that morning. After the reading, I did something I'd never done, and loathe in others who so indulge themselves. I "walked off the set," that is to say I stomped into my canvas dressing room and slammed its fabric door. Not very effective or satisfying, but a statement. Dick's assistant, Frank Adamo, rapped gently on the door (which didn't make very much of a sound), opened it, and passed through a drink. I think it was brandy, and that it was still morning, but I drank it anyway.

Remembering the words "The play's the thing," I placed my tail firmly between my legs and slinked to the set. For the rest of the day, I gave a good impression of an unwilling actress going through the "moves." Well, it was a start. It wasn't until Carl called me at home that night to reaffirm his belief in the script and the positive impact it would have for me that I reminded myself, as I drew deeply and with great pleasure on a Kent, how freaking lucky I was to have a script at all.

I continue to hear from industry people and fans alike how impressive I was in that episode. Not so long ago, I gave Carl a token of that, now, humorous memory. I found an enormous brass faucet in an antique shop, which I had mounted on a plaque that contains an engraved inscription. But if you want to know what it says you will have to contact Carl.

The Dick Van Dyke Show's prop room was a twelve-by-twelve kitchen/storeroom with shelves that contained everything from a Parcheesi set to a first-aid kit and all the twenty-seven thousand other things one can think of that might be required for a particular scene. An oilcloth-covered table held a radio that looked like a relic from the forties. It was a cozy place. Glen Ross and Jimmy Trainor, the property masters, supplied all the general stuff needed to make the Petries' house look the way our director, John Rich, saw it. They made the office set a functioning place of work—typewriter, legitimate-looking papers inside a filing cabinet, notepads, ashtrays. They also had edible food for either set when that was needed. They could create, through their magic, the most unlikely items, such as a lady's brooch in the shape of the United States, with gemstones to mark certain cities. This monstrosity was needed in a story about an heirloom that Rob gives Laura, much to her dismay.

It was their design and hand packing that also produced, on cue, the self-inflating life raft that brought Laura's snooping days to an embarrassing end.

Looking for all the world like Laurel and Hardy and bickering with each other in much the same manner, this duo became loving uncles to the actors, protectively defending us (albeit under their breath) should one of us be singled out for criticism by anyone.

Each week we gathered to read a new script around the long worktable that stood between the set and the bleachers. It was flanked by two imperatives, the telephone at one end and at the other the coffee machine, which gurgled and hissed its readiness to contribute to the work all day long.

Glen and Jimmy would scurry between their prop room and the worktable with our necessities—pencils, extra scripts for those who'd lost track of the ones they'd been given at the start of the week on Wednesday, gum, the trade papers, ashtrays, and a fresh pack of each one's favorite brand of cigarettes. We all smoked except for Morey Amsterdam (wasn't he the smartest one of all?), and we smoked a lot.

Kent had become a sponsor of the show, which saved us from a threatened cancellation that year. We were all grateful for their having come to our rescue, but not enough to outweigh our commitment to personal choice. P. Lorillard sent each of us two cartons of Kent a week, which we immediately had our husbands or wives or aides exchange for our regular brands at the store. Having filmed commercials for Kent, it would hardly do for any of the cast to make the switch in person.

Rehearsals started at ten, but that actually was the gathering hour. By the time we finished the small talk it was ten forty-five, and Morey was just arriving, so we could start.

Mid-week, Dick and I would be still carrying our scripts as we walked through the scenes we'd blocked a day earlier. Then a run-through for the writers would be held that afternoon so that the final rewrites could be made and then memorized by the cast over the weekend. Dick and I were usually familiar enough with our lines so that our eyes could leave the pages and meet, triggering, as it often did, a fit of giggling. It was sometimes simultaneous, and at other times I would look at him, thinking he was about to laugh. I'd give in and go with it, only to realize his mind was behaving itself. But that would be all he'd need to start thinking about breaking up, which would set him off shortly thereafter.

One day, as we were in this normal rehearsal routine, Glen uncharacteristically walked up to our director, John, as he stood watching us make fools of ourselves and said something in his ear. John
said, "What?" to which Glen replied, ". . . just now, on the radio."
"Kennedy's been shot," John announced. "Thank God!" I quipped.

As soon as I said it, I was ashamed of the thoughtless instinct to
make a joke. The atmosphere on our set was in part made up of
rapid-fire one-liner knee-jerk responses to anything. I will never forget hearing myself say that. I have often wondered if anyone on the
set heard, too. I pray not. It would have been intolerable when a
half hour later he was pronounced dead, and sorrow vied with
anger for primacy.

The TV had been turned on in the prop room and we gathered
around it to listen to the bulletins and try to understand what we
were hearing. The unthinkable ending came when the man who had
always made the news a little easier to take, Walter Cronkite, failed
us this time and said, "From Dallas, Texas, the flash apparently official. President Kennedy died at one p.m. Central Standard Time, two
o'clock Eastern Standard Time, some thirty-eight minutes ago."

We disbanded without anyone saying, "There will be no further
work today." We just silently followed our instincts to seek the security of our nests in the face of this unfathomable atrocity. I think
it was a fairly common reaction. There was no official directive for
offices and schools to close. They just did.

Richie opened our front door, saying, "Mom, what happened?"
I gave up trying to be properly reassuring and wept with him.

When Grant got home the three of us began a four-day vigil with
the rest of the nation, the montage of Mrs. Kennedy so stoic as John-
son was sworn in, her blood-stained pink suit, John-John saluting
his father's coffin, the riderless horse, watching the incredible shooting of Lee Harvey Oswald, going about the routine of eating, sleeping, bathing, and then returning to the television set which seemed

to remind us that the world was continuing even as we watched a part of it curl up and die.

We would never be the same again as a nation, or individually, but we did manage to return to school, work, watch soap operas, do crossword puzzles, and argue over parking spaces.

Back on the set, we still had a show to be filmed, and an airdate to meet. For the first time, we shot on an empty stage with no audience to react to us. It was too soon to expect laughter, and so we guessed where the laughs were, waiting a beat or two for the laughs that would be created in postproduction. The silence that surrounded us, as we said and did the funny things that were a part of that script, was eerie.

I suppose every age has its moment during which innocence is lost. The assassination of John F. Kennedy spanned a longer time frame for everyone as the single most destructive blow to our country.

Nuts!

❧

$\mathcal{T}$HE EPISODE IN WHICH
Rob dreams we've been invaded by aliens from the planet Twilo,
creatures with four eyes who subsist on walnuts and steal your sense
of humor along with your thumbs, ranks high among the audience's
all-time favorites. The cast loved it, too, because it allowed us to do
some science-fiction bad acting in the roles of newly converted followers of Kolak (played by Danny Thomas), the evil ruler of Twilo
and Rob's antagonist.

No one knows it's a dream until the final scene when Rob opens
the coat closet by the front door and is knocked to the floor by a
thundering avalanche of walnuts, with me sliding down its seven-
foot slope. It had a gasp-producing effect on the studio audience and
the cast and crew as well.

Jerry Paris, who played our neighbor, Jerry Helper, was the director that week. While he knew where the comedy was and how
to make the most of it, he didn't have an idea how to make this visual stunt a reality. It was not the kind of setup that had precedent
or guidelines.

The first problem was finding a source for a half ton of walnuts.
Glen and Jimmy never disappointed us, and by day two of rehearsals

❧

they had an enormous truckful of walnuts backed up to Stage Eight, looking for a bowl. The triumph, from the producer's point of view, was that, instead of having to buy them, they were rented nuts.

A three-sided, seven-foot box was built against the back of the closet door into which would be poured one thousand pounds of walnuts. Because of the time and manpower required to collect the nuts after their release, a full-scale rehearsal was out of the question. A lot of guessing and praying had to suffice.

The first practical difficulty they found was that even with the closet only half filled, the pressure on the door was so great that Dick was unable to turn the knob. So a special slide bolt maneuvered off-stage was designed to be pulled in perfect synchronization with Dick's action at the time of release.

When Dick opened the closet, what would happen as the force of the rushing nuts at seven feet high showered down on him? we wondered. Would they slide and disperse at his feet or smack him in the face? This was a physics problem that was not easily answered. Every time we got to that point in the rehearsal, Dick would open the door to the empty closet, and Jerry would say, "Cue the nuts and nuts, nuts, nuts, nuts, nuts, nuts. Cue Mary," and I'd walk in and lie down on the floor.

During the week, we kept reassuring each other that it would work smoothly and kept munching away at the ever-present walnuts that were scattered all over the set, indicating the aliens' presence in the office, kitchen, bedroom, people's pockets. They were everywhere, and so we kept eating them, despite the plaintive reminders from Glen and Jimmy that they were rental nuts and had to be returned. The air was pierced with the sound of cracking shells. People were massaging the heels of their hands bruised from the constant crushing. Walnut shells were overflowing the ashtrays and could even be found on the sinks in the rest rooms.

By Monday night, we all had indigestion and were gaseous from the excessive diet of walnuts.

Tension was building as zero hour approached, everybody wearing those falsely encouraging faces that flight attendants put on during severe turbulence.

Rob enters the empty living room, calling to Laura. He checks the kitchen and bedroom and then crosses the stage toward the closet. A final "Laura" was the cue upon which all action would commence: Dick turns handle of door. Glen and Jimmy pull the bolt in back. Two men on ladders pull a canvas flap, releasing the torrent of walnuts. Two seconds later, a side door halfway down the seven-and-a-half-foot chute slides open, and I do a swan dive onto the still dissipating nuts, and glide to the floor safely on my belly. So proud of our combined efforts and my bravery in particular was I, that I managed to end chin on hand, one foot in the air at a jaunty angle.

The most exquisite timing of the whole business was the roar of the audience which covered the tiny freep unmistakably heard from my general direction—the sound that spelled relief.

Movin' on Up

❧

$\mathcal{T}$HE SHOW COLLECTED
a number of nominations for, and winning of, Emmys in its first
season, 1961. That freshman year saw John Rich nominated for Best
Director and Carl Reiner win for Outstanding Writing Achievement in Comedy.

I began to realize that this was something very special, this work.
It was more than a regular job (actually, I never thought of the parts
I played as jobs, rather like honors bestowed).

The *Van Dyke* series became a phenomenon in television—successful and meritorious. The producers had made me what seemed
a fair deal at the time, but I now wanted my payment adjusted to
more fairly reflect my contribution. (Isn't it amazing how one
minute you will work for nothing but the honor, crying yourself
to sleep for want of expression, and the next you are keeping score?)
Well, we all do it, and one day it would be done unto me as MTM
chairman by fledgling series stars.

When I signed my *Dick Van Dyke Show* contract it had been for
scale. But because Screen Actors Guild had by then raised the minimum, I was now earning $450 per show. I was being represented
by the William Morris Agency then, who also represented Shel-

don Leonard, Danny Thomas, Carl Reiner, and Dick Van Dyke, as well as collecting a commission for having put the package together. So it was with less than the expected enthusiasm that my agent approached the big guys at the agency and came back to me with "We can't afford to give you more money." It is now against the law for an agency to represent both the show and the actors. Had it not been for some coaching from Grant in what to say directly to Sheldon and Carl, I would have been pulling down $2,000 a show in its final year. That's a decent amount of money, especially for the sixties, but other actors in comparable roles were being paid that amount for their first year, plus a percentage of ownership as well.

I got a slight adjustment, with improved escalations yearly. Richie was going to private school, Grant and I had bought a larger house with a pool, and I was buying my pants at Jax. Jax was the first store in Beverly Hills to carry classically casual, designer-look ready-to-wear. Jack Hanson, its owner, created the sought-after look in suits and dresses, too, but it was the cut of the pants that everyone went mad for. And you had to be mad to pay those prices! Wow! $12.95 for cotton pants with a lining, $24 something for pants and matching jacket! Some really rich people would actually spring for $150 to sashay through an important party in a Jax dress with matching jacket. It was considered an investment in futures.

It was very sad for me, and any number of long-legged types, when, after converting us to the Jax uniform he got tired of it all and closed shop. The women of Beverly Hills have yet to find an equal to the fresh and sexy look of what was then a talisman of understated chic.

In the second year, Dick and I were also nominated for Emmys. Flush with success and high hopes, I attended the ceremony wearing a long, silk Jax gown. I lost to the star of *Hazel,* Shirley Booth, which seemed appropriate, if disappointing.

Our show won Outstanding Program Achievement in the Field of Humor. And though it is better to personally feel that cool metal in the palm of the hand, we all took a little of the credit in our minds, knowing it was award-winning work we were doing.

The following year, 1964, was a triumphant Emmy sweep—Best Show, Writing, Directing (Jerry Paris), Dick, and me.

Tears welled up, making it impossible to speak. They were the release of all the hurts, slights, and failures I'd encountered on the way. Winning that Emmy was the equivalent of a momentary breakthrough with a psychiatrist. Unfortunately, it had no long-term benefits. Through the years, subsequent awards have produced the same catharsis, but I always return to my normal insecure self within hours. For the moment, though, it sure feels good to stand there and accept that huge compliment.

I wonder if, at this point in my life, insecurity hasn't morphed into a stance of self-defense—if I admit I'm a fake, it won't hurt so much when someone finally declares it to the world.

Rob Reiner, later the co-creator of the density that was "Meat-head" in *All in the Family,* and who was to become the gifted director of such movies as *This Is Spinal Tap, Stand By Me, The Princess Bride, Misery,* and *A Few Good Men,* was, at one point, a rather lost-looking, kind of hunched-up twelve-year-old. His father, Carl, allowed him to hang around the set of *The Dick Van Dyke Show* when school was out. He was quiet and wore a serious face, but if you looked closely, you could see a jester peeking out at you.

I was still in my Kate Hepburn mode, demanding respect with my every gesture and word. This hauteur now invaded my off-camera personality, as well.

I don't know what got into this usually shy and retiring boy— some unpredictable hormonal eruption in the boy-to-man process, I suppose. But one day, as he passed me backstage, he reached out and swatted my behind, saying, "Hiya." I, of course, being ever the lady, and having no way of predicting the power seat he would hold later on, told his father on him.

Carl called him into his office and asked if he had, in fact, committed this crime against gentility. When Rob hung his head and nodded his confession, Carl just smiled at him and said, "Well, don't do it again."

At this writing, I feel like an ancient lady of the night recalling with pride and affection the transition she facilitated for a man of greatness.

Millie

✦

FIVE YEARS SEEMED
like a good long run for the *Van Dyke Show*. Remember in the sixties a series produced thirty-two to thirty-six episodes each season
as opposed to the eighteen to twenty-two of the nineties.

We were pretty much "talent-to-watch" now and as such, those
only-dreamed-of opportunities were now a definite "could-be."
Movies and Broadway were the new frontier.

Dick had already begun to enter that larger-than-television world
with the success of *Mary Poppins,* and now Universal Studios had a
multipicture contract for me!

It was with the same feelings that one leaves home to go into the
world that we said good-bye. Boy, it hurt as those ties pulled at the
hearts of everyone from writers and actors to those dear propmen.

It was time, though.

Grant and I were blissfully writing our own real-life saga, "The
Golden Couple at Work," while Richie coped with writer's block.
I wonder if he resented that perfectly "always there" mother I portrayed. My recollection is that he grew up thinking everyone's
mother had a television show, and he just wasn't impressed with
mine one way or the other.

To quote Lew Wasserman (still chairman of Universal Studios as he was then) I was to be the next Doris Day. Fine with me! I wasn't enough tuned-in to know that you are not supposed to be the next anyone. You are yourself. I should have known it, and more important, the people making the movies should have.

My first assignment was to play the intriguingly vapid Miss Dorothy in the movie *Thoroughly Modern Millie*. When Julie Andrews was tagged for "Millie," Universal wisely started writing songs and adding dances to what was originally a straight comedy. While we were already shooting, it became a musical. I saw the part of "Miss Dorothy" with me in the role as a good example of miscasting. It was expedient, I thought, for Universal to use me since I was already on the payroll and somewhat well known. However, I thought of myself as an exuberant, spirited type, not the shy, well-mannered (to the point of being insensitive) rich girl opposite Julie Andrews, Carol Channing, and Bea Lillie. Creating a new character was not then in my repertoire. Today, it's the whole point.

George Roy Hill, the director, agreed with me but the studio had apparently forced me on him. And with so many give-and-take arguments with the producer to deal with, George caved.

We met for lunch, George and I, in the studio commissary, where a huge photograph of me graced the walls along with many of its other stars both past and present. George said that he, too, was unhappy with the situation, but was willing to work toward making this character real for me and right for him. I said, "Let's do it."

But I lacked an approach to that task, a method to use. I carried an empty bag that drama training could have filled with tools. I kept saying Miss Dorothy's words as though she were Laura Petrie caught in a time warp. I had always played parts (except for "Sam") that were not too far from my own demeanor. If I had been doing a dramatic role, it was basically the same, just done slower and with meaningful pauses.

In working with me, George described in detail the life and feelings this girl might have, how contained and innocent she was. He stopped rehearsals many times to try and reach me, but the more he would talk the more inept I felt, which led to a real block—resentment. What had I been doing all these years that now was no good? I cried almost every night when Grant asked, "How'd rehearsals go today?"

Then one day, George asked me if, as an experiment, I would go through the whole day's work never taking my eyes off my shoes and speaking only in a whisper no matter what the scene was about. I felt so unable to give him what he wanted, so guilty about not delivering, that I gave up trying and simply did as I was told.

It worked. It worked because the ladylike WASP young woman was one of quiet reserve, and the looking down and whisper facilitated that. It was the correct demeanor. Going through rehearsal that way gave me the *feeling of shyness*. It was the platform I needed to reach Miss Dorothy, and within a few hours, I nailed the bitch! Everyone on the set applauded my work at the end of the day, and so began the process of finding Miss Dorothy. He further augmented my character-building experience by having me watch Lillian Gish films in a screening room whenever I wasn't involved in rehearsals. It was like the scene from *A Clockwork Orange* where Malcom McDowell, eyes held open, is forced to watch brainwashing film as part of his rehabilitation. But it had a glorious effect on me. Miss Dorothy became complete to George's and my delight.

I found myself not only comfortable with the script as written, but also contributing ideas to add my own take on her.

During all this, negotiations were ongoing for me to star in the musical stage version of *Breakfast at Tiffany's* on Broadway. David Merrick, whom I have always affectionately referred to as the warlock of theater, was producing the show based on the novella by Truman Capote. The movie, which starred Audrey Hepburn, had been an enormous success, immortalizing the story and its heroine, Holly Golightly. And now, ladies and gentlemen, in a once-in-a-lifetime opportunity, all her dreams come true, Dad has to love her now—Mary Tyler Moore on Broadway!

Both my parents were pleased for my success, if a little startled by it. I was aware always of the need to keep my place on the ladder, guard it from takeover, and prove to them both that I wasn't the fake I knew myself to be. It's a wonder I kept my footing, at all.

Convincing Lew Wasserman that he should share my enthusiasm for a sabbatical on the stage and let me defer all those movies his studio had planned for me was the hardest battle I'd ever fought. In so winning, I gave up my right of approval of those films. At the time, I thought when *Breakfast at Tiffany's* had finished its run I would be so big a star they wouldn't dare ask me to do a less-than-great script, so, not to worry.

I must have been feeling the power of my newly flexed muscle to have pulled off what happened shortly thereafter. A change in our shooting schedule meant that I would be working on the day Richie was to have his tonsils out (a date that couldn't be changed because of summer camp). I was told that they could not do anything about the change, because the day's shooting would take place on the backlot of Warner Bros., the only day their old New York street set was available.

I've sometimes thought of what I did next with pride, and a little affection for the mom who wasn't always the best in the field. I saw Less Wasserman in his office and asked if he would try to arrange something so that I could be with my son before, during, and after his tonsillectomy. When he said there was nothing he could do, I told him I'd be at Cedars-Sinai on that date until mid-afternoon, and left.

I may be the only person who ever said no to Lew. Not one to lose a battle gracefully, he called the doctor's office asking him to be unavailable for surgery on a certain date. Dr. Kantor also said no. A man of principle.

The tonsils came out and the scene got shot that afternoon.

Julie Andrews, whose talent was the focus of almost every scene and who was rehearsing the added production numbers after a full day's shooting, managed to make me feel like a sister. I turned to her for the fervor boosters I needed to sell Broadway to the studio, and when we said good-bye she gave me a beautiful silver box from Tiffany's, with my name engraved on it, filled with her favorite throat lozenges.

I was disappointed that I didn't have a solo in the film, but the director pointed out that it would have been wrong for the personality of the character. In any event, I was thrilled to have been in such a grand musical production.

Out to Lunch
at Tiffany's

～

*M*OVING TO NEW YORK was a difficult adjustment for everyone. Grant, who had been head of NBC West Coast Programming, was able to negotiate a sideways move without much loss of prestige within the network. But he hated New York City with uncharacteristic passion.

Richie, who was a ten-year-old California innocent, had been given a few going-away dollars. In an effort to feel important, he made the big mistake of flashing his wad in Central Park, and was immediately mugged by a pair of like-aged boys. I think he enjoyed it in the long run because the cops took down lots of information from him and called him to police headquarters to look at mug shots, all well worth the twelve bucks.

He rode to school on a bus by himself, something New York kids do by the time they are four. For one who'd never been on public transportation, much less alone, it was unfamiliar and a bit daunting despite his bravura.

Max and Maude, our six-year-old German shepherd and five-year-old miniature poodle, had always lived their lives and taken care of their functions in the privacy of our backyard, and at their own discretion. You can imagine their confusion when leather straps were attached to their collars, and they were commanded to "get busy" (a phrase suggested by a dog trainer) on cement and with strange people walking back and forth. Since I was out of town in rehearsals, it fell to Grant to take the late-night walk. "Get busy!" he would be screaming in desperation as it got later and later.

On occasion, Richard Nixon, who lived in an apartment one building away, would come up from behind, completing his evening's constitutional, pass the trio, and glance back in amusement. However, Grant was not amused. Once the dogs were back in the carpeted, more grasslike apartment, they would immediately relieve themselves, proud that they hadn't soiled that lovely cement outside.

When we started rehearsing *Breakfast at Tiffany's,* Abe Burrows, the writer/director, had given the cast (Richard Chamberlain, Art Lund, Sally Kellerman, and me) the first act *only.* The second was to be written by him at night, after directing us all day. At best, it was a long shot, and for Abe, an extremely talented but now weary man, it was a disastrous approach. He gamely tried to stage the show, but succumbed more and more to reminiscences and theater lore, while questions from the cast went unanswered. And since director and writer were one and the same, no help came from the writer, either.

I felt very uncomfortable in most of my scenes, but I put it down to lack of experience on stage. Chamberlain, too, lacked personal knowledge and had little to base his judgment on except the belief that this legend (Burrows) would pull it off. In the meantime, we learned the music, did the dances, and at night absorbed the new second-act material when it was given to us.

There is a creepy feeling that emanates from the dancers who, when not dancing, might seem to be paying no attention, but are a pretty good barometer of how things are going. They wanted it to work, they were definitely on our side, but the word on the street was, "Look for shelter."

Just before we boarded the train to Philadelphia for the out-of-town tryouts, I got word from Bertie that Grandma, eighty-three, had suffered a stroke. She died shortly afterward. I could not imagine her not being there. I had planned to call her that night for some encouragement. She had always been the one to help me find sanity in chaos.

At the opening night in Philadelphia I had a temperature of one hundred and three degrees, and a vocal range of about six notes. But believing the self-serving saw of producers—"The show must go on"—I did, and what a mistake it was. The critics, never having heard me sing, thought that what they were hearing was my normal voice. With a preset resentment of a television actress daring to invade theater, they declared me awful.

Well, I was. I shouldn't have listened to those voices in my head telling me it would be all right once I got on stage. I should have waited a couple of days, letting Sally Kellerman, my understudy, go on. I might even have found some sense of what was wrong with the show by sitting in the audience. But, I'd chosen the path I had seen taken in movies about Broadway. Again, the battle between optimist and doomsayer.

The reviews mentioned a few other names besides mine as being culpable, but the word was that I was the problem with the show. And despite reassurances to the contrary, I convinced myself that I was. One rumor that preceded us into Boston, our next stop en route to the Great White Way, was that Merrick was going to replace me with Diahann Carroll. When I asked him if it were true, he said, "No." When I asked him to say so to the press he again said, "No. This kind of publicity is good for a show. I like it."

I told him I understood, which was a big stretch. I just wanted to believe that this was going to have a happy ending.

My voice had recovered enough in Boston to warrant some vindication, but the show was still being panned. One of the problems peculiar to Boston was the "proper" reaction to the inescapable fact that Holly was a hooker. It was complicated, too, by my own good-girl image from *The Van Dyke Show*. My opening line on stage was

"I can't find my goddamn key," the "goddamn" evoking an intake of breath from the blue-haired ladies.

Just before we were to open in New York, Merrick decided that a major doctoring was necessary. It is sad to note that this function had been Abe Burrows's forte in his early years. Carl Reiner was sought, but he was on an uncharted vacation in France and no one knew how to find him. For ten days they played tag with hotels he had just that morning checked out of with no forwarding address. I was in agony, as I knew he could locate the problems—anyone could find the problems, but he would have the answers.

Edward Albee was the next choice for God-knows-what reason. A brilliant writer, he gave not one indication of understanding this story. On one of his visits to the theater, he was overheard remarking to someone, "I hate the musical form."

We closed for two weeks, and day by day learned an entirely new play, new songs, new staging, and learned to live with an absence of dances. The play had become the avant-garde experience that one could expect from Albee, and in preview drew responses from the audiences that I have nightmares about today.

They talked back to us, yelled things at the actors. At one point, Richard Chamberlain looks at Holly as she lies in a hospital bed and asks the rhetorical question, "Where did I go wrong?" "When you left *Dr. Kildare,*" came the response from one angry audience member who provided a much-needed laugh. They left in clumps (I don't know what droves look like), and by the middle of the second act, perhaps fifty people remained in the theater.

After the matinee performance on the night before the opening, Merrick gathered us all on stage and broke the news. It must be like the last blow you remember before losing consciousness. We would close after that night's performance.

It was a relief, at first, knowing that we would suffer the indignities of an irate audience only once more. The dream had been replaced by the desperate need to survive with dignity.

I called Grant, who was in LA on business, to tell him what a miserable mess I'd made. He flew home immediately, joining me at a hastily put together wake at Sardi's. He says he walked in expecting to find me sobbing. Instead, I was lending my shoulder to the dancers who'd returned to mourn a second time.

Word of closing moved rapidly through the neighborhood. Tickets for the final performance were scalped at outrageous numbers, but we had a full house and received a standing ovation when the curtain mercifully came down. Abe Burrows was not in the audience. He would spend the next several months recovering from the trauma.

From the very beginning, the Broadway community had sneered at the casting of two television stars in the leading roles of this show, saying things like, "They've had it easy. They don't know what real work is." Well, I'm proud to say we were thanked and praised by everyone involved for the examples we set for work under pressure. In fact, Dick Chamberlain and I were about the only two left standing when the dust cleared.

When the *New York Times* hit the street that night, we had made the headlines: BREAKFAST AT TIFFANY'S, MOST EXPENSIVE MUSICAL IN BROADWAY HISTORY CLOSES—$350,000.

POSTSCRIPT

David Merrick and I remained friends, and one night when he visited us for dinner, I was able (unwittingly, to be sure) to exact punishment in return for the pain he'd caused me when he refused to stall the replacement rumors. As we sat having drinks, a thirteen-year-old Richie asked David if he'd like to hear him play the drums. He actually was pretty good, having undertaken the hobby on our return to LA. Richie took the kindly gentleman into his room, closed the door, and for fifteen minutes made scrap metal out of his full set of drums. I didn't interrupt.

My Affair with Elvis

❧

$\mathcal{B}$Y THE TIME I EMERGED
from the *Breakfast at Tiffany's* nightmare, Universal, for whom I was
supposed to carry the sophisticated-comedy banner, had changed
its focus and was no longer putting thought or big budgets into small
comedies.

One of the movies I was asked to do was an intended breakaway
for Elvis Presley called *Change of Habit*. He was looking for a film
that would require none of his typical rock-star gyrations but would
illuminate his acting ability. He chose an unfortunate vehicle.

The premise was that a ghetto doctor (Elvis), while straighten-
ing out the lives of some young people, falls in love with a nun (me).
In order to be more effective with the ghetto kids, she has abandoned the drab church habit *(Change of Habit)* in favor of smart little dresses and matching handbags and pumps.

Apparently, the studio was able to convince Elvis that this choice
would pave the way for dramatic recognition. In fact, the studio's
approach seemed more like: "Let's see what happens when we toss
all these elements into a paper bag and shake it up. Maybe, when
we spill it out, it's a movie."

It was a dud, but the experience of working with Elvis was a nice one. He was in peak form during that time, careful about what he ate and exercising as if he enjoyed it. He was a thorough professional: always prepared, and willing to spend extra time with the little girl in the piece, a seven-year-old, to make her feel comfortable.

He confessed right from the start that he'd had a crush on me since *The Dick Van Dyke Show*. He was so shy about it he was literally kicking at the dirt below him as he talked. He had a tendency, even though I was younger, to call me "ma'am" out of respect: "Yes ma'am. Be right there, ma'am".

I was his last leading lady. The King would slyly say later on, "I slept with every one of my leading ladies but one." I don't want to bust anyone's cover, but I know who the "one" is.

4

With Grant and Richie.

MTM and GAT.
Immediately after the final scene of the last episode.

Four, Less One

c~~o~~

S HORTLY AFTER OUR
return to LA, I became pregnant. I was joyously two and a half
months along when one day I felt those familiar cramps that tell of
uterine passage.

I called my doctor, who told me to go on about my business. If
I were going to spontaneously abort, he intoned, there was a medical reason for it, and we would have to let it happen. He then asked
that if I did go so far as to deliver something, that I save it for examination. Not the reassuring response I was looking for.

I had a luncheon interview that day with a writer for one of the
women's magazines. I had to excuse myself when the pain became
so strong I couldn't hide it anymore. I could feel moisture between
my legs as I walked to the car.

When I got home, the cramps had become one long, insistent
pain. I made it to the bathroom, and as I was removing my hose, I
moved instinctively to the toilet whereupon some fluid and a mass
of some sort emptied into the bowl.

After my breathing returned to normal, I stood up and reached
into the bowl to find what, in my mind, was my child. My fingers
found something, and trembling, I pulled it out. It was flesh-col-

ored and about the size of my thumb. I cupped it in both my hands, remembering what the doctor had said about saving any tissue. I was crying as I made my way to the sink. I turned, catching a flash of silver from the corner of my eye. My poodle, delighted to find me at home, bounded to where I stood.

At that moment the fetus slipped from my hands to the tile floor. The dog made a dash for it, and began gleefully nosing it back and forth, before my horrified eyes. He moved it halfway across the room with playful curiosity before I could finally capture the life that had met a very early end, and place it in a glass.

When Grant got home that evening he asked how I was feeling, and I told him a less descriptive version of what had happened. Throughout our marriage, Grant and I had an unspoken understanding that part of what we admired about each other was the strength and positive determination with which we both faced life. We would comment on other people's frailties, but never our own. In effect, we had contrived an agreement that nothing untoward or ugly would ever enter our lives.

I'm not certain what impelled Grant to want a fifth child, but I most surely felt the instinct to have *his,* and though unplanned, it felt ordained somehow when the pregnancy was confirmed.

It had been just a day or so since he'd called all the family with our news. There had been no mistaking the happiness he was so typically holding back. We held each other in a rare acknowledgment of our vulnerability to loss and sorrow.

Sweets No More,
My Lady

A FEW DAYS LATER, as I lay in a hospital bed, recovering from the routine dilatation and curettage procedure that usually follows such circumstances, I opened my very tired and swollen eyes to see, at the foot of my bed, my gynecologist surrounded by several other doctors who were unknown to me. They asked quite a few questions about things like the frequency of my urination during the last few weeks, as well as any unusual thirst and dryness of mouth I might have noticed. Had I felt more than a little fatigued? My answers, all of which were yes, seemed not surprising to these men who checked their charts and regarded me, as well as each other, with grim, knowing looks.

"Mary," my doctor said in a falsely reassuring tone, "you have diabetes." He then introduced me to the men on the team—an endocrinologist, an internist with a specialty in diabetes, a diabetologist, and a few residents along for the education. What astounded them was that I hadn't gone into a coma. They spoke with alarm about my blood test, which revealed a glucose (sugar) level of 750. Normal glucose levels run from 70 to 120.

Diabetes. The picture in my mind was that of a reclining, semi-invalid, draped in a comforter. No one in our family had ever been diabetic. Wasn't it genetic? How could this be happening to a strong person, a dancer! I was told I would be staying in the hospital for several days while they balanced insulin doses with a controlled diet. The fundamentals of the disorder would be carefully explained to me, and I would learn to give myself insulin by injection.

For the next several days, my head and my emotions floated through someone else's movie as I learned about the illness. Diabetes is a genetic disease that affects the production of insulin, a hormone needed to sustain life. Insulin is manufactured by the pancreas to handle sugar (glucose) for energy.

There are two kinds of diabetes: Type I, or insulin dependent, is usually diagnosed in a person from time of infancy through their thirties. People with Type I cannot produce insulin at all and therefore must take injections, as many as five times a day, to control the glucose level in the body. Type II diabetes, non–insulin dependent, typically begins showing symptoms in later years. Obesity sometimes initiates the condition. These people don't produce adequate amounts of insulin, but can be controlled with dietary restrictions, exercise, weight control, and/or oral drugs.

I was a Type I diabetic, and for the rest of my life I would be self-injecting insulin several times a day.

Diabetes has been a leading cause of death throughout history. Today, fourteen million Americans suffer from the disease. Over time, it can present serious complications which make it a leading cause of end-stage kidney failure, amputations, heart disease, and strokes.

Diabetes can also lead to blindness caused by vascular death in the eyes. Smaller, inadequate blood vessels grow at nature's bidding to compensate for the loss. These "stand-ins" very often burst from the intolerable demands placed on them, filling the eye with blood. Today there is an effective treatment. Had it not been for the use of the laser treatment on several occasions in both my eyes, I would be blind now.

The latest studies show that with Type I diabetes, a genetic marker appears at birth, and the disease may or may not present itself later. Often a trauma, either physical or mental, will bring it on.

Years following my diagnosis, I would be included as patient Mary Tinker in a medical textbook because of the question that arose: Did the diabetes kill the fetus, or did the pregnancy precipitate the diabetes?

Anticipating my return home, I asked our housekeeper to rid the kitchen of all things high in sugar. I found an ally in Richie, who was eager to help and didn't mind dropping a pound or two himself. Since birth he had always been on the chubby side.

When he began taking tennis lessons a few months before and then seemingly lost interest, a little probing uncovered the reason. "I don't like wearing shorts," he said. "When I sit down my thighs bulge out and touch each other. I hate that." It was a moment of openness between us. And so we made a pact, the two of us.

My new education required knowing which food could be substituted for another to produce correct amounts of carbohydrates, protein, fat, and calories. These levels must be maintained and balanced daily, as part of a program including regular exercise and the administration (one or more times each day) of the requisite dosage of insulin.

My sugar was high more often than not. I could test my sugar levels with urine litmus strips, which weren't totally accurate, but were within range. I tended to keep it that way in an attempt to avoid the opposite condition, hypoglycemia (low blood sugar), which quickly affects the nervous system, making the diabetic perspire, shake, and become disoriented. It can, in the short term, be more dangerous, and certainly more uncomfortable, than its counterpart, hyperglycemia. I can tell, by the symptoms, when I'm hypoglycemic. Not everyone is so fortunate to have the tip-off, though.

Any life adjustment requires all the shoring up from family that's available—the more one has, the better the likelihood for success.

One of the qualities Grant admired was my ability to slog through life's muck. How could he know the degree to which I was afraid much of the time? There wasn't much comfort or support offered.

Handling diabetes was my assignment. It was expected that I'd succeed.

After several days of frustration at not getting my levels right, and with not much in the house to comfort me, I caved in to an assault of self-pity. I jumped into my car and zeroed in on the local grocery store, where I bought a dozen glazed doughnuts and drove around Beverly Hills eating every one of them.

Feeling quite pleased with myself, if a little dry in the mouth and dopey, I got out of the car, empty box in hand, looking like I'd been walking through a snowstorm—flakes of glazing were everywhere on my clothing. I sneaked around to the kitchen door and silently opened the large metal garbage can. I plunged the evidence to the bottom, so as not to be discovered by the housekeeper. She had become a convert to healthy living and was now a soldier dedicated to a "world without sweets." Needless to say, my sugar level went berserk, and I nearly ended up back in the hospital.

While our cocktail consumption hadn't reached the danger level, it certainly was more consistent than it should have been. The long-term effects of alcohol on the diabetic can be serious, but for the moment drinking simply warranted an adjustment in calorie intake and insulin dose. By the way, no doctor would have imagined the range of possibilities interpreting the phrase "moderate amount." So I was never scolded. I wouldn't have listened, anyway.

Diabetes is an especially difficult disease to take as seriously as it warrants, since most of the time we feel fine. It is hard to connect viscerally that what we put in the face is a direct threat to life. In my defense, I'll say that monitoring devices were not available for home use in the late sixties. I never really had a clear picture of what my blood sugar level was except at the doctor's office. Urine tests were the only home indication (and not a very accurate one) of what the body chemistry was.

Richie's discipline with the new diet was way ahead of mine. I wish I'd relied on him a little for support. What benefits might have occurred in both our lives. However, I never thought to share my feelings of uneasiness and self-disappointment with my twelve-year-old son. What a shame. I wonder about the good that might have come from his seeing that the mother he believed to be very strong and seemingly indestructible was not so sure of herself after all.

It took some time before I was ready to let it be known that I was anything but a perfect person, and certainly not one with a condition ending in "ic."

*Y*ears later, I was asked to be the International Chairman of the Juvenile Diabetes Foundation (JDF) to which my husband and I contribute money and time. It involves my going on camera as a diabetic and asking for dollars to aid in research. I had a dilemma: Could potential benefactors grasp the life-threatening aspects of the disease when they saw before them someone so vibrant and healthy-looking? Conversely, I wondered, if I were identified as someone whose health was compromised, would my ability to disappear inside a character before an audience be threatened?

I finally just said, "The hell with it," and I'm proud of the work I have done.

Besides public-service announcements, I travel to Washington, appearing before Congressional committees, asking for help in the passage of bills that will enable further funding in the search for a cure. I also help extract large donations from corporations for this cause by paying visits to the offices of their CEOs.

My husband Robert has also joined the battle on two fronts. A cardiologist with experience in the development of preventive therapies, he has become involved in the research that will one day find a cure for diabetes. He is also chairman of JDF's Government Relations Committee, which is broadening understanding in Washington of the important role the National Institutes of Health and other federal programs play in getting closer to arriving at a cure.

I feel somewhat hypocritical about my advocacy of animal rights, when I do not object to the use of animals in experimentation. In fact, it is a terrible dilemma. I do question our right to kill other animals in an effort to save our own kind—medical experimentation. But I know that if it were my child whose life could be saved, I'd probably sacrifice my fellow man, as well, to rescue him, let alone an animal.

Ironically, my gray poodle, who made the move across the country to New York and back, died of diabetes. She showed the same symptoms as I had. If, in my mind, I can justify an act to protect my own, I can also accept the use of animal experimentation to provide a cure for other creatures as well. This rationalization will have to do for the moment. It's what I come up with in the insoluble struggle between what I've been taught and what feels right.

Maybe one of the irresistibly strong motives for my supporting research is self-preservation which, despite our nobler attempts to put it into perspective, emerges in first place.

5

The cast of The Mary Tyler Moore Show, *clockwise from bottom left: Valerie Harper, Ted Knight, Ed Asner, Gavin MacLeod, Cloris Leachman, MTM.*

With Ed Asner—The Mary Tyler Moore Show.

The Mary Tyler Moore Show—The Beginning

❧

$\mathcal{I}$N 1969, THREE YEARS after I wailed my final "Oh, Rob" to Dick Van Dyke, Bill Persky and Sam Denoff (the writer-producers under Carl Reiner on *The Dick Van Dyke Show*) asked me to join Dick Van Dyke in a musical-variety special. They wanted to write a show that would be called *Dick Van Dyke and the Other Woman*. The premise was that everywhere Dick and his then wife, Marge, went people were surprised not to see me and more often than not made Marge feel like an adulteress.

I saw it as an opportunity to clear my name of self-diagnosed malperformance in *Breakfast at Tiffany's*. I decided that no matter what the outcome of this romp with Dick I'd be with people I trusted, and at the very least have some fun again.

In typical Van Dyke style, he tossed a lot of the show my way, delighting in our song-and-dance numbers, especially. I think he knew how much it meant to me to get back on the horse and he was glad to provide the paddock.

The show was a big hit with the critics and the high ratings it garnered caught the CBS eye. They offered me a half-hour spot on the network, with a firm commitment for twenty-four episodes. No pilot. My, how times have changed! It was to be a situation comedy, producers and writers to be chosen at my discretion. Grant was working for Twentieth Century–Fox Television at the time, but he extricated himself so that a production company of our own could be formed to shape this project. It was he who laid all the groundwork and chose the people who created our tiny empire, MTM. It was, over the years, what would come to be referred to as the "Camelot" of independent television production.

I think our marriage was in the same high gear as our work lives—coursing energy, mutual appreciation, and shared laughter. In the beginning, Arthur Price (who had been my manager for some years) was given the responsibility of the nuts-and-bolts part of building a creative company. Arty was sometimes referred to as Dr. No. He kept everyone's budget within economic feasibility. He also had fine creative ideas not only for my show but for *The Bob Newhart Show,* which we produced, among others.

The two people Grant hired to be the hands-on producers of my new show couldn't have been more dissimilar. Jim Brooks was an electric personality in his ability to change tracks without warning, tightly wired, speaking so quickly you sometimes wished for subtitles. Allan Burns, by contrast, resembled Clark Kent, always turned out in breezy, yet conservative, togs. In words and image the master of quiet good taste. (Yet it was he who would, over time, become the master of double entendre and sexually motivated stories.)

They liked the work ethic that Grant more or less invented for television: give the writers autonomy. Hire the best, and then step back and allow them to create, make the choices, hire and fire. (It's a system that worked well at the time but was to backfire on the industry years later. Writers became so powerful and demanded so much money and royalties that independent companies could no longer afford the few with track records that the networks would approve.) But in the early days of MTM, it was a setup that produced some of the most adventurous and truthful comedy on the small screen.

"The boys," as the producers were to become known, gave us a story outline that made the executives at CBS rigid with fear. I was to be a recently divorced assistant to a gossip columnist (the last bit a CBS suggestion) who was building a new life for herself, after a failed marriage. "Well," these executives said, "she can't be divorced! Not only is divorce an offensive life choice, but they will think she's divorced from Dick Van Dyke!" So away the boys went to rethink.

What they came up with over the next few months is pretty much the show that aired. Instead of being divorced, Mary was putting the pieces of her life together in a new city, Minneapolis (culturally alive, urban, but lots of nearby cows), after being dumped by her live-in doctor-in-training. It's always amused me that the network had a problem with an ended marriage but found it acceptable to have Mary "living in sin" all those years.

*E*veryone had agreed on MTM as the company's name. I didn't dare luxuriate in the tempting satin comforter that the name offered my ego. But, God Almighty, it was me. I had earned this opportunity. If I'd known the extent to which the company would grow, I would have insisted it be called something else, probably GAT. And yet, I loved the dignity and intelligence it implied were mine throughout the years to come.

As we hunkered down in that office, someone said, "MTM—does it sound too much like MGM?" "Oh, yeah," I concurred. At which point Allan said, "Maybe we should follow through with that. MTM's a small company so we could have an orange kitten meow in the same setting as their lion."

A few days later, a visit to the local animal shelter produced the kitten that would roar. It was her one and only foray into show business. Taking her memories and dreams with her, she lived out a life of seclusion in the San Fernando Valley in the home of an MTM staffer. Over and over he recalled her glory day until, many years later, she slipped into the twilight of her memory, ready always for the close-up that never caressed her face again.

MTM Show—The Casting

❧

$\mathcal{G}$RANT ASKED JAY
Sandrich to join us as director. In his youth, Jay had served time as
an assistant director (a mostly technical experience) on several series, one of which was *I Love Lucy*. There he had the opportunity
to observe some masters, and begin to formulate the concepts and
standards that would eventually make him the first choice of everyone in television at pilot time.

It was during his experiences on the *I Love Lucy* show that he'd
honed his diplomatic skills as well. Jay told us how, toward the end
of that series when Lucy and Desi were not getting along very well,
neither one would emerge from his or her dressing room on opposite sides of the stage until the other one was toeing the mark on
the set. So, poor Jay found himself running from dressing room to
dressing room promising each star that the other had already opened
the door and was now making his/her way to the set. It required
exquisite timing and diplomacy to get them there together, egos in-
tact.

From the first auditions for the cast to the filming of the last
episode, Jay was the actor's champion—always prepared with ideas,
while at the same time encouraging experimentation. He never let

us feel foolish for having tried an approach to a scene that ultimately failed. And he never flinched at a head-on confrontation with Jim and Allan when he felt a scene needed to be rewritten a bit. When all efforts by the cast failed to produce the desired effect, he'd take them on. He had an undeniably strong story sense.

We referred to him as the "Little Tank." No matter how many technical complaints or arguments that were all going on at once—"Where's camera B's mark for move fourteen?"; "Sound was no good on Mary's third speech, page nine"; "Jay, when do I cross to Ed?"—he would let it continue until some of us figured out a few answers ourselves. Then with a wide stance, arms outstretched, and a loud, short whistle, he would get everyone's attention, and in an orderly fashion answer all of the questions of the moment as he trudged ahead.

Ethel Winant had her own casting agency when she joined us. She also worked for CBS, so she was a strong force in getting approval for her unpredictable suggestions in casting.

Dave Davis was a quirky, wonderful writer who was added to the team, as was Lorenzo Music. They wrote stories of friendships and situations that had never been considered fodder for television. We were indomitable.

When Ed Asner (a Grant Tinker casting inspiration) came in to read for the part of Lou Grant, everyone expected him to find the comedy in the script as easily as he was charming us during the usually awkward small talk that precedes a reading. He had never done comedy on film, but there was a definite imp within his dramatic heart. We were certain, just as the clown is very sad, that this actor who spent most of his professional life scaring the hell out of us could become an adorable stuffed animal.

We were all making knowing, confident eye contact as we settled in for the reading. It was the scene where Mary is interviewed by Lou for the job of associate producer at WJM, a scene dependent upon excellent timing and sense of balance. He asks questions, the answers for which are always a few beats behind.

How many beats? How fast the next questions? What level of
impatience and when does it peak? Tipped one way, the scene can
be a kaleidoscope of humorous misunderstanding or simply miscues
between bully and wimp:

LOU

How old are you?

MARY

(NOT BATTING AN EYE?) *Thirty.*

L O U

(SURPRISED) *No hedging? No "How old do I look?"*

MARY

Why hedge about it? (BEAT) *How old <u>do</u> I look?*

L O U

Thirty. What religion are you? (HE OPENS DRAWER AND
POURS A BLAST OF WHISKEY INTO HIS COFFEE.)

MARY

(UNCERTAINLY) *Mr. Grant, I don't know quite how to say this,
but you're not allowed to ask that when somebody's applying for a
job. It's against the law.*

L O U

Wanna call a cop?

MARY

No.

L O U

*Good. Would I be violating your civil rights if I asked if you're
married?*

                                    MARY
(THINKS IT OVER) *Presbyterian.*

                                    LOU
(REACTS) *Huh?*

                                    MARY
I decided I'd rather answer your religion question.

                                    LOU
Divorced, huh?

                                    MARY
(QUICKLY) *No.*

                                    LOU
Never married?

                                    MARY
(EMPHATICALLY) *No.*

                                    LOU
(STRAIGHT OUT) *Why?*

                                    MARY
Why?

                                    LOU
(LOOKS AT HER, THEN SMILES AS IF HE KNOWS THE ANSWER)
Do you type?

                                    MARY
(FEISTY) *There's no simple answer to that.*

LOU

Yes, there is. You can either say 'No, I can't type' or 'Yes, I can.'

MARY

(POINTING OVER HER SHOULDER TO THE QUESTION BEFORE
THAT) *There's no simple answer to why a person isn't married!*

LOU

(DISINTERESTED) *How many reasons can there be?*

MARY

(CLIPPED) *Sixty-five.*

LOU

(POINTS AT HER) *. . . Words-per-minute. My typing question.*
(MARY NODS)

LOU

*Look, Miss . . . why don't you try answering the questions as I
ask 'em?*

MARY

(HER BACK UP) *Well, I would, Mr. Grant, but you've been
asking a lot of very personal questions that don't have a thing to do
with my qualifications for this job.*

LOU

You know what? You've got spunk.

MARY

Well, yes . . .

LOU

I <u>hate</u> spunk. Tell you what. We'll try you for a couple of weeks *and see how it works out. If I don't like you, I'll fire you. If you don't like* me *. . . I'll fire you.*

MARY

(GRINS) *That certainly sounds fair. What's the job?*

LOU

The job is that of Associate Producer.

MARY

Associate Producer?

LOU

Something wrong? (MARY LOOKS UP AND WE SEE THAT THE FUNNY LOOK ON HER FACE HAS BECOME A BROAD SMILE.)

MARY

(QUICKLY) *No . . . I like it!* (TRIES IT ON HERSELF) *Associate Producer!* (SMILES)

LOU

The job pays ten dollars less a week than the secretarial job. (HER SMILE FADES A LITTLE, THEN SHE DOES SOME QUICK FINANCIAL FIGURING.)

MARY

I think that'll be okay.

LOU

If you can get by on fifteen less a week, we'll make you Producer.

MARY

(QUICKLY CONSIDERS IT, THEN SHAKES HER HEAD) *I'm afraid all I can afford is Associate Producer.*

LOU

You start tomorrow.

MARY

Wonderful! (STANDS UP) *Well . . . see you tomorrow!* (SHE
RAISES HER HAND IN A WAVE, THEN EXITS.) (AS SHE EXITS,
BUBBLING) *Associate Producer!*

Ed lumbered his way through it, now that I think about it, as
though it were a scene from *Silence of the Lambs,* Anthony Hopkins
with an intense appetite for Jodie Foster's liver.

Everyone let a moment pass before the compulsive chatter took
hold. Things like "Hey, interesting angle on the character," "Thanks
for coming in" brought him to his feet and backed him toward the
door he had so expansively entered just a little while before. Then
he stopped and said, "I'd like to do it again."

In the second reading, he soared. He was another person, surprising us at every turn. He brought nuances to Lou's bluster that
made us laugh where no one else had before, delighting everyone,
including himself.

During the next few months the bad Ed, the dramatic Ed, tried
to emerge once or twice, but it was always a futile attempt. Lou
Grant was set on a course that Ed was driving. He twisted and
curved, and sped along, sometimes opting for a quiet Sunday drive.
It was always an interesting route.

Gavin MacLeod had been in to read for the same part earlier that
day.

To everyone's surprise he asked if he could read for the part of
Murray. With the emerging of Ed Asner as the Messiah that afternoon, Gavin's request gave us a new possibility for the character who
was to sit next to Mary for the next seven years.

. . .

Ted Baxter was always conceived as a self-important news reader, but he was to be about my age and the source of some romantic antics with Mary. We'd been visualizing tall, dark, and handsome types when Ted Knight—shortish, white-haired, and the epitome of self-absorption—entered the room as though with an entourage and bellowed in his most resonant voice, "Hi, guys." He brought more colors to the image and notes to the voice (produced from a part of the body not known to medicine) than had ever been thought of. He created in everyone's mind images of buffoonery, and pomposity that hadn't been imagined before. He was doing things with his body that were impossible to reconcile in anyone but a Shakespearean character. However, it came in truth from a frightened aberration that was Ted Knight's creation. The dialogue preceded his entrance that day, but Ted Knight gave Baxter a soul.

What we were to learn about that audition was touching. Apparently, he wanted the role so much that he went out and bought a light-blue blazer to help him look the part. He was working so seldom at the time he was barely making the rent.

Cloris Leachman entered the office with a mission to convince Jim Brooks that she wasn't just a brilliant dramatic actress, but that she was Phyllis. (The following spring she won the Academy Award for Best Supporting Actress in *The Last Picture Show*.) Jim had serious doubts that she could be the zany wood nymph who was married to Lars Lindstrom in our show. Before anyone had a chance to rise to his feet in greeting, she demanded to know in that breathless neurotic voice which one was Jim. Whereupon, she flew to his lap and remained there for the conversation that followed, never once referring to her unlikely position. Everyone was laughing, especially Jim. But she continued to chatter on as though it were the most appropriate place to sit.

The reading that followed was an unnecessary test. Her tempo, flights from topic to topic, precision of speech, and that ability to control our attention and make us laugh were enough. The script and how to play it would be simply a matter of choice, and with this actress the avenues were limitless.

That most people think she was in every episode is a great tribute to Cloris Leachman. In fact, she never made more than six appearances per season.

We were so pleased with our merry band of players, but time was edging toward the June start date and we still hadn't found Rhoda. We were looking for someone to make the kind of impact the others had for the roles of Lou, Ted, Murray, and Phyllis.

Valerie Harper was portraying several fairy-tale characters, including a duck, in a stage show called *Story Theater*. Somehow Ethel Winant could see the potential through those feathers and collared us.

Valerie came in and read for the part and the boys loved her immediately. The only problem was that Rhoda was written to be a self-made loser—not good with hair and makeup, overweight, and self-deprecating. Valerie, to Jim and Allan's anguish, was the perfect actress except for one thing: she was beautiful.

They asked her to come back the next day to read with me, and to try to frump herself up a bit beforehand. No matter how hard she tried, she couldn't hide her beauty. Once again the boys had to rethink a character, and they did. So what if she were attractive, the important thing was that, like so many women, Rhoda didn't *think* she was. As such, that great self-deprecating aspect of her humor was preserved no matter what she looked like.

I'll never forget her reading of the line "This is going to be my apartment." No one else had given that sentence such determination and hostility, while still getting a laugh. We clicked immediately, and I knew I'd made a friend.

The Dress
Rehearsal

~∾~

*T*HE REHEARSALS WERE, from the first to last episode, the sculpting sessions of our work, and our fond support of each other nourished that work. Often Ted and Ed and Gavin would sit and observe the women bringing their roles to life in scenes that didn't include the men. They'd howl their approval when one of us made a line work, and when we were through, would make suggestions about difficulties we might have. The ties that would become our mortar were delicately weaving themselves around and under the easy friendships that were forming already.

During the first week, Valerie said to Cloris, "Mary is so nice." To which Cloris replied, "Well, of course she's nice. She's happily married and she's got her own show. Why shouldn't she be nice?" Cloris was right. I've come to believe that a person's mettle can't be judged until her back is against a wall.

Grant reinforced a truth I had learned on the *Van Dyke Show*. He often reminded me that if the leader can remain fair and calm through difficult moments, a tone is set for all to follow. I had to find myself before the others could follow suit. Even though I was a figurehead, really, I did feel a responsibility to remain objective

~∾~

and not take sides when small eruptions in the group tempted me to intervene.

Through the years, the press would occasionally refer to me as the "Ice Princess." I was brought up to be a perfect person, or to look like a perfect person. So I never wanted anyone to know that there were any of the dark shadows I now can talk about. It was an image that drove some journalists crazy. I think they covered themselves, when not being able to write interestingly about me, by calling me an Ice Princess.

For the first episode it was decided that we'd do the show twice. We had taken more than the usual five days to rehearse since time was plentiful, and as insurance they put tape in the cameras for what would be a kind of dress rehearsal on Tuesday night prior to the filming that would take place on Friday.

Canned laughter might be used for a single-camera filming of a show without an audience. We never used that technique. The routine for the multiple-camera technique, with audience, begins with the reading of that week's show around the table with the producers, actors, staff writers, director, network representatives, and the script supervisor, who in our case was a woman named Marge Mullen. She had worked on the *Van Dyke Show* in the same capacity: the one who times the script, keeps a record of the camera coverage, makes sure the action matches if any retakes are needed—a meticulous observer and log keeper.

The show is rehearsed for five days and filmed in front of three hundred people on the evening of the fifth day. If anything, a live studio audience will laugh louder and longer than one or two people sitting in the den, watching a small screen. So the trick was to reduce, through editing, the amount of laughter to help move the show along.

There were very few problems indicated from the reactions at the table when we worked over the lines—laughs in all the right places, and a sense that you'd want to know these characters better. The rehearsals were productive, each actor finding more layers and shadings to shape the person he or she would be playing. We used the director, the writers, and each other to become comfortable in our new skins and grew confident that this was a very good show with excellent potential.

It was with as much confidence as it is possible for me to muster that I dove into that first episode dress rehearsal before an audience. The cameras that we used, behemoths designed to cut cost, had a double-decker arrangement—film on the bottom and a tape cartridge on top. They were dinosaurs that all but obliterated the view for the people in their bleacher seats. It seemed like a good idea to save the film (which is more expensive) for the Friday-night actual performance and utilize the tape for dress rehearsal. It also enabled instant review and assessment. I think ours was the first and last show to try it.

The show opens with Phyllis and her eleven-year-old daughter, Bess, showing me an apartment. Rhoda is claiming it to be already hers. I think Bess garnered a laugh or two, but you could feel the audience's growing dislike for Rhoda, whose combative demeanor made them defensive on Mary's behalf. Here, too, there was some confusion. Who is this Mary? Where's Dick?

The temperature was in the high eighties outside, and although the antique air-conditioning system was inadequately whirring away, it had to be turned off while shooting was in progress. The next scene, the now classic Mr. Grant and Mary interview scene, got only one laugh, and it was a lifetime in coming, at the line "I hate spunk."

In a multicamera-audience show, the audience has a chance to go outside in-between takes to stretch their legs if they want, as one set is moved to the side and another put in its place. Meanwhile, the actors change costumes for the next setup. No one is sure if it was the heat, the inability to see, or just general disinterest that caused it, but each time people wandered out, fewer came back. By the end of the evening, there were perhaps seventy-five people left and most of those were family and agents.

Today, I can see all the elements that combined to work against us that evening; but at the time, that experience was a nightmare of personal rejection. A view of nearly empty bleachers or theater seats is a recurring nightmare to this day. I guess I'll never be rid of *Breakfast at Tiffany's*.

Fix It

*O*NCE HOME, I TUCKED
Richie in and told him the dutiful lie about how fine the run-
through had been. I wondered, as I brushed my teeth, if the face I
was looking at was so different now because the makeup was old,
or because the musculature had fallen from fatigue. My eyes moved
from the mirror to the wall that supported it, and I thought how
much more room I would have for clothes if the sink and drawers
were placed on the opposite wall and a long hanging closet with
shelves were put there instead. The terrace outside the bedroom
could then wrap around the tub wall, which would be floor to ceiling glass, bringing the garden inside.

I got into bed, waiting for Grant to set the alarm and turn off the
lamps on both sides of the bed from the single control on his side,
a ridiculous system. It seemed particularly bright as I lay there trying to picture the terrace if it were made two feet deeper.

Tears came to my eyes. I waited for one of them to find its way
down to an ear. I tried directing its passage with minimal head
movements, but then gave up and gave in. Grant heard the first sob,
which was more like a foghorn. It must have unnerved him, until
he entered the room and saw to his relief the twisted, wet face that

lay there, not the monster he was imagining. He put his arms around me, gave me some pats and hugs, and then excused himself saying, "I'll get them to fix it."

According to the writers their phone rang. They picked it up simultaneously and heard Grant say, "Fix it." That was all. Grant came back into the room and said, "It's taken care of." I thanked him, and slept like a baby.

The Filming

❧

OR THE NEXT THREE days of rehearsal and camera blocking, morale was high, even though nothing specific was added or deleted from the script. It touched us and made us laugh. We believed more than we did Tuesday morning that we had a smallishly great show.

Friday night finally walked in and smacked me between the eyes with a left hook. I felt a hand on my shoulder and heard the assistant director say, "It's time to go to makeup." Like a shade descending over a window, I felt a transformation inside me go from a confident, eager actress to defeatist—the young dancer whose headwork "seemed stiff." I was cold, several of my fingers had no blood in them, and as I brought the magnifying mirror from the table to my lips, it slipped out of my hand, breaking on the cement floor into seven pieces. The legend dictates seven years of bad luck for merely breaking a mirror. The seven pieces were not only breaking superstition but a prescience of our good fortune's run.

There were three makeup chairs in the room, so there was nervous chatter aplenty. The actors ran lines with each other from scenes that had been changed, amid urgent discussion about the hue

❧

of an amber eye shadow or the tension of a curl, and the muted eye contact that screamed our tension.

Flowers were arriving all day for all of us, overflowing our dressing rooms and spilling into adjacent hallways. Every arrangement of flowers became a veiled reminder that there are expectations to be met. As their numbers grew, so did the telegrams which sang the sincere hopes of my colleagues that I wouldn't humiliate myself on this, the most important test of my life.

Time to dress now, take a few deep breaths, and make a bargain with whatever or whoever hovers skyward and controls your destiny.

The show played better than any of us had imagined for him- or herself, and surpassed even the well-wishing we'd heaped on each other. From the moment Bess confessed her palship with Rhoda (a suggestion of our script supervisor, Marge), the audience was free to delight in the neighbor's steamroller attempts to get her way. Every character was so well understood right from the start that the fun for the audience seemed to be in anticipating expected reactions and then being surprised by the outcome.

Afterward, Grant and I and all the people who were MTM went out to celebrate and eat the dinners none of us was able to consider before the show. We stayed out late—a happy clan of chimps shrieking and chattering our triumph.

Everyone who was present for the filming, as well as those who saw the episode, agreed that it was a winner. The cast had the easy chemistry that usually evolves after years of working together. Individually, each was (as time would prove) a star.

The writing was fresh and inventive without calling attention to itself. CBS was pretty sure it liked it, too, but had to wait for the test results before they could venture an official opinion. And so they got about thirty people together and showed our first episode to them. The honored evaluators (people taken from the street with the promise of coffee and doughnuts) were asked to fill out questionnaires regarding the potential for the series and its characters.

The results of that test have gone down in the annals of CBS as the most negative reaction to a show in its history.

The questionnaires revealed that they thought the premise of the show was wrong. "There should be a lot of problems in the newsroom Mary should solve for everyone." "And by the way, Mary is a loser. Over thirty and still not married!" "Rhoda shouldn't be so Jewish." "And Phyllis is annoying."

*I*t was at this point that MTM was asked to make a settlement with the network, calling the whole thing off.

The Little Engine That Could comes to mind when I think of how Grant refused to give up even when we were given a death-sentence time slot—7:30 p.m. Tuesday, preceding *Hee Haw* and opposite the huge hit *Mod Squad*.

Fortunately, there was a changing of the guard at this time with a new president, Robert Wood, now making some very grown-up changes at CBS. He was determined to act like a broadcaster and take some risks in order to bring intelligent programming to replace old standbys that had the network in the number one place, but the object of some ridicule.

Grant marched himself over to Wood's office to personally show him our piece and won him over immediately.

To think how close we came to never having had the chance to make the impact we did is almost as frightening as the fact that they still test shows in the very same way.

A Basket
of Rolls

*HE MARY TYLER MOORE
Show* was coming to the end of its second season, and Grant and I
were enjoying each other as well as the success of our work. We
liked our weekend life in the small rental beach house so much that
we undertook the building of our own home in the Malibu Colony.
We had purchased half of Lana Turner's old house that at one time
spanned a double lot. Well, to be a little more precise, the original
house had been torn down except for the stairway. We were going
to build our house around it. I'm not sure if it was based on the
novel idea of entrances and exits I could make—the vision of descending Lana's stairway—or some horribly mistaken idea that in
recycling it we'd save some money. But it was a catastrophe from
start to finish.

Saving was not our priority that year. We were hemorrhaging
money. For two relatively conservative people, we managed to
convince ourselves that "expensive" was merely a matter of se-
mantics, as we unwaveringly chose the most costly items on the architectural menu. Having established this level of extravagance, it
didn't seem ridiculous at all when we bought a pale-blue Rolls-
Royce Corniche convertible for me to drive. It was a near sexual

experience putting that magnificent piece of machinery into gear. The whole chassis would slowly undulate as I completed the shift, in much the same way an Otis elevator will add a final slow rise as it settles onto your floor.

There are other things that separate this car from the bunch. I remember the first time it rained on my blue chariot. I watched in amazement as raindrops bounced off the hood and I arrived at my destination the only car dry. I was never relaxed in it, though. Every time I took the wheel, I felt myself to be the object of maniacal bumper-car drivers, each yearning to be the first to place a gash in its twenty-three layers of pristine lacquer.

All my friends connected with the show ooooed and ahhhed as I drove my ego-extender onto the lot that first day. They cheered me on saying, "Good for you!" "And you deserve it." Within the month, every actor had begun proceedings to renegotiate their contracts.

Literally every two weeks, my Rolls was in the shop for one major breakdown after another. And these generally required an automotive sleep-over of at least one week's duration.

The director John Frankenheimer, who also lived in the Colony and who had been driving his own new Corniche for a bit longer than I, would ask whenever we saw each other if I'd had a particular failure yet. "Well, I had it three weeks ago, so you'll be getting that soon," he would say, and off he'd drive in his loaner.

It was a fifty-thousand-dollar joke that ceased to amuse when one night, in the middle of a left-hand turn on Sunset Boulevard, it died.

The company had *The Bob Newhart Show* on the air now as well as mine with several others in development: *Rhoda, The Bob Crane Show, The Texas Wheelers* (our first hour-long project) with Gary Busey starring, and *Three for the Road* with one of the Van Patten brothers in the lead. Paul Sand in *Friends and Lovers* evolved from the actor's single performance on my show as a nervous IRS auditor who had a crush on Mary.

Some did better than others but MTM was decidedly turning

heads with the champion caliber efforts it was making. What began as two men (Grant and Arthur Price) sharing a secretary in a three-room suite was becoming a complex structure, requiring a full-time legal department, financial office, and publicity staff.

What is unique here is that while it grew, Grant never allowed the quality to be obscured. He cared about each fledgling show as though it were his only one. The producers, writers, and directors were given the same nurturing atmosphere and attention as the first-born.

Fish Gotta Fly

RICHIE LOVED THE beach, and would comb it for treasures hour after hour.

He once rescued a baby pigeon that had fallen from its nest at the end of the pier, into the surf. We took it home wrapped in a towel and nursed it with an eyedropper filled with a concoction from the vet. Richie named the bird "Murf" after a rock singer or murderer of the time, Murf the Surf.

Murf quickly graduated to tasty morsels and tidbits that Richie and I dug up together in our backyard, and he seemed quite happy in his cardboard box. Richie was a devoted nurturer. The first thing after school, he was through the door and into the playroom, scooping up Murf to a resting place under his chin, where he remained—the two of them cooing to each other—as Richie undertook a reading assignment, or read whatever it was he was reading that passed for one.

He sometimes carried the bird around like an ice-cream cone, all head and shoulders emerging from the gentle fist that held him.

As time inevitably advanced, so did Murf's need for space to test his wings. Richie had become so attached to him that any hope Grant and I may have harbored of setting him free was gone now.

"He wouldn't survive on his own, Mom." And those big brown eyes worked their magic. Richie could talk his way in or out of almost anything, so engaging and ingenuous was he.

We got a large crate to accommodate Murf's adolescence, but eventually that, too, became inadequate. We finally gave up and just turned the playroom over to Murf, leaving him free to his fanciful swoops from drapery rod to chair back, to snare drum (his perch), freely leaving reminders of his flight pattern.

We tried to keep up with the droppings, Richie doing his part as well, but in time it became so raunchy in the bird room, that had the board of health ever paid us a visit, I'm sure the house would have been quarantined.

I'd been working on *What's So Bad About Feeling Good?,* a movie with George Peppard. It was another of those crowning mistakes to come out of my contract with Universal. Here's the plot: a toucan, an exotic bird with a beak like a lethal banana, flies to New York from its natural habitat in Brazil, infecting all of Manhattan with a euphoria-causing virus. Everyone starts being nice to each other. Without hostility, however, business begins to suffer, and the city quickly collapses into economic rubble. Well, despite the movie's failure, its bird wrangler, upon hearing of our dilemma, volunteered to take Murf into his aviary of feathered stars and hopefuls.

It was Richie's decision to make, and, with a maturity beyond his twelve years, he turned Murf over for his greater freedom.

Deep-sea fishing was also a passion of Richie's. He went out whenever he could talk one of us into driving him to the pier at 5:45 a.m. to catch the local excursion boat on a weekend. Off he'd go, the only twelve-year-old on this big old fishing barge made up of white-haired retirees and hungover sea slugs.

The boat would return about four hours later. So weathered was he from the salt and sun and wind, I could have sworn Richie had grown stubble on his face.

I could see from a distance the happy signs that he'd made a catch. As the boat approached the dock, I'd spot his form wriggling through the others to a position at the rail, where he'd stand so puffed up and pleased with himself it seemed he hurled his smile at me.

I understand his love of the sea and the sand. You know you're alive when you live at the beach. It heightens all the emotions. You feel exhilarated as you walk through the surf; deeper, darker, and colder when the rough edges are making themselves known in your mind. All of life's drama is heightened.

The ocean released many treasures to Richie that amazed and haunted us—bits of colored sea glass, worn smooth and dull from years of tumbling against the sand in the turmoil of surf; a rusted, barnacled iron hook measuring two feet by one foot, which I used to support the dining-room chandelier; a day's collection of some one hundred or so starfish, which, we sadly discovered, melted into one gelatinous mass when heaped in a corner of the deck overnight. And a shark that made Richie think a little about sport fishing.

One afternoon, he brought his first shark to the kitchen for cleaning. He was thrilled. It wasn't very big, maybe two and a half feet, but he'd caught it himself in what sounded like the struggle from *The Old Man and the Sea*.

As he held it by the belly against the bottom of the sink, knife in hand, our attention was drawn from the teeth to the other end of the shark. Tiny, fully formed babies popped out each time Richie depressed its middle. They were motionless. I can't imagine what we'd have done otherwise. But now "it" became "she," mother, and our dinner plans changed. The entire family was given a burial at sea. I think we ate pasta that night.

Camelot Days

❧

*T*HE SHOW WAS ENJOY-
ing great success. Despite its Saturday-night time period, a high per-
centage of those who stayed home did so to watch our show.

Valerie Harper's "Rhoda" had become such a strong force that
a series of her own had been suggested by CBS. Corporately, Grant,
Arthur, and I celebrated what was sure to be a terrific opportunity
for the company and for Valerie. Privately, it was a big loss for me.
Not only would she be missed in my living room by the public, but
I'd miss her friendship as well as the inventiveness she brought to
every scene, every conversation.

We don't see each other often. I sometimes don't even call if
we're in the same city, but the connection is solid. She's stood by
me at graveside on four occasions.

Friendships are not come by easily. Most of my buddies are performers—palships that began on a set or in a dance class. The relationships I like best are those that begin with an objective, a common
goal that's important to both. It takes the heat off. You don't have
to be clever or sensitive or wise, you just do the work and lo, you
know each other pretty well; the foundation is laid, and you can
relax.

❧

At different times I suggested two people who I felt could help fill the void created by Valerie's departure. The first was meant to be a one-time-only appearance by a blond "babe" type who would have a flirtation with Ted during one of Mary's parties. The high-pitched innocent squeal of the sexy-looking Georgia Engel in this brief exchange had a big impact. I'd never seen anyone so unaware of her sexuality, nor had I seen anyone take so seriously a basically one-dimensional character. I asked the boys after dress rehearsal, "Can't you bring her back?" By the end of that night's filming, they'd come up with several story-line possibilities for her.

The other time involved casting the part of a TV Household Hints Lady who, when not creating new and exciting uses for toothpaste, was nibbling at the ear of every available man, including the not-so-available husband of Phyllis, Lars Lindstrom. The character was described in the script as being a man-eating bitch who laid out her victims with the sweetness of a Betty White. Well, they'd read every actress they could think of. I asked Jim and Allan why they hadn't seen Betty White herself. "Because she's a friend of yours," came the reply. "What if she's awful?" "If she's awful, don't use her," I ventured, wondering to myself how such intelligent men could come up with such cockeyed logic.

What testimony to Betty's ability that she could take a role requiring her to sleep with the husband of a series regular and have the audience eating "Veal Prince Orloff" from her hand. And so Betty White, with her syrupy, silver-forked tongue joined the cast and carved an even deeper spot for herself in my heart.

During the third season Ted came to see Allan Burns, our producer, in his office one morning before the start of rehearsal. He entered, as Allan remembers it, with an expression of pain on his face. He stood there wordlessly, extended both his arms in a helpless gesture, and as he slowly shook his head from side to side, unable to speak, Allan came around from behind his desk. "Ted, what is it?" he asked, and as he reached him, Ted flung his arms around Allan's neck and sobbed, "I can't do it anymore. I can't play Ted Baxter. Everybody thinks I'm stupid and I'm not. I'm an intelligent, well-read man, and everyone treats me like I'm a schmuck." His tears were real. Who knows what tipped him over the edge at that moment, but Ted was actually considering leaving the show, he felt so humiliated by what he saw as character takeover.

With all modesty, Allan recalls delivering an inspired talk, using examples of the great comedians throughout time whose intellect and soul brilliantly shone through the clowns they'd created and whose contributions to the hallowed halls of laughter inspire reverence for their commitment. Ted was ready to go out there for the Gipper, when co-producer Jim Brooks walked in and, unaware of what had transpired, slapped Ted on the back saying, "Ah, Ted, Ted, Ted, the world's favorite schmuck."

Chuckles Bites
the Dust

$\mathcal{T}$HE ALL-TIME FAVORITE
episode of actors, production people, and fans alike is "Chuckles
Bites the Dust."

When Chuckles the Clown, a character seen a few times on
the show, joins in a local parade, dressed as a peanut, he dies vi-
olently, shelled to death by a rogue elephant. After word of this
tragedy reaches the newsroom, Lou, Sue Ann, Murray, and Ted
soon begin exchanging double entendres and jokes about his
demise.

INTERIOR NEWSROOM:

MURRAY

*Can you imagine the insurance claim? Cause of death: a busted
goober.*

LOU

*Lucky more people weren't hurt. Lucky that elephant didn't go
after anyone else.*

MURRAY

That's right. After all, you know how hard it is to stop after one peanut. (STAGE MANAGER GIVES TED "ON THE AIR" CUE.)

TED

Chuckles the Clown died today of—(FLOUNDERS, CAN'T THINK HOW TO PUT IT) . . . *um, died today a broken man! . . . I don't know his age but I'd say he was in his early sixties . . . of course, it's hard to judge by a guy's face—especially when he's wearing big lips and a light bulb for a nose. . . . Chuckles had a motto he used to recite at the end of his shows. It was called the "Credo of a Clown." I'd like to offer it now in his memory.* (RELIGIOUSLY) *"A little song—a little dance—a little seltzer down your pants." . . . That's what he stood for—that's what gave his life meaning. . . .*

Mary becomes indignant at what she deems bad taste and insensitivity from the dead clown's colleagues. Instead of recognizing that they are using comedy as a pressure valve against their shock, she takes the staff to task for not showing the appropriate solemnity.

Then comes the funeral, and in the hush of the moment, surrounded by all who have come to mourn Chuckles, she gets the giggles and cannot stop. All heads turn to her, aghast at her bizarre behavior. The minister calls out to her and asks her to stand. Mary is humiliated by her inexplicable behavior. Then the minister praises her, reminding everyone that Chuckles loved laughter, hated tears, and asks her to let go and "laugh for Chuckles." Mary collapses in sobs.

It was an unconventional premise for a situation comedy in 1975. I mean, what's funny about death? What if some viewer had just lost a mother or an uncle that week?

We usually read our scripts two weeks in advance of filming so that rewrites could be done without a lot of pressure. There was

173

enough time for everyone to grapple with what we knew we were about to launch on an unsuspecting public.

When this script found its way to the table, our director, Jay Sandrich, fearing the subject matter, decided to take that week off. Suddenly we had a problem finding a director. Ultimately, a relative novice named Joan Darling directed the problematic "Chuckles," for which she won an Emmy Nomination.

From the moment we began to block this show on Monday, I giggled (that kind of out-of-control thing) at the mention of Mr. Fee-Fi-Fo, one of Chuckles's characters. And, of course, every time I did, everyone else having been bitten, too, by this contagion, laughed at me.

By the run-through on Wednesday night they had stopped, however, and I was now laughing alone, completely in the grips of this insanity that struck me every time the name was uttered. I think the crew was scared. It must have been like seeing "mother" lose it.

Everybody at one time or another approached me, asking if there was anything they could do to help. I kept promising that I would have myself under control by the time the audience came in, and we were rolling. At this point, I was barely able to talk about the issue without smiling, so I doubt I communicated any confidence.

If I were to laugh before the audience, all would have been lost. The laughing that takes Mary Richards by surprise during the funeral scene would have been confusing to the audience, instead of the huge shock and subsequent laugh that it was written to be.

I think it was sheer terror that finally won my attention when the "Fee-Fi-Fo" line was uttered—terror of losing the faith the cast had placed in me. Maybe that's why I set myself up for this little test: to prove that ultimately the show bore my name because I was deserving of it.

Looking back on it, I realize that I have always chosen work that challenges me, because if I don't go in to work a little scared, I don't have interest in it. I need to go to work thinking, "Oh my God, how am I going to play this?"

I don't have confidence in myself, but I am able to respond to a need, a challenge. Like a fireman, I must achieve whatever it is I set out to do. I must save the person from the burning building, reach the goal. I learned that drive, professionally, from watching movies about movies. The understudy always goes beyond what is necessary. I had a strong identification. The necessity to push myself became part of my rules to live by.

MTM, Incorporated, was growing at a good pace. *The Mary Tyler Moore Show* was, of course, its central strut, but other programs were climbing nicely in the ratings.

For a number of years, MTM dominated the airwaves. Viewers were beginning to realize that when they were looking at *Newhart, Rhoda, Phyllis* they were watching shows we produced. In later years, MTM produced *Lou Grant, Hill Street Blues, WKRP in Cincinnati, St. Elsewhere, The White Shadow,* and *Something for Joey,* a TV movie hailed for its excellence.

The best writers loved the breathing space that Grant created for them in a business where "Hurry!", "make it cheaper," and "because I said so" were the bywords. As a result, the creative people knocked first on MTM's door when they had an idea. Everyone wanted to enter Camelot.

On the professional side of my life, things were blooming.

My father, George Tyler Moore.

With my mother. I was about six months old.

With George Melville Moore, my grandfather, who said, "This child will either grow up to be on the stage or in jail."

My parents, George Tyler Moore and Marjorie Hackett Moore.

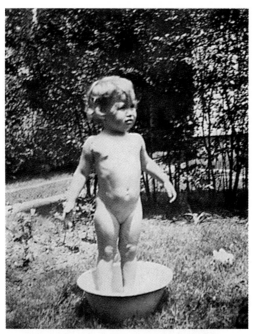

Me and my belly, at age one and a half.

*At age six. Already the ham
and would-be dancer.*

Grandma Mabel
Burgess Hackett.

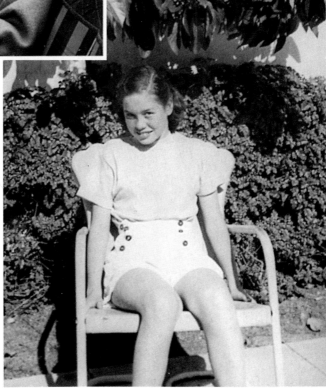

At age twelve.

*With Dad, after the Christmas tree trimming and
the meticulous draping of the tinsel.*

My early dancing days.

Cor Mariae 1955 Yearbook.

```
MARY TYLER MOORE

SAG - AFTRA

Hair:  Brown
Eyes:  Brown                    Dialects:
Height:  5' 6 1/2"
Weight:  120                    Southern
36-23-36                        Midwestern
Size:  10                       Bronx
Age Range:  17-25

TELEVISION:                     MOTION PICTURES:

   JIMMY DURANTE                   ONCE UPON A HORSE (U.I.)
   EDDIE FISHER SHOW               OPERATION MAD BALL (COL.)
   GEORGE GOBEL SHOW
   CLUB OASIS                   MODELING:
   OSCAR LEVANT
   GEORGE BURNS SHOW              MARY WEBB DAVIS
   BOB CUMMINGS                   PHOTOGRAPHIC, live commercials
   BOB HOPE SHOW
   JERRY LEWIS SHOW            INDUSTRIAL FILMS:

COMMERCIALS:                      J.C. PENNY CO.

   39 WKS AS "HAPPY HOTPOINT" (appliances)
   ON FILM FOR OZZIE & HARRIET SHOW

   6 LIVE MODE O'DAY

   GILLETTE RAZOR WITH ROCK HUDSON

   WHITE KING LIQUID DETERGENT

TRAINING:

   BETTY LOU GERSON (Drama)
   AMERICAN SCHOOL OF DANCE
   HARRY FIELDS STUDIO OF MUSIC (Singing)
```

An early publicity shot and my résumé at the time.

At eighteen with my first husband, Dick Meeker.

With my son, Richie, and my sister, Elizabeth—nineteen years younger than I was and just three and a half months older than Richie.

With Danny Thomas, who gave me my big break.
He thought of me for the role of Dick Van Dyke's TV wife.

The Dick Van Dyke Show.

With Rose Marie in The Dick Van Dyke Show.
She was to be the leading lady by virtue of her billing alone.
When my character grew, an ever-present wariness set in.
Today, we can laugh about what seemed career-threatening then.

The Dick Van Dyke Show—*The ingenious "Nuts!" episode.*

*With Danny Kaye,
Dick Van Dyke, and
my hair at the
Emmy Awards for the
1963–64 season.*

*With
Dick Van Dyke
and our Emmys.*

Laura Petrie changed the look of TV wives.

The Dick Van Dyke Show—
*It's a miracle Laura became pregnant
given the twin-bed setup.*

The Dick Van Dyke Show—*The memorable "Toe in the Faucet" episode; one of the most popular shows we made.*

The last episode of The Dick Van Dyke Show.

*With Lew Wasserman. He said I'd be "the next
Doris Day" when I signed my multipicture deal with Universal.*

With John Gavin in Thoroughly Modern Millie.

With Richard Chamberlain in Breakfast at Tiffany's.

With Elvis Presley in Change of Habit.

Dick Van Dyke and the Other Woman.
*The premise of the show was that everywhere Dick went with
his then wife, Marge, people expected to see me,
and often made Marge feel like an adulteress.*

With Grant Tinker.

With Betty White and Gavin MacLeod—
The Mary Tyler Moore Show.

With Valerie Harper,
Georgia Engel, and Ted Knight—
The Mary Tyler Moore Show.

With Ed Asner and Walter Cronkite—
The Mary Tyler Moore Show.

With Jay Sandrich, The
Mary Tyler Moore Show*'s
director. Always the actor's
champion, he was
unanimously adored.
No one else lived up to his
directorial talent.*

*With First Lady Betty Ford, during the shooting
of* The Mary Tyler Moore Show *episode in
which she appeared.*

With Valerie Harper, on the cover of Time
*magazine in 1974. "The MTM touch had
become synonymous with Midas'."*

Tinker kids and Richie, clockwise from bottom left: Jodie, Michael, Mark, Richie, John.

Perched on the Lana Turner stairway. This was all that remained of her Malibu house when Grant and I bought it, determined to build our house around it.

Grant and me, at one of many business-social events.

With David Letterman, Michael Keaton, and Swoosie Kurtz
for support, who needed a star!

With Ben Vereen in Mary's Incredible Dream.

During my short-lived variety show.

With Sam Waterston in Gore Vidal's Lincoln.

With Richard Crenna in First You Cry.

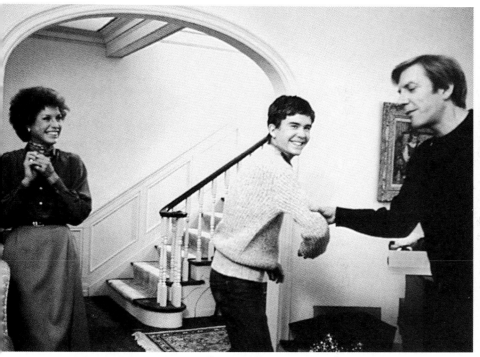

With Timothy Hutton and Donald Sutherland—Ordinary People.

With James Garner in Heartsounds.

Aunt Bertie, Wind Stalker, and Robert.

THERE'S NO EXCUSE! FUR HURTS

My sable coat—the extremely expensive disgrace I donated to PETA just months after I bought it.

My mother and me during our audience with Pope John Paul II.

My brother, John.

With my husband "the cowboy," Dr. S. Robert Levine.

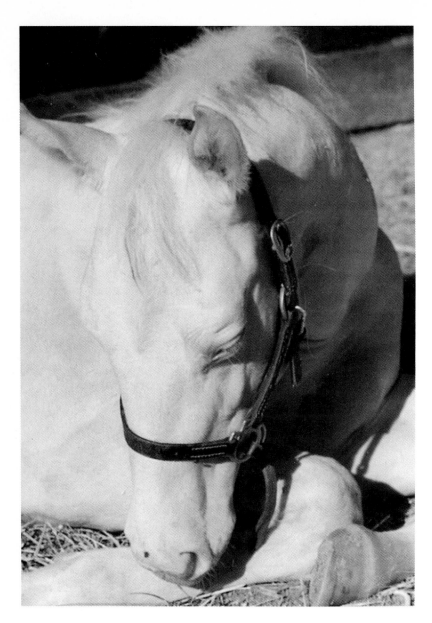

John, my brother's namesake.

With Donald Sutherland and Robert Redford—Ordinary People.

In Russia.

Elizabeth

❧

$\mathcal{I}$N THE SPRING OF
1978, before her twenty-second birthday, my sister, Elizabeth,
died of an overdose of the narcotic Darvon, combined with alcohol.

She was looking forward to a future in journalism and worked
in the newsroom of KNXT television in Los Angeles. She lived with
a young man who was the love of her life. I can't help but see a
similarity between us both seeking rescue in a man.

If I barely had the time for my son, I had even less for Elizabeth, and so we were more like aunt and favorite niece than sisters. She and our father had always shared an open affection and
deep love with each other—so much so that as I now use the term
"our" father it seems ill-chosen. He was a different person with
her—easy.

I was to learn, later, that there had been a huge rift between them
over this man. Upon finding out that Liz was sleeping with him,
Dad went into a Catholic rage and gave her an ultimatum. "Either
stop it, or leave my house." Without hesitation she moved in with

her boyfriend, but carried the loss of her father's esteem as though it were a heavy wooden cross.

Two years later she was shattered by the declaration of her live-in: he no longer loved her and had found someone new.

She returned home, but our mother was bedridden with another knockout punch from alcohol. Liz was uncomfortable with the circumstances there, and went to Bertie's house for the night.

The next morning, Bertie found her, still in bed, dead.

That night Joseph Benti, who co-anchored the news with Connie Chung at KNXT, spoke the following eulogy on air:

I hope you'll forgive me for being personal in this report. . . .
A young friend of ours died this morning. Elizabeth Moore . . .
We knew her as Liz. She was just twenty-one. I knew her from the time she was a freckle-faced teenage schoolmate of one of my daughters at Corvallis High. . . .
But, Liz was also a co-worker on the overnight shift. . . . She was very eager, sometimes moving too fast and making a few mistakes.
But she desperately wanted to find a place in the world, and she believed she could begin finding it working here.
Her aunt Bertie worked at Channel 2 for many years and is a dear friend to many of us. It's possible you may have heard about Liz's death because she has a famous sister, Mary Tyler Moore. . . .
But, I wanted to tell you about it because she was Liz Moore.

When I remember Liz, it's her humor that stands out. She was really funny by herself—no dialogue necessary. And she didn't use it to distract from any deficiencies she might have imagined.

She was the only Moore child who loved school and she excelled at it.

I think she'd have taken television journalism to a level that would have made us proud. She'd have made us smile, too, at her sign-off, feeling a bit more optimistic about the world.

She'd have been my good friend.

The King and I

❦

I CAN SEE *NOW* THAT
it was difficult to live with Grant, his moods overriding his best intentions. At the time I thought it was normal. When we were with
people, he was a very warm and witty man, and an appreciative audience of other people's wit and observation. When we were alone,
he didn't have much to say. "I don't want to have to *work* at marriage," he'd respond when I suggested we talk about why we
weren't talking.

We cheered each other's ability to stride over life's potholes
without looking down to see what repairs could be made.

The Golden Couple didn't have very much of a life. We both
hated parties and attended them only if they were work related.
Most weekends found us at the pool or the beach house lying in
the sun, Grant surrounded by stacks of scripts. A not unfamiliar sight
from my childhood, only the reading material itself being different.

I think I must take responsibility for having let Grant down one
way in particular. Politics and world events held little more than
passing interest for me, while he read the papers forward and then
back again if time allowed. The nightly news broadcasts captured
his attention completely. How nice it would have been for us to

❧

share some questions and opinions about Washington and the rest of the globe—at the very least.

He played tennis for fun, friendship, and relaxation, just as I took my ballet classes to fulfill the same needs. We traveled to Cap-Ferrat in the south of France for two weeks each summer and spent most every Christmas in Hawaii. Our friends knew they were our friends because we'd go out to dinner with them occasionally, not because we confided in them. We didn't. We wisecracked and laughed and talked about the art of putting on shows in the business of television.

Grant and I were the blind leading the blind—two people so much alike we could have come from the same litter. Admired each other—certainly! But not different enough to lead the other in new directions. And so, like Richie's starfish, we stayed in the corner and melted into one sodden mass.

Anytime we erupted in disagreement (and after stifling so much for so long, it could indeed be explosive) we ruefully regarded the unpleasantness as erosion, not a cleansing process of discovery. It was a strange dynamic for a marriage.

I walked on eggshells and so did he, neither of us able to just stoop down and pick the damn things up.

Then there was the beach house. What had begun as a project that would allow us to come home at night, walk on the sand, and to sleep with that complete awayness that only the surf bestows, ended up as a Beverly Hills house set back from the sand, and separated from the sound of the ocean by a glass wall. It also took an hour to get to the studio in the morning and an hour and a half to return at night. By the time we'd done battle with traffic and digested the day's mistakes or no-shows on the parts of the carpenter, landscaper, and plumber who were still finishing up, there wasn't much left.

Whenever Grant and I had separate cars and were heading home at the same time, he always insisted on following me in case I encountered trouble of some sort. By the time we got home, but before the front door closed behind us, what had been intended as a caring, thoughtful act on his part turned into a matter-of-fact review of my driving skills: "You pulled into that lane without signaling on Ventura and Laurel"; "Didn't you see the broken pavement on Coldwater?"; "You anticipated the green light at Sunset and Bundy." The longer the trip, the more opportunity for mistakes and corrections. I dreaded those "tailing" trips. The minute I got into the car I self-consciously evaluated everything I did as though seen through his windshield. I was so tense behind the wheel it is amazing I didn't have a major accident.

It was a metaphor for a rather basic problem we had: the effect his ever-present certainty had on me. I allowed myself to be treated like his student, taking every one of his lessons on people, places, and driving very, very seriously.

I would get into our king-sized bed feeling a little self-conscious at its strange intimacy given our non-relationship. In all our marriage, except for the act of making love, we never casually viewed each other undressed. If a trip from the shower to the closet were necessary, a towel discreetly placed belied what had happened only a few moments before in bed.

I was becoming as cross as Grant was and matched him, upping the ante with sharp words for his silences.

The sameness of the process was something he mentioned to me once. He was talking about the company—the development and selling of product that varied little. I suggested that he try a movie to shake things up a little, but he didn't have the energy—or was it the nerve? Maybe the whole thing was a metaphor for our marriage.

The most unrestrained display of anger I ever witnessed from Grant came during an argument at the dinner table. He was a powerful and articulate adversary in business confrontations, but surprisingly without the weapons of self-defense and expression needed at home. Silence and brooding were his methods for dealing with what should have been some good, constructive arguments.

This particular dispute was over something irrelevant. Reaching for a banana from the centerpiece, with a "Well, what do you think of this?", he peeled the thing and made a Zorrolike slash with it across a five-by-five-foot abstract oil painting that we were both very fond of. What did I do? Did I throw something at him? No. Grant got up from the table, went upstairs, and got into bed and read. And a few minutes later I followed, got into bed, and read. We never discussed it again.

Looking back with the perspective of intervening years, I smile at Grant's then horrifying outburst. I still have the painting. Over time, the oil from the banana has darkened in the minimalist desert scene to provide, in the same stroke technique, the suggestion of a far-off road.

The closest thing to a discussion of a fight that had taken place would be Grant coming to me and saying, "You really are stupid. You know that, don't you?" And I'd say, "Yes, I do." And then we'd smile at each other and hug.

And that's how we resolved our differences. Or didn't.

One night after Grant and I had watched the news through dinner, I got up to take our plates to the kitchen and said with exasperation, "Can't you remember to put your knife and fork together on the dish when you finish?"

I returned, putting our coffees in front of us. Calmly and deliberately, he said he thought we should separate, that we had "poisoned the marriage." Perhaps eleven and a half years was all we had in us, he concluded. My face flushed and my mouth went dry as I tried to respond.

He put his hand on my shoulder and said, "I think we should wait for the hiatus in May so that we don't upset everyone at the studio." It was at this point that I headed upstairs and found myself in my bathroom. I wanted something against my chest, and so I dropped to my knees and then flat out on my stomach. I began crying—loud childlike sobs—and screaming, "No!" over and over.

After a while, I became aware that I was pounding on the carpeted floor with my fists. It was the mother of all tantrums, exploding now for all those I was never allowed to throw as a child, I guess.

After reassuring the dogs who'd come rushing to my rescue, I got up, heart aching but ready to face my demon. I was almost excited by the enormity of what was going to happen. I joined him for a Grand Marnier at the bar. "I don't want to pretend until May. Go now," I said. "I'd like you to have your clothes and things out of here in two days."

As we got into bed that night I asked him if he would put his arms around me for a while. He did.

The next morning, except for having had separate breakfasts, we left for the studio as always. This time, though, I followed him.

We didn't see each other for six weeks. This was at my insistence. It would have been too sad for me. Keeping out of each other's way for that long was an amazing choreographic challenge for two people who worked on the same small lot. During this time, Grant leased a house in Beverly Hills.

As the news spread, those at MTM were solicitous of us both, while covering their own reactions. Frightened, stunned, and sad, they could be seen standing in small groups off to the side or exchanging quick glances at odd moments. Just as no one was aware of our drinking, so were they blind to the emptiness in our marriage. It came as a huge shock to us all.

One rainy night the phone rang in Malibu and it was Grant. "There's going to be a terrible storm tomorrow. Maybe you should plan to spend the night in town rather than driving back to Malibu," he said.

And so we started seeing each other for dinner. He was allowed back on Stage Two for rehearsals, and we spent several very physical nights a week at his house. Before long, without ever discussing the cause of our troubles, or how we might avoid them in the future, we decided to have another go at it.

I had missed him terribly during the separation and remember thinking, "This hurts so badly. I wish I could talk to my best friend about it." But that would have been Grant.

Taking the
Megaphone

⟊

*B*Y WAY OF A FEW
connections, I won a much sought after (and rarely bestowed) directing assignment on *The Mary Tyler Moore Show*. This series was held in such high regard that directors with top credentials vied for a chance to add the credit to their résumés.

Grant, in particular, was eager for me to give it a go, but I think his encouragement was based on corporate thinking. As chief executive officer of MTM, he was looking to tomorrow. He may have arrived at the conclusion that in years to come I would be more valuable as a fledgling director than an aging actress. At least that's what I sensed. And I took it in the same defensive way I reacted to my mother when she suggested that a typing course would be a good safety net if the acting business didn't work out. I didn't embrace the idea.

Usually, when a new director innocently arrived on the set to do his work, he'd be met with a barely hidden attitude on everyone's part of, "Oh yeah?" We didn't mean to be so rotten, it's just that Jay was our favorite and no one else could fill the imprint in his chair.

During my week in the power seat it was like being surrounded

⟋

by a pride of golden retriever guide dogs. Every time I was called on to make a decision, whether technical or artistic, several answers would be lovingly voiced before I had time to digest the question. I was so well supported by caring professionals (from camera operators to the guy ordering the snacks), the whole thing became a meaningless exercise.

One specific and laughable difficulty I seemed unable to overcome was remembering to say "Action" during rehearsals, and when I did remember I lacked the confidence to say it with the energy actors expect from their director. It seemed to require a belief on my part that I knew what I was doing. I'd say things like "Okay, go." Or, "Yes, start." Anything but "Action," the one Pavlovian cue actors respond to.

However, I learned or began to sense an essential self characteristic: despite my fondness for being number one, I wanted no part of the responsibility that sometimes goes with the distinction. The mantel of leadership is not one that rests easily on my shoulders.

Nonetheless, the episode was filmed, and thanks to the efforts of everyone around, "A Boy's Best Friend" looks pretty much as professional as the one hundred sixty-seven others.

Mary Tyler Moore Explains the History of the World

❧

*I*N 1976 JACK GOOD, the creator of the Broadway show *Catch My Soul* (which was later to be made into a film), and the producer of the television series *Shindig,* approached MTM with an extraordinary vision of an hour-long special. He wanted to depict the history of the world through music, song, and dance only. There was to be no dialogue. It was a unique premise, and avant-garde for television to say the least—scary as hell, just the thing to get my adrenaline going.

The story began at the book of Genesis, with Arthur Fiedler as God conducting a symphony orchestra while sadly expelling Adam (played by Ben Vereen) and Eve (ta da) from Eden.

We were in trouble right from that first scene. Production went well over schedule, and members of the orchestra who had been hired only for the day started leaving one by one to go to their evening jobs. So, as God cast us out, it appeared on screen that he also cast out nearly three-quarters of the musicians on camera.

Eve is next seen as cave woman, a pathetic wretch who must now exist throughout the violence that is our history. She sings the rueful "Nobody Does It Like Me."

The Manhattan Transfer acted as Greek chorus to the world's

❧

events that included, at various times, appearances by the devil himself. He was portrayed by Cajun singer and electric fiddle player Doug Kershaw.

I was nearly shivering with excitement throughout every moment of the three weeks of demanding rehearsal and ten days of exhausting taping. Every moment was chaotic. One night we worked outside until three a.m. to capture the musical depiction of the surge West, and the fallen Indians who lay dead in its wake.

The Great Flood, the Renaissance, World War I, the Depression, Hiroshima, all were represented in fantastic, diverse forms of ballet and song. Among the musical pieces were "On Your Toes," "Sh-Boom," "I'll Make a Man of You," "I'm Still Here," Aaron Copland's "Rodeo," "Java Jive," "Running Wild." The show's final moment was taped at Malibu Beach, the waves crashing on the rocks beneath my feet as I stood there in my lox-colored chiffon gown, bravely and optimistically singing "Morning Has Broken" to the cormorant circling above.

I felt it was a wonderful piece of abstract art—a comment through music on the indestructibility of the human spirit.

Some pretesting of it, however (they just don't learn), produced negative confusion, such as you might expect when looking at a contemporary artist's work for the first time. Instead of standing firm as MTM had done with that first episode of *The Mary Tyler Moore Show,* when testing showed that we'd deviated from the expected, the kitten caved. Wraparound segments were taped, establishing the premise of the show as a dream (I guess so no one would be scared). Instead of an impression of life, we gave the audience a little book of instructions—interruptions showing a sleeping Mary so that they wouldn't worry. Where it once was humorously titled *Mary Tyler Moore Explains the History of the World,* it was now a very safe *Mary's Incredible Dream.* I remember one MTM executive saying, "We've done some research that shows anything with the word 'incredible' in the title sells more." (Than anything with it not in the title, I guess.)

As it was presented, it met with a hostile response from both critics and audience. We were tarred and feathered—I find bits of fluff in the odd shoe or coat pocket to this day.

If it were economically feasible to rerun it today (which it's not because of union regulations), I bet it would be considered brilliant.

Death and the Spice of Life

❧

*T*HE SUMMER I FOUND myself missing the wedding ring that was *The Mary Tyler Moore Show* hit me with the same force I'd later feel at the ending of my marriage. I was lost. I had no other life. Party-giving wasn't on my agenda, I didn't have any interest in cooking, my friends had been the people involved with the show. Daily ballet classes and some less-than-productive analysis made up the larger slice of my time "pie" starting with Grant's breezy good-bye in the morning until he returned at night.

After concluding that the filling of the enormous hole inside me might be more realistically accomplished with a less direct approach, I arranged to spend some time at UCLA's pediatric division, volunteering myself for some observation by, and occasional conversation with, the youngsters who were old enough to have watched television. It wasn't fulfilling exactly, but I made a bit of time easier for some pretty sick kids and their parents, and that made me feel that I mattered, even without the show.

There was a ten-year-old boy fighting leukemia and the side effects of his treatment again, after what was to be a final remission. We became pretty close, sharing some laughter, feelings, and events from our very different perspectives.

It takes a strong person to live through a child's death. When the call came telling me that he didn't have but a few hours and that he wanted to see me, I ran to the car and wondered how I'd manage the two miles without driving off the road. I tried to remember how I'd gotten involved. I couldn't. What desperation was it that had produced this strange friendship?

I was grateful that I'd been there for him, but I knew it was the last of my visits to UCLA. That night, I'm afraid, I listened to the part of me that shrinks from people, the voice that cautions against loss.

I spent much of the next year reading (nothing that might illuminate), shopping for the perfect tennis outfits (I could erase the bulk of an afternoon in pursuit of socks trimmed in a particular shade of blue to match an outfit). Oh, and yes, tennis lessons.

I'd been so caught up in the series all those years that, given my reticence to aggressively pursue work, I watched Jane and Goldie and Sally make picture deals, and simply waited like a jilted lover for the phone to ring.

$\mathcal{A}$ year and a half after *The Mary Tyler Moore Show* went off the air, we began to talk about the kind of vehicle that would be good for my television return. And I breathed again. Since we had done the definitive situation comedy, and since I had singing and dancing abilities, it was decided that a variety show would be the best way to break away from Mary Richards.

But what we failed to recognize was that the genre was fading from the horizon of television. I don't know why I didn't reflect on the decision of my Saturday-night neighbor of many years, Carol Burnett, who abandoned the variety-show format. They'd been falling like great old dinosaurs, these shows of my youth, the gray cloud of music videos and what would become MTV shutting off the sun. Why we thought *I* could revive the formula of sketch comedy and music I don't know, unless it was that everyone's ego was unduly expanded from the success we were coming from—and yes, running from.

It was the hardest work I've ever done, mounting a one-hour show with song and dance, in the same five days it takes to do a half-hour comedy. But it was the best, most terrifying fun, too. Gene Kelly, my adored dancing sex symbol from the forties and fifties, was my guest, for God's sake, as well as Lucille Ball, Hal Linden, Johnny Mathis, Bea Arthur, and Dick Van Dyke, among others.

And if the old MTM show had a great cast, how about this one: Dick Shawn, Michael Keaton, Swoosie Kurtz, and David Letterman. It was one of David's earliest network appearances, his previous experience having been limited to some weather reporting for a local station in Indiana.

We did sketches and musical numbers, sometimes so complicated we would have to pretape them the night before the show. Everybody did everything—sing, dance, monologue. Wrong. David did not sing and dance. He would not sing or dance. He was, then, painfully unimpressed with himself, admitting only that he had a comedic edge. His role on the show was to pester and undermine me, and, of course, he did it brilliantly. But, he wouldn't allow funny costumes or silliness for himself. We gave him a hard time about his unwillingness to make an ass of himself. Looking back, he was right. Even then, he was defining the aloof shyness that distinguishes him as a comedian now. I loved the inept attempts at sparring he triggered in me as he does when I guest on his show today.

I watch his show now with a feeling of propriety, that I was a part of his beginning. I wouldn't dream of calling him "Dave," though, as he refers to himself now. I think he knows that Dave, as opposed to David, gives the connotation of friendly, down-home approachability, qualities that surely elude him, either by choice or just plain fact. I can see him luring us into his trap with the same devilment as when he would have us believe he takes the subway to work. "Dave" is his secret smirk at the rest of us.

Michael Keaton was the first young actor I'd worked with to make me aware of a new pace and rhythm potential in sketch comedy. He always surprised me and broke the rules right and left. For example, tradition dictates that a comedian should never move during the delivery of a punch line. Forget it. Michael proved if you walk funny you'll get an extra laugh. So what if they laugh harder at the walk than at the line? Even his breathing was different from everyone else's. And he seemed always to scuttle into place—all angles and bobbing, like a fighter.

Mary ran for only eight episodes. I was decimated. So there are the two sides of me, once again: the ridiculous ego that made me think I could pull it off in the first place, and then feeling that I was responsible for not making it a success.

School Daze

~♦~

WHEN HE WAS FOUR-teen, word of a school was brought to our attention that seemed tailored to Richie's needs. He was doing poorly academically, wasn't taking much responsibility around the house, and was pretty bored in general since sports weren't of particular interest to him.

This school was a ship, the largest privately owned sailing vessel at that time—a three-hundred-and-fifty-foot converted yacht that would sail around the world with the kids acting as crew and in-termingling with the people whose countries they were studying, all under the able guidance of teachers and seamen.

He had all kinds of adventures, from being on board when the ship was suddenly seized in the Panama Canal by armed soldiers, to withstanding a few typhoons. It was an enlarging experience for him, if a little lonely for me. There was a Christmas vacation, but other than that, it was a long time from September to May when my four-teen-year-old goof-off returned a seasoned sailor. Sea tales aside, he was now a year older, but even further behind in his schoolwork than when he'd left. It had been a great idea with good intentions, but disappointing results. He had to return to regular high school a

year behind his pals to sit in class with an almost uncontrollable feeling of claustrophobia.

The next couple of years were tough for him. After failing to complete his junior year in high school, Richie was seriously thinking
of dropping out of school as a solution to the pressure he got from
me and his teachers. I was so scared that he was going to find himself with very few options when maturity called for some decisions.

Dick Meeker, his father, was married again and living in Fresno,
a small farming town in central California, where he worked at a
local radio station. We'd been communicating regularly about our
son through the years. The hint that money and success were the
fomenters of Richie's problems always colored Dick's comments.
In my heart, I feared he was right.

I'd always found it difficult to foster in Richie a sense of responsibility. Chores like mowing the lawn, taking out the garbage,
washing the dishes, were easily taken on when I was growing up.
But in Beverly Hills I had a hard time selling Richie on the notion
that he should contribute to the family's routine when there were
people who were being paid to do those things.

I know there are answers to the question of how to motivate a
kid who has everything, but Grant and I surely didn't know what
they were. I also found it difficult to follow through on statements
regarding consequences. He could always talk me out of the punishment or limitations that were threatened.

So when Dick suggested that Richie come to live with him, I
found myself with very little steam to come up with a rebuttal. The
decision was made, and I prayed that Dick could give his son the
best of himself and instill in Richie the curiosity and determination
needed to define a personal ethic.

Richie did complete his junior year, and cheers were heard from
central to southern California. There was no question that he took
to the quieter, slower pace of the town. He'd also made some
friends who Dick told me were good kids. He and his dad had connected all over again, too.

However, a rather large fly landed in the ointment. Dick was being transferred to another town a few hundred miles away, and Richie still had his senior year ahead of him.

When he came home to Grant and me that summer, he turned up the voltage on his powers of persuasion and asked us to prove our heartfelt belief in him by letting him remain in Fresno in his own apartment, with drop-in supervision from his friend's father. He promised that the outside changes in him were only half the story, that he'd found himself. He could do this! He'd graduate from the school that had finally turned him around, and the next step on this road to a rewarding and full life would be COLLEGE!

And so, the grand experiment was initiated that fall with an outcome that anyone (except us) could have forecast. Disaster.

Richie succumbed to all the temptations that can overcome even a kid who's living with supervision. On his own, he was a kid at a carnival, and pitifully short on the self-discipline to get to school, do the work, and stay out of the way of drug dealers. Apparently Fresno, for all its small-town charm, held the same threats of destruction of its youth as Los Angeles or New York or any other metropolitan area. The people we'd counted on to watch over him fell victim to his mesmerizing promises to do better, if only they'd give him one more chance before "ratting" on him.

But, it wasn't until a frantic, sobbing Richie called home in February, begging sanctuary from a cocaine dealer who had threatened to kill him over some unpaid debts, that I realized the extent of the tangle that was now my son's life.

Drugs had, even then, become so frequently the means of that most tragic end, early death, that psychiatric counseling just for teens on drugs was a specialty of its own. We were fortunate to find such a doctor who had the time in his overbooked schedule to treat Richie. It was on the condition that he see this doctor as often as was deemed necessary (it turned out to be five days a week) that my emaciated, frightened prodigal came home.

There's no question that my own habits had an influence on

Richie. Just as my particular addiction was different from my mother's, so too was my son's different from my own. But the bizarre lesson was the same: if it hurts, don't look for the source; deaden the pain.

During the next two years, he got himself straight and finished high school.

Because we were both so scared by how close he'd come to the edge, Richie and I found ourselves experiencing each other on a here-and-now basis, no recriminations or expectations; just show up, which we both did. I wasn't able to attend the graduation ceremony that was such a triumph for him. I was taping my show. Well, we do the best we can.

Ordinary People

❧

I READ THE NOVEL
Ordinary People when it was first published in 1976. Like most people whose appreciation put it on the best-seller list, I was moved by the story of a family who seemingly had everything but was shattered to bits by the death of a son. The character of the mother, Beth Jarrett, a woman trapped by her expectations of self and family, was of particular interest to me. She made me think of my father and his rigidity. I never thought of it becoming a movie while I was reading the book, so I certainly didn't see myself in her skin.

Yet two years later, when I was told that Paramount was going to film it with Robert Redford directing the Alvin Sargent adaptation, I knew it was going to be a modern masterpiece, or the next thing to it, and that I was meant to be a part of it. Redford himself thought of me for the role, saying later that as he occasionally caught sight of me walking Malibu Beach, he wondered about what might be the "dark side" of Mary Tyler Moore.

I was very much aware that this icon trod the same sand as I. On the rare occasions that our footprints crossed, I was so respectful of his much talked-of need for privacy that I made staring at my quickly moving feet a prime concern. So I cannot say what he appeared to be thinking or how he seemed, at all. I saw nothing except for his feet, which revealed little.

I guess I don't handle meeting celebrities very well, at least not at the beach. One day while dozing facedown on a towel in front of my house, I was jolted awake by the unmistakable voice, directly above me, of Cary Grant. It sounded like he was saying, "I admire your work." I whipped around too quickly to remember that I had unhooked the top of my bikini. I tried to say thank you while at the same time diving back down on the towel to preserve my modesty. Balanced on my stomach, while vainly trying to connect the clasp in back, I craned my head around and tried to speak. I never got more than half words out (certainly no vowels) as he backed away apologetically for having disturbed me. To this day, I agonize over the lost opportunity to have had a conversation with the man I had most admired for his comedic ability, and on whom I had had a major crush, along with most of the female population of the world. I had a blissful week feeling like a champ because of what he'd said to me, though.

But that was long before *Ordinary People* became the Holy Grail of my career. I was not feeling at all confident as I drove to the studio to meet Robert Redford. But he was warm and funny, and so charming that within minutes I forgot who he was. Reality, however, would call to me from time to time. I would be immersed in his vision of the story and its characters, even making an intelligent comment or two myself, when I would feel a thunk in my chest as my mind screamed out—THIS IS ROBERT REDFORD! Then I'd have to summon all my discipline to return to the conversation we were having, without revealing my little lapse.

He told me I was the one whose face he saw as he read the book. There was, however, the issue of whether my television image (Mary Richards) might in some way impose itself on the piece, causing people to think, "Ah, she's going to be funny" or "Look, she's not being funny" and "Where's Asner?" Beth was the character he most cared about, and he wanted her to be portrayed with sensitivity. It was she who drew him to the project. Her non-relationship with her surviving son was the mirror of the non-interaction Redford had had with his own father. He certainly didn't see her as a villain, rather a victim herself.

I flew out of that meeting convinced that whether it was his father or my own who would drive the characterization, I wanted that part. I was going to find out what rooted her resentments and lifted her dreams. I knew he would supply any answers that eluded me during the rehearsal period. There was just this tiny problem of having been too successful at what I had been doing for the last seven years.

I never wanted anything so much. Time stretched interminably on—three months of mental jousting—"He'll go with his first instinct"; "You'll never be anyone but Mary Richards, again." The pain was compounded by the trade talk about the various women being considered for MY PART. My agent, John Gaines, made as many calls to Paramount as he could without seeming to be as obnoxiously single-minded on my behalf as he in fact was. The feedback was always a little hazy and noncommittal.

One day John received a phone call from producer Emanuel Azenberg regarding the replacement of Tom Conti in his award-winning role in the Broadway play *Whose Life Is It Anyway?* It is the story of an artist, a man, whose life has become intolerable after a car accident leaves him a quadriplegic. Having determined the permanent inability to move anything but his head, which is throbbing with torturous scenes of all that will never be, he undertakes the all but impossible legal actions necessary to be granted the right to die.

Tom Conti had given notice after having played the role in London for two years and on Broadway for a third. Mr. Azenberg was inquiring about the availability of another of John's clients, Richard Thomas. John told him that Thomas was going to be working on a film and then added, "But what about Mary Tyler Moore?"

I'll never know what caused John Gaines to leap from a male dramatic actor to me, except that I was never far from his thoughts those days. Perhaps the stalking animal in him sensed the possibility of leverage. Manny Azenberg liked the idea right away.

John's thinking, as presented to me, was this: "It's a great play and a wonderful vehicle for you to show the industry that you're an actress of greater range than they may have considered. Plus, once Paramount and Redford realize that after the filming of *Ordinary People,* but before its release, you will be starring on Broadway in a role strong enough to cast a shadow or two on that bright, happy-ending visage from TV, they'll be on their knees!"

It was a big commitment to make. I would be risking bad reviews simply because I came from that all-too-easy medium called television. Furthermore, who could be sure that changing the sex of the leading character wouldn't adversely affect the dynamics of the play?

*A*nd what about the marriage? Could it withstand this kind of separation? Hell, I was so unsure of our marriage that I'd already turned down two plays to be done right in Los Angeles, fearful that our different schedules would create a chasm.

Grant and I had begun hesitantly to talk about the great silence that had fallen on us. We always made these feeble attempts at self-counseling during the so-called happy hour, the only time we had courage enough to broach the subject. And so the edges of what should have been painful recognition were blurred. Drinking gave us strength but then quickly snatched it away, replacing it with anger. Thus, we were emotionally battered by dinner time, and even more resentful of each other by breakfast. There was nothing in-between.

In case there's any doubt about the acute state of my alcoholism, and the insanity it produced, I can recall with sickening clarity that on more than one occasion I played Russian roulette with my car, and what's more, some unwary, innocent people played with me.

Upon meeting the wall with Grant in a besotted argument after dinner, I'd vent my furious frustration by storming into my car, slamming it into reverse and out onto the street. After I'd crossed Sunset Boulevard, which was an amazing achievement in itself, I'd hit the accelerator and run each stop sign in the residential area called Brentwood 'til I reached Santa Monica Boulevard. It was the certainty of a collision at that juncture that would finally bring me, heart wildly pumping, to a halt and the tears would reduce the force of my anger.

We went to a therapist once, but the thought of entering into a process of truth-telling in front of a complete stranger was more than Grant could allow. The day before we were to have our first real counseling session together he said, "I can't do it."

My answer, partly in disgust at the sense of loss I felt and in recognition that as it stood now *there was nothing more to lose*, was, "We follow through with this or end it." He turned his head away, but not before I saw how shiny his eyes had become. With a curt wave of the hand, he said, "Whatever you want." And then as he walked out of the room, "But you're crazy."

I agreed to do the play. It was announced and solemnly confirmed to the skeptics at Paramount by my dedicated and crafty agent that I would, in the tradition of all great actors, be standing (or in this case, lying) on the boards in the ennobling glare of the spotlight that is theater.

Three months after the first meeting with Redford, I got a call from John Gaines. "He wants to see you this afternoon! He wants to hear you and Donald Sutherland together." "But isn't Sutherland cast as the psychiatrist?" I asked. "He was, but he talked Redford into letting him play Cal, the husband, instead. They want to see how you two interact." I'm pretty good at detecting tension in people's voices, and John was used to playing verbal poker, but I could sense that there was the definite possibility of his succumbing to a stroke over this meeting. This was it!

As I sat in front of the mirror in my bathroom trying to decide how I should look, and what I could do to look like that once I'd figured it out, my face began to take on the grotesqueries of a funhouse reflection. All my flaws were magnified, and I looked like I could play Sutherland's mother more easily. But there was no such character, and it was time to flex all those emotional and physical muscles I needed to win. There was no place for the whining, insecure voice that demanded to be heard.

I tried on and then discarded on the floor, the backs of chairs, in the bathtub, all my fresh-from-the-series knit dresses and pantsuits. Finally, I chose a faded-blue denim skirt that I don't remember buying, or even seeing before. I threw on a white tee shirt and, shod in tan loafers, ran down the stairs, jumped into the car, and backed it into the edge of the garage door.

I reminded myself that I had to get there to win the part and tried to come back to earth enough to make that happen, without corkscrewing myself into a bleak, never-gonna-happen state of mind.

I don't have the kind of looks that stop traffic. I say this from my most well-analyzed and now relatively secure heart. But as I waited at a red light at the corner of Sunset and Beverly Glen, trying to modulate panic and insecurity, the best-looking man I'd ever seen pulled up right along beside me and said, "Hey, babe, you look great." I took it as a sign, and felt myself becoming a racehorse, confident, trained, and ready to win.

I smiled at him, kind of shook my hair the way great-looking babes and horses do, and turned left to what was to be the beginning of the rest of my life.

Chicago

❧

*I*T'S NOT POSSIBLE
to compare directors any more than one can compare people in general. The big screen demands a depth of portrayal much greater than does television. The scenes are structured so that the hidden feelings a character possesses become as important as the dialogue. An actor's mind will have its own thoughts, feelings, and reactions that form during rehearsals, and which are felt but never displayed on film. Bob (that's what I called him then, although I always referred to him as Redford) touched more responders in the process of character development and integration of that person than I'd ever experienced. By the time filming began, there wasn't a situation in which I couldn't imagine just how Beth would feel and how she might behave.

He had to watch me constantly for instinctive "Mary-isms" that were by now a part of me but incongruous for Beth. He systematically stripped me of familiar body language and gestures that were the trademarks of Mary Richards.

He was a perfectionist. He would keep at it take after take, until he saw what he wanted. Then he would turn the last take over to the actors. We could do whatever we wanted to. The blocking re-

❧

mained the same, but we could play it angry, if it had been a tender moment, or stare at the ceiling, scratch anything, as long as it was unexpected. This gave him a treasure trove of options and gave the actors a rich and broadening experience. It involved trust, but I would have entrusted him with my soul, so in awe of his ability was I.

There was just one scene that proved elusive, and drove us both crazy during the entire filming. We tried to shoot it every time we were filming something in the kitchen set and were lit for it. It had no dialogue and only one actor, me. Here is the scene: I stand next to the open refrigerator, holding a cake with a single row of cherries encircling the top. I look at it carefully for some seconds, adjust one of the tiny fruits, place the cake back on the shelf, and close the door.

Redford shot the scene with every lens from every angle, always with the same direction, "Just look at the cake you've made." And every time I would have a thought about it—it was a good cake, it needed more cherries, would it taste as good as it looked—he would stop me and say, "No, no. Clear your mind. Let's go again." We did a total of twenty-six takes over the twelve weeks of filming. If we had an early day he'd say, "Mary, let's try the cake scene again." Off I'd go to put on the required wardrobe, to return feeling naked and resigned to the ritual that was going to take place once more before a mystified crew.

When I saw the final cut, I knew why it had never, in any of its versions, made it. Bob was looking for a glimpse of the woman's soul.

Otherwise, I was pleased with my interpretation. Beth Jarrett's ready smile and cheerful demeanor hid the contempt she felt for weakness, self-doubt, and disorder, all of which lurked inside her. The woman was constantly struggling for the survival of all she'd been taught to hold dear—winning, self-confidence, and pride.

Every seemingly graceful step she took on the road toward happily-ever-after was warily calculated with her family's best interest in mind. There was very little room for spontaneity in Beth's life.

She was a product of her own upbringing, a demanding mother who was so concerned with the externals of a loving home, there simply wasn't the energy left to comprehend the unplanned for, sometimes unattractive, needs of the people she loved.

Everything Beth despised she was herself. But no matter how far down she pushed it, she recognized herself in her surviving son, Conrad. He was the embodiment of her failure as a woman and as a mother. Conrad had fallen apart; his attempted suicide was the prophecy of her own unworthiness. She couldn't forgive him for betraying her.

It's not that she deserved our sympathy, but I've always resented the meant-to-be compliments of "I hated you." "What a bitch." She wasn't. She acted out that which was cultivated in her. It takes good fortune for the opportunity, and then hard work, to break a cycle.

When I began the discovery process before filming, it occurred to me that Beth and my father were not dissimilar in their unrealistic expectations, my father's demands of John in particular. I felt lucky, indeed, to have such a hard-to-find role model right in my family.

It took a few years before I recognized someone else in Beth. *Me.*

*O*n one of my days off, Joel Israel, my hairdresser and friend of over a decade, and I decided to take a limo into the city and have a lovely grown-up lunch at Crickett's, Chicago's elegant sister restaurant to New York's '21.' I called ahead to make a reservation and identified myself to ensure a good table, but since I was to be Joel's guest, I told them to make it in Mr. Israel's name for one p.m. I must have underestimated the impact my presence at the restaurant would have. The maître d', upon receiving a cue from the doorman as we pulled up, came rushing out to our car. His hand, as I took it, was like melting ice and his voice a kind of continual vibrato without music as he said, "Miss Moore, it is an honor to have you here," and then to Joel, "Welcome, Mr. Jew."

I knew I had heard it, but I wasn't certain that my ears hadn't sustained a kind of aural stroke, rendering me incapable of sorting data at that moment. I didn't dare look at Joel, just in case. But as our host led us to the table, he beckoned us to follow, "Miss Moore, right this way. Mr. Jew, I hope the table is to your liking." We collapsed into the banquette, barely containing our shared hysteria. But when the sommelier appeared and asked Mr. Jew if he'd like to see the wine list we then lost it all together. "Manischewitz," Joel replied.

It was during this time that I had my first affair. At age forty-two with the third man ever to enter my body and, for a time, my life.

I met him on the set after the shooting had begun. When he touched me that first time with such intense passion and curiosity, I thought I'd die from pleasure. And I was pretty sure it would be God or Grant himself who would enter the room and do the job. In our lucid moments, we reminded ourselves that this was the heartfelt yet temporary phenomenon of location shooting. He had a longtime commitment and wasn't interested in changing that life.

As for me, there was no question but that my marriage was over. The emotions in Chicago brought me into ownership of my own life. The whole experience of *Ordinary People* led me to anticipate a change. I was loving a man who desired me and who awakened an appetite I'd never experienced, and the world was not coming to an end because of it. The Catholic in me was convinced that I was committing a mortal sin so grave that hell would erupt right here in Chicago as punishment for us all. Worse, it would be written that I was the one who lit the match. On the other side of the ledger was the undeniable affirmation that I was an appealing woman. I had forgotten.

When I returned to Los Angeles for Christmas, however, I did the only thing a guilt-ridden good girl would do about the course I knew I must take—I waffled. Upon going to bed that night, I put my arms around my husband and pressed myself against him. I was told to go to sleep. What a deeply odd feeling that rejection was. Grant didn't know what had happened on location, and was never going to experience the change in my sexuality. What I didn't know was that there was someone else in his life now. We'd moved on in mute concert, once again.

Christmas day, the day before he moved out of our house for good, was pathetic. Even though we had decided that it was over, neither of us could forget the fondness that prompted gift-giving. And so on a day which, even under the best of circumstances, can produce melancholia, we sat side by side on the couch, opening what we knew were the last presents to be exchanged on Christmas or any other occasion. We hugged each other and the dogs, and cried.

*B*ack on the set of *Ordinary People,* we had only a few more days left to finish the picture and for me to finish the affair. My heart was well beyond aching at the thought of saying good-bye to the man who had taught me to see the possibilities in myself. It was bursting. I had known that the relationship was finite from the very beginning; but as time went by, a part of me wanted to believe it could somehow continue, that real life with its expectations and other people's needs could evaporate, leaving the two of us innocent and free.

"Do you know I'll always love you?" "I will never forget you." "I'm going to miss you." Everything he said over the last couple of days that was intended to comfort me confirmed, instead, that I wasn't enough of a woman to manage a miracle.

It was difficult for him, too, but he'd suffered this kind of parting a few times before. He was such a giving lover, I envy all the women who have known him and those who will in the future. And I marvel at the wisdom of his companion, knowing that it is she who gives him his foundation.

When Ordinary People opened in Utah, all of the actors were invited to stay for the weekend at Sundance, Redford's home set amid a thousand private acres of horse trails that lead up steep rocky mountains. The vistas overlook waterfalls and rivers through meadows edged by trees of every shade of green, and quaking Aspen shake their tambourines in abandoned delight to the tempo of the breeze. There were endless views and sheer sudden cliffs that made you suck in your breath and pray that the horse you were riding really was as wise and as practiced as he seemed.

We came to a place where the view was so wide and high and deep, it was too beautiful to exist. Redford stopped, pointed to a huge rock frighteningly near a thousand-or-so-foot drop that was part of this wonder. "Mary, that's where I spent a lot of time thinking about you, almost every day for weeks, trying to make the decision to put you in the film or not." I thought of the wrenching time I'd spent hoping that he'd choose me, never dreaming of the effect that decision would have on me personally.

I wondered what became of *The Lost Princess of Oz*. I couldn't remember the ending from my father's long-ago reading of the book to me as a child in Virginia.

Whose Life Is It Anyway?

❧

I THINK PRODUCER
Manny Azenberg and the Schubert Organization liked the idea of
my name attracting an additional audience. Television fans might
be more inclined to go to the theater if they were going to see an
old friend.

With not much more than the changing of a few pronouns, history was made. It was the first time that a character's gender was
changed during the life of a play. Women have played men and vice
versa. However, in this play the lead character was written to be a
man. But now, suddenly with a woman in the role, the play was
given a new perspective. "Hey, maybe we should see this one,
again"—sound effects of the cash register.

I memorized the play before I left Los Angeles and began to de-
velop the iron will I'd need to remain immobile for two hours. My
character was never offstage so it took three or four rehearsals before I could finally resist every excruciating urge to scratch a phantom itch on my nose or knee, and to resist the instinctive arm thrust
or shoulder shrug to make a point.

People have said it must have been hard for me, a dancer, to re-
strict all movement. But, on the contrary, it was my control of

movement and lifelong attempt at the mastery of muscles that helped me through it. A few set-dressing tricks with pillows and sheets helped, too.

I knew that in New York it would be necessary to devote the rehearsal time to character development and interaction with the other actors, some of whom had been in the play from the start. I was determined to be excellent. I was going to prove to the New York theater community that its "cousin" television could produce an actress of self-command and some surprising depth. I also wanted to dazzle them so that in their memory of *Breakfast at Tiffany's* I would be exonerated of any culpability in the legend of its fall.

I'd heard that the talk in the street was negative in reaction to my coming to this play. I'd been told a few of the jokes going around: "The reason Mary Tyler Moore was cast in this play is that it is the only way they could get her to stop singing and dancing!" and "They're changing the title to *Mary Richards Goes to the Hospital.*"

The rehearsals went fairly well, except that the director, Michael Lindsay-Hogg, seemed to be searching for something more than I gave. He never really articulated his dissatisfaction and, in fact, says he never was unhappy with what I was doing. He simply wanted a performance devoid of female vulnerability or hints of self-pity, and he was guiding me toward that choice.

I remember the epiphany so well. It was a run-through for the Shuberts and a few invited guests shortly before our opening. I was as nervous as a nine-year-old girl in her first recital. Gone was any recollection of our rehearsals and the decisions made, the subtle shadings, the nuance—all gone.

I'd become helpless, the very antithesis of what I knew we'd worked toward. I remember thinking that if I could at least keep my voice from giving me away, I wouldn't lose it all. So I lowered its pitch an octave and *pretended* to be the character. (Funny how often that works.) I pushed the first scene into overdrive and it felt strange at first, but the stronger I became the more everything

Michael had been saying, and not saying, was translated into a language the sculptor in me knew.

I was on top of it, and it felt great. It became clear to me that this was an "adventure play." This woman was digging herself an escape tunnel from prison. No time for sadness or grief. There was a lot of legal digging to be done before she was set free. The small audience applauded with gusto. Michael, now grinning like a new father, took me aside and said, "If you ever play it any other way I'll break both your legs."

We opened to mostly great reviews. It was the triumph I was looking for. And it was to be repeated night after night, and twice a week at matinees. On all but two or three performances during our four-month run I received standing ovations. One of those exceptions was the night my mother and father came to see the play. But that didn't seem to bother them at all. When they came back to the dressing room my mother had tears in her eyes. Really, she was almost unable to speak and my dad was moved to utter, "Well done, chum." I know they were proud.

But what a task! I'd always said the multiple-camera technique in television is very much like the theater, in that you rehearse the show and then perform it from beginning to end in front of an audience. That's the way both the *Van Dyke Show* and mine were filmed. Even though the object is to get it on film the audience certainly boosts the adrenaline. Actors time the lines and physical moves to the reactions the audience gives them. It is a terrific give-and-take.

So naturally after twelve years of experience "playing to the crowd" I thought I was prepared for the theater. What I hadn't counted on was the challenge of repeating the same material night after night without becoming locked into a "by the numbers" performance. In television we had a new story each week. It was the way repertory theater would be—same bunch, different stuff to do. Always fresh!

It took tremendous control to free myself of the sameness I felt lurking in my eight-times-a-week performances. If I got a laugh on a well-delivered line, the tendency was to ensure the laugh by always doing it the same way. And when I reached that peak in a dramatic scene so fine I could hear a silent gasp from that dark place beyond my sight (and the applause that followed convinced me that I could act after all), why, I wanted to do that scene the very same way next time. But giving in to that temptation doesn't work, because only rarely can one mimic one's self convincingly. So, I would sit in that quadriplegic's bed waiting for the curtain to rise, wondering how I would get through it. It seemed as though I were at the base of a very high, very steep mountain that had to be climbed. Once we began, however, I always became involved and focused. And I enjoyed the trek.

GIRDLES

Three weeks after opening, I came down with laryngitis. That was something else peculiar to the stage that I'd not been prepared for—the vocal projection required to reach the back rows. No microphones. The extra volume needed to be heard at a distance of fifty yards as opposed to three feet can cause a small war between your vocal cords. I could hear the raspiness creeping in, and I could certainly feel it, almost like slipping a gear.

I was sent to see the best voice man in New York, Dr. Wilbur Gould, now gone, savior to opera singers, public speakers, and at one time or another, most all of Broadway. First he wrapped my tongue with a strip of gauze, which he used to pull it from its mooring and straight out of my face. After about twenty minutes of probing with some very strange-looking instruments so he could see any and all enemies hiding in there, he gave me his diagnosis and remedy. The problem, it seemed, was caused by a lack of support from my stomach muscles for the diaphragm, which is an important part of amplifying the voice. Because I lay on my back for the entire performance, I wasn't using my stomach muscles as I would if I were standing. So the effort was coming entirely from the throat. He then prescribed what I'm sure is the oddest Rx of all time—a girdle! He said its tightness would remind me to contract those muscles, and soon all would be well.

I wonder if anyone can imagine how self-conscious and defensive I was as I, a former dancer, Laura of the Capri-pants fame, approached the saleswoman in the lingerie department of Saks Fifth Avenue and told her I needed a girdle—for my throat! After that initial trauma to my ego, I recovered pretty nicely and bought girdles in every color! My throat got better, too.

My Assassin

I began receiving life-threatening letters at the Royale Theatre soon after opening. For a time, we dismissed them as being the harmless, if ill-advised, attempt at contact on the part of some twisted fan or someone who just strongly disagreed with the critics about my performance! But then I was paid a visit by two New York detectives. They told me of a phone call they had received from a Catholic priest. He had heard the confession of a man who had seen the play and said he loved me so much he was going to grant my (stage) wish to die. This was followed by a call to them from a bartender who heard a man sitting at the bar muttering to himself about the same wish fulfillment. They asked me a lot of the same questions we hear on television, who I might know who "had it in for me," etc. I told them that I once walked into a laugh of Ed Asner's in the last year of the show, but despite his tough demeanor, I didn't think he'd take revenge this far. And so began the search for the would-be "perp," and I said farewell to the last vestige of privacy I had. From then on, a plainclothes detective followed my every move while I wasn't on stage. A guard was stationed outside my door at the Waldorf Towers, where I lived. Frank Sinatra kept an apartment on the same floor, and when he was in residence there would be a sentry posted at his door full-time. I wondered if they ever chatted after we were tucked into our beds for the night.

There is a peculiar sensation in being guarded. I was constantly reminded by the police presence that my life was in real danger. At the same time, I was forced to carry on inane chatty conversations with these strangers for most of my waking hours. I did get to know a couple of them pretty well, and will forever be grateful to them.

At the theater, each time the curtain went up, the oddest sight presented itself to me and it was all I could do not to laugh! On either side of the stage at the balcony level were two boxes seating four to six people each. In addition to the theatergoers in those boxes were two plainclothesmen. However, unlike the ticket holders, they were not facing the stage. They sat with their backs to me so they had a clear view of the audience. The police felt that if the would-be killer made his try, it would most likely occur while I was onstage. The other actors were, of course, horrified at what was going on, but did their best to make me feel more comfortable. They were in danger, too! But I pointed out to them that at least they could try to dodge the bullet, while I could move only from the neck up, with a spotlight on my face!

After ten days, he emerged one afternoon from the shadowy area just outside the stage door as I was entering the theater for a matinee. He made a lunge for me, arms outstretched, but was captured and cuffed so quickly by my new best friend that I wasn't really sure what had happened, much less the gravity of it. It wasn't until the curtain went up and I saw those two empty chairs that I realized my personal police saga was over. That evening, as I walked down the long corridor to my apartment, I was sad not to see the now familiar figure of my nighttime companion. Frank still had his.

HELLO, IS THAT YOU?

When the play closed, I was suddenly without my mountain, without anything to give my life structure and purpose. I was on my own, single, no obligations to anyone. Richie, via telephone, was showing signs of growing up, of pride in himself and his accomplishments. We had developed a still unsteady but growing tolerance for, and gentleness with, each other since my separation from Grant. In Richie's eyes I was now vulnerable. The mother who'd always seemed to exhibit willpower as the source of fulfillment was not so sure of everything. He became very protective of me, cautioning me on the wicked ways of men with divorcées. A paternal tone crept into his voice when he asked, "How are you doing, Mom?"

I was seeing some real changes in him. He had been drug-free and working for a year as a bank teller in downtown Los Angeles— getting himself there and home by bus to an apartment he shared with two others in West Hollywood.

He had a girl who lived in Fresno who, despite the distance between them, obviously made him happy from the way he spoke about her. We talked often, and coming through those conversations was an affection for each other that pushed expectations to the side for a while. It was as though this major change in my life provided an avenue for retreat from stances long held by us both, namely, "You care too much about work," and "Why don't you get to work?"

He was being considered for a full-time job as an assistant to the CBS photographer Tony Esparza, who had used him from time to time. Tony had watched him grow up from the beginning of *The Dick Van Dyke Show,* and he admired his fight to survive as an adult. He was willing to be a mentor to this still rough but promising young man. I'm not sure that photography was Richie's goal so much as it might have been an entry into acting. I was concerned that acting might have seemed too easy from his vantage point growing up in Beverly Hills. But a part of me was pleased to know that I hadn't made so many mistakes with him as a working mother that following my career choice was out of the question for him.

Put on a
Happy Face

❧

*L*OOKING AT NEW YORK
City from my thirty-second-floor window at the Waldorf, I felt the
anticipation of someone about to be released from prison. Not just
from the play, but my whole adult life, which I saw as having been
lived with my arm around someone else's neck. It was 1980.

My routine as television star and Mrs. Grant Tinker was so narrow and protected I didn't even know what to do in a bank! I had
never experienced any of the situations around which *The Mary
Tyler Moore Show* had been based—independent young woman
carving a career for herself, finding her way in a strange city, making new friends, choosing, rejecting, saying, doing exactly what I
wanted for myself, by myself, ALONE!

I decided to stay in New York for three months and try everything I could in that time before heading back to Los Angeles and
my now empty house with its vaulted ceilings, long shadows, and
deserted tennis court. Newly solo, I was going to do everything I
should have done had I gone to college. So what, if I were now
forty-three years old. It's never too late. We must walk, jeté, spin
through all life's stages and take the opportunities if we are lucky
enough to be given a second go-round.

Living at the Waldorf had removed any hint of self-management I had arrived with. It had been five months of a luxurious existence there, just push a button—"Bring me an omelette and take my laundry." I was like a middle-aged "Eloise." Now I was determined to make it on my own. I rented a house on East Sixty-fourth Street where I could recapture that sense of self I'd flirted with in Chicago, and experiment with my impression of the hard-to-beat gal, Mary Richards. But before I left the shelter and privacy of the Waldorf Towers, I decided to get myself a new face, or at least a very much younger version of the one I had.

It embarrasses me to have denied by my actions what I believe to be true: that women deserve the same consideration in aging as men. To perpetuate the stigma of wrinkles by having them erased is not in the best interest of females who seek equality based on integrity, intelligence, and talent.

Carl Reiner once told me that when his then fifteen-year-old daughter, Annie, asked if she could have a nose job, her mother, Estelle, put an end to the brief discussion by saying, "Annie, it's not what a nose looks like that counts—it's what's in it." I carry that exhortation tucked away but easily retrievable because it makes me laugh and it's basically sort of true. (I doubt my mother would agree with Mrs. Reiner. She said that when I was presented to her at birth she was concerned about what appeared to be the absence of a nose on my face—just a small bump with two holes in it, no bridge. So every time she held me, she gently pinched and shaped that area until it became a nose. To those who've always suspected I didn't come by my nose naturally, it is true. I had a nose job and at a very early age.)

I made the appointment for my lift, paying particular attention to the details of secrecy. I figured I'd be better off recuperating at the hotel because I could have room service and wouldn't have to encounter anyone until I was presentable.

The procedure went very well. My handsome cosmetic surgeon was grinning from surgically pinned-back ear to ear.

The morning I was to leave the hospital, my face resembled a bruised tomato. My eyes were slits and my entire head was swathed in bandages. I'd been told what to expect, but I wasn't prepared for the apparition that squinted back at me from the mirror. I was a gargoyle.

A friend who was to accompany me home had dutifully brought along the disguise I'd planned—dark glasses, a long chiffon scarf, and a wide-brimmed floppy hat, which, it turned out, didn't come close to fitting over my bandage helmet. The item I was most proud of coming up with was a large empty dress box to hold close to my chest so that only my glasses would be visible peering over its top—well, my glasses and the oddly shaped chiffon turban, with the hat precariously resting on top.

I thought it important to take a cab rather than one of the chauffeur-driven limos I used, for fear I'd have a driver who knew me. That proved to be a mistake. As luck would decree, the cab we hailed had long since lost its ability to absorb even the smallest of shocks, and its driver seemed determined to confirm this by finding every pothole that existed on that very long (ten blocks) drive home. I braced to protect my sensitive head area as best I could, and kept adjusting the box so it didn't jab me in the face as I tried to hide from the lunatic who was in command of this ride from hell. When at last we pulled up to the Towers, with its discreet entry on Fiftieth Street, the driver turned around and said, "I hope you feel better, Miss Moore. You don't look so good."

What happened next was right out of a script. The private elevator that was to whisk me to the sanctuary of the thirty-second floor was broken. Tower residents had to use the main-lobby elevators! Holding on to my hat, I crouched and hurried around the windy corner to the main Park Avenue entrance of the Waldorf-Astoria Hotel. Up the marble stairs I crept to find more people milling around than I had ever seen—obviously a convention of some sort. When I glanced at the event easel at the top of the stairs, I nearly passed out: WELCOME SOCIETY OF RECONSTRUCTIVE SURGEONS it read. Never did the walk from the door to the bank of elevators on the other side of the lobby seem so endless, nor was it ever traversed so quickly. Of course, all the doctors recognized my pathetic post-surgery disguise and guilty body language. I was certain that if I raised my eyes from the carpet, I'd find every one of them winking at me with knowing grins on their own all-too-perfect faces.

I don't know when it was I lost the hat, but I'll be forever grateful to whoever might have seen me lose it, and tactfully chose not to bring it to my attention.

Liar, Liar,
Pants on Fire

❧

*T*HERE ARE STRANGE
consequences when lies and truth share the same bed, I have learned.

When I lied and said it was the right thing to close *The Mary Tyler Moore Show,* it was the truth for corporate-planning purposes. But it was also the truth that closing the show was a crippling moment for me.

There was an ironic backfire from a lie I chose to tell in order to hide a truth about myself. Since this incident, which occurred in 1980 with Gloria Steinem, I've made it a policy never to lie unless it not only serves, but also covers every possibility of entrapment.

When Gloria asked me to fly to Washington, DC, with her to attend a rally to support passage of the Equal Rights Amendment, I reluctantly agreed. The reason for my reticence was my perennial sweaty-palmed, knee-shaking fear of standing at a microphone and speaking right to people's faces who are staring back at me. It doesn't matter whether it's ad-lib or a prepared text. It doesn't matter whether it is before ten people or two thousand, it is terrifying. I became Mary the person who, without a role to play, might finally be seen naked and judged to be the fake she is. Simply having to read the list of nominees and announce the winner at the

❧

Academy Awards sends more adrenaline through me than opening night on Broadway. It's the absence of the mask. I know that someday I will accept who I am with a measure of pride, but by that time, I'll be too old to stand at a microphone. I'll be in the long wooden crate at the base of one, while someone extols my past virtues.

As the date for the DC trip drew nearer, my nervousness increased. I had also been asked to have dinner in New York on that committed day by a man who was a potential cause for sweating palms and shaking knees of the sexual variety. I called Gloria, certain that they didn't really need me. I told her, with what I'd hoped was convincing disappointment, that because of an ear infection, on doctor's orders I couldn't consider flying for the next few days. She was understanding yet devastated. "Tip O'Neill has agreed to see our contingent, which will get us good press. But he only agrees to see us if you're there." Having already told a lie, there was nothing I could do but try to maintain a reasonable balance between guilt and glee at having pulled it off. Within a half hour she called back to say that the solution to my ear condition was an easy one. Instead of flying to DC, a forty-five-minute trip, "We could save the day, if not time, and the movement, by taking Amtrak."

EIGHT HOURS BY TRAIN round-trip instead of an hour and a half! All because of a badly told lie!

For the most part, the rally was peopled by a few hundred well-intentioned intelligent women waving placards and generally behaving like angry children. Which is, in my opinion, one of the reasons the amendment didn't pass. Along with others on the podium, my speech was to those who were already on our side. So, what was the point?

The capper to that long, seemingly purposeless day, before the four-hour train ride back to New York, was the still-not-understood meeting with Tip O'Neill, an avowed supporter of the ERA, anyway. He entered his office which was peopled by well-spoken advocates of women's rights—tough, no-nonsense women, including Bella Abzug, Gloria Allred, Shirley Chisholm, and Frances

Lear, and said, "Where's that little cutie? I want a big hug from Mary Tyler." Redfaced, I stood in demi-crouch and presented myself for the encircling: his payment for the audience granted to these hardworking well-credentialed women.

It wasn't a wasted experience. Afterward, I went through the room-to-room process of lobbying congressmen to listen to our pleas for funding day-care centers, equal pay for equal work, all part of the process that makes this country of and by the people. Gloria was off to points elsewhere and I took the train back to New York alone. I was pleased that my little speech was well received. And even though I had missed the date with frog number ten, who could have turned into a prince, so what? I was a member of a group who fought for equality and was proud of myself for making a contribution to that goal. Still, eight hours on a train *is* a big price to pay for inept lying.

Here's Lookin' at You, Kid

༄

$\mathcal{T}$HE THIRD FLOOR OF
my new digs on East Sixty-fourth Street had a balcony off the bedroom in the back which I used to try to regain my now faded California tan. The shadows cast by the surrounding tall buildings made
it impossible to receive the rays for more than about eight minutes
a day. But each day shortly after ten a.m., when the sun made its
brief yet seductive appearance, I donned my bikini, lay down on
the wooden floor of this five-by-six ledge, adjusting the potted
plant so it would shade my face, and began to reclaim the leathery
skin California had so easily produced.

Sometimes, this porch provided an interesting glimpse into the
backyard of the house Richard Nixon and his wife had bought on
East Sixty-fifth Street. It abutted the house two doors away from mine.

I remember that Fourth of July in particular, when the temperature rose to 103 degrees. I watched in amazement as this man,
wearing a dark blue suit and tie, stood for a long, long time with a
garden hose in his hand and concentrated quite earnestly on filling
a plastic wading pool (for his grandchild as it turned out). Mrs.
Nixon, dressed for a formal tea party, sat quite upright on a chair
and silently watched.

I never saw either of them out of their strangely formal attire all that summer, but I was pleased to see how often the little ones visited and the ready smile on the face of the man who was "not a crook." It was touching.

A woman came three times a week to clean, but that was all she did. I relearned how to operate a washer-dryer, and lugged my own clothes to the dry cleaners. I even kept track of the claim checks.

I quickly picked up the New York habit of delicatessen take-out food. If it didn't come from room service or a live-in cook, I convinced myself at least I was moving in the right direction. I didn't dare go much farther than that.

Years earlier when I was still married to Grant, I had tested new ground in the kitchen with an old recipe of my grandmother's: "made from scratch" french fries. I was confident that I could duplicate her special crunchy-on-the-outside-soft-in-the-middle English recipe. Grant stood guard at the barbecue, armed with a water pistol to control the heat of his coals under steak.

I remembered my grandmother's preparations, such as cutting the fries thick, soaking them in water for a time—why, I don't know. I'd remembered the subtleties but had forgotten, or never knew, the obvious: You don't wait for the oil to boil before putting the potatoes into the pot because it will burst into flames. And it did! But reacting surely and quickly—no panic here—I grabbed a towel and put the flaming pot into the sink and, yes, turned on the water! There was, of course, a miniature atomic explosion radiating flames everywhere, including the ceiling, which I had just, that week, covered wall-to-wall with overlapping baskets of all shapes, textures, and tones—a process that took days of planning, purchasing, arranging, nailing, and which transformed a closet-sized dull kitchen into the kind of cozy room *House and Garden* would have lusted after. I remember leaping away from the inferno now blocking the only exit and finding myself backed against the re-frigerator, which I opened and reflexively made a feeble attempt to enter.

How I escaped joining the walls, shutters, and the beloved bas-kets in their charred fate could cause one to reconsider the existence of the old guardian angel. But, in fact, it was Grant who uncharac-teristically broke eye contact for a moment with his ever potentially threatened steaks to give me an encouraging wave through the glass door. He charged in, still carrying the water pistol, I noticed, along with a stack of towels that did the trick. He saw, he came, he con-quered, and never let me forget it.

Designing my single life in New York, I took friends to lunch and dinner, confident in my recently acquired ability to figure out the appropriate tip. This was a big deal for me when you consider my inexperience with the role of host, plus a teensy brain disorder I have called dyscalculia. It's the mathematical equivalent of dyslexia.

The reason that I know there is such a condition and that I have it is because of my conviction at the time that I'd never be invited back to the big acting party. So I decided to seek the council of a psychologist who specialized in testing for hidden talents, and mak-ing career evaluations. I spent four days taking a lot of tests, the re-sults of which revealed dyscalculia: a glitch in the brain that prevents one from dealing with numbers at the proper level.

And after all that testing, it turned out that I was best suited to be either a model or a member of the armed forces.

In 1981, the weight of Grant's dissatisfaction with television pro-duction was lifted from him, along with what I'm sure was his dis-comfort in running the company that bore his ex-wife's initials.

RCA asked him to become chairman of the board of its sub-sidiary, the National Broadcasting Company. This meant he'd have to divest himself of his interests in MTM Enterprises, Inc. The ethics of a network president possibly buying shows from his own company would be frowned on by FCC standards.

It was the final cut of any tie I might have had to him, and oddly, it hurt.

An assessment of the company's value was made by an outside auditing firm and, based on their findings, Grant called the numbers he wanted for his buyout.

It was to Grant's dismay and our pleasant surprise that seven years later when MTM was sold, it brought a greater amount than it was earlier thought to be worth.

Despite my resolve to be fiercely independent, there were times I thought it would all be so much nicer if I had a man to accompany me on this crummy journey. Without someone to validate me, I saw myself as a failure. When I went to the Metropolitan Museum of Art and looked at the Impressionists, for all their beauty I saw myself alone in a corner of a Renoir, or wished that I were in that park Seurat painted, with a lover of my own. Everything seemed to focus on my being painfully single.

There had been only six months in my life that I'd lived by myself, and that was between my two marriages. And even during that period, Grant and I were in love and it sustained me. I was coupled—safe.

I began to feel that half my body was missing—Grant. Seventeen years is a long time, even if the relationship is fraught with problems. There was the familiar strong face to reassure me that the world would not come to an end. Grant brought out the adult in me, while comforting the child.

Feelings of helplessness are common to every woman I have talked to who either leaves or is left by her husband. And I am told it is even worse for men. I love the apocryphal story of the newly divorced man wheeling his cart through the supermarket in a daze, who finally asks for help, "Where will I find the toast?"

The Tarzan approach to coupling makes life easier. Don't let go of one vine until you have the other firmly in hand.

So, in the beginning of my solo existence, I was really looking for another man to comfort, distract, and consume me. Oh sure, I would be my own person, but was there any reason I couldn't be in love, too? It got to the point where I would evaluate every man I met on his looks and qualities for mating potential.

It's amazing that so many of us, men and women alike, are so undernourished emotionally that despite all evidence to the contrary, we feel that we are unattractive to those who attract us. I have never allowed myself second thoughts about my talent, judgment, or looks in front of a camera or on stage. But that is the only sanctuary from self-criticism I can count on. The self-doubt is still there, I just don't think about it so much.

Not surprisingly, during that summer the distillation of what had been, for many years, my growing alcoholism took place. Even though I was accomplishing things by myself, it was all so uncomfortable for me that instead of investigating those feelings, I anesthetized myself at the end of the day. Nothing was so tough I couldn't get through it until five-thirty or six. Then the anticipation of the effects of my two fishbowl–sized glasses of vodka on the rocks made it all go away. I replayed a very different version of the day for myself as I drank the elixir: one well spent, and accomplished easily.

I'd been laying the groundwork for full-out alcoholism for some time. But when you have company, the destination of that trip isn't so obvious. There's no doubt in my mind that the essential problems between Grant and me (our inability to reveal ourselves to each other) were aggravated by alcohol-provoked arguments. They were never resolved as neither of us could remember them the next morning. So the only residue of these alcohol-veiled evenings was a sureness that we fought more than we laughed.

The death knell of our seventeen-year marriage was sounded by ice cubes.

I grew to prefer isolation at night in New York, because then I could get as fuzzy as I wanted without anyone to see the distortion. And the sad thing is that, in part, I was drinking because I was so damn lonely.

At one point, in the spirit of the grand adventure in Manhattan, I took to making margaritas in the blender. (Hey, a little kitchen experience, too.) My recipe was a quarter of a blender of bottled mix, one-quarter of ice, one-half of tequila, and shake it up, baby! It had the consistency of a milk shake and the effect of morphine.

I loved to take it to my bed. It was right by the air conditioner, which the City of New York had made almost ineffectual in an attempt to conserve the energy output that summer. But if I stayed on the side of the bed next to it and built a baffle on the other side of me with bed pillows, it resembled a kind of soft igloo that was quite comfortable. The phone rested on a large table as did the TV. Everything I needed was within reach. My life from six till eight p.m. was spent looking at pictures of people in magazines doing the things I thought would be fun—boating, skiing, dancing with the new man who would allow me to soar, as I did now from the drinks.

There would be moments when I'd recognize the irony of my drinking and fantasize about what could have been reality (what I had hoped to do in these three months); but sitting up there at the North Pole with the margaritas was so much easier than risking life.

Drinking was part of my upbringing. They weren't all addicted to it, but all the family used alcohol, and pretty constantly, too. While Gail and I were putting on those little shows, everyone was drinking. There was never a 5:30 p.m. when individually, or as a group, my whole family didn't go to the liquor cabinet and pour themselves a drink.

I saw nothing unusual, let alone wrong, with the style in which I was living my life, secreting myself in that bedroom and watching television until I couldn't make sense of it anymore. It is another indication of my problem that it never occurred to me to want to change my behavior.

On the infrequent occasions when I was out with other people, I was able to judge the level of their sobriety and never outdistance them, a classic characteristic of an alcoholic. Mostly, however, those evenings at home, alone on that bed with its pillows, became a pattern that didn't vary. The phone would ring occasionally, but I never answered for fear my speech would betray me. Eventually, I would nibble on the ever-present cold delicatessen California-barbecued chicken-with-coleslaw dinner.

I didn't pass out, and I never had hangovers. At least not as others described them. I did have a little trouble putting on my eyeliner in the mornings, though. The tremor in my hand was a nuisance, so I simply put a little more time into it.

*A*fter my rewarding summer experiment in homemaking, I returned to the Waldorf.

Along Came Bill

*H*OPE LANGE HAD
played Dick Van Dyke's wife in the second, shorter-lived *Dick Van
Dyke* series. Jay Sandrich, the director, kept saying to us both, "You
two gals have to meet. You'll love each other."

We had lunch one day in New York, and laughed so much that,
when the restaurant closed only a week later, we took it to be the
result of our bad behavior and laughed some more. Hope became
my big sister. She's a great cook and liked nothing better than to
have her small coterie of lonely New Yorkers over to her cozy Tur-
tle Bay apartment for a few drinks, laughs aplenty, and lotsa pasta.
I generally reciprocated by having her come to my suite at the Waldorf for room service. We liked that better than going to a restaurant because it allowed us the privacy that two ladies who drink a
tad too much find so comfortable.

One evening, as we sat in my living room, going through the
room-service menu that I knew by heart, the phone rang. It was
for Hope, a friend who had been given my number by Hope's answering service. He kept me on the phone longer than necessary,
I thought, but I enjoyed every minute of it. I handed him reluctantly to his rightful owner. "Nonsense," she laughed at the half-

hearted apology I made for having flirted with this charmer, and I left the room to give her privacy.

When I returned, she was glowing. "This is great! Bill wants to meet you," she squealed with delight. She proceeded to fill me in on the artist who was, for a short time, her lover. They saw each other now as friends whenever he was in the United States, which was seldom.

"You've got to meet him," Hope said. "He's magnetic. You'll have the time of your life. He's intelligent, knowledgeable, a raconteur, and a magical lover. Just don't take him seriously," she threw in. "And ask him if he's got anyone for me while he's in town."

He called me a couple of days later and asked if I wanted to take a walk sometime. "Why don't we have lunch?" I asked, to which he responded, "I'm afraid of long-term commitments. What if you're bored with me by the salad?" He was masterful at playing the stallion, and the first to laugh at his clichéd come-ons. He was as engaging as anyone I had ever talked to, male or female.

I recalled a party several years prior when he had been surrounded by several people. As I neared him, there was a powerful moment of connection between us, in spite of the fact that he didn't appear to miss a beat in the conversation he was conducting. That had been at least eight years ago, but I could still remember the impact.

We met for a walk. He was waiting at the designated spot and opened the taxi door just as it came to a halt. He paid the driver, which was good, because I was so taken by the warmth of his smile, the comfort it offered, that I seemed to have lost the reflexes needed for such things. I was barely able to find the curb with my foot. Despite the threat his flirting had posed on the phone, I was now looking into the eyes of a boy who had just opened the one Christmas present he ever in his whole life wanted—me.

As we walked, he wanted to know everything about me—childhood, Richie, my work, how I felt about the ending of my marriage. The man was fascinated with my answers, too, never letting an offhand comment go unanalyzed. We took delight in each other's sparring abilities, views on life, and theories about nothing important.

After an hour or so of aimless meandering, we found ourselves in front of his hotel. Warning lights brought everything back into sharp focus. I had a very serious, if brief, conversation with myself about what possible harm could come from following my very strong instincts. A broken heart? A social disease? Do it. I obeyed.

We saw each other almost every day for about three weeks. Our lovemaking was all-consuming and our appetites scared the hell out of me. The more we were together, the stronger my passion for him grew. His mind could tackle everything from politics to movies. And I loved going to galleries and museums with him serving as my personal guide.

I slept alone at the Waldorf one night. He went to a party given by a man who was a partner in the New York gallery that represented his work. It might have been awkward for me to be there. So, I spent the evening alone doing "girl things" like an avocado mask, deep-skin moisturizer, and hair conditioning, complete with a Saran Wrap turban, and then off to sleep I went, feeling in that "Cosmo woman" way that the results might make me more worthy of this man's attentions. We would see at lunch, tomorrow.

Richie

෨

$\mathcal{A}$T FIVE A.M. THE phone awakened me. It was Grant. "I waited so you could get some sleep first," his very strange-sounding voice said. "If you're standing, you should sit down."

"I am sitting," I said. That's what they always say when they're afraid you will pass out. "It's Richie. He's dead." I stood up and shouted into the phone, "What do you mean?" My body and mind were struggling to stay calm to comprehend what he was saying. His housemate had told Grant that Richie had been sitting on his bed, watching TV with a gun in his hand. Then the gunshot.

The reaction I felt was one familiar to all mothers on occasion. I was furious with Richie. It was like the time he wandered off as a youngster. At first finding him was blissful relief, then anger with him took over for having put himself in jeopardy.

It could not be true. There was a mistake. This was not happening. I so disassociated myself from the horror that I went through an experience of feeling badly for his mother. Could he be here for twenty-four years and then irreversibly cease to exist? My sobs were those of panic.

෨

Then I recognized a primal feeling from my childhood: if I let my pain out, if I were very truly sorry, maybe I could change it. But the tears wouldn't deliver me.

I called a friend to help get me on a plane to Los Angeles. Maybe when the plane landed it would all be different—a mistake.

I called Grant back for the details that are better left unknown, but essential to hear. He had been holding a gun. The wound, where? Face. Did he live for any time? Death en route to a hospital, in the ambulance.

I had an appointment with my analyst for that afternoon. It was now seven a.m. I wasn't expecting him to be in his office at that hour and was planning to leave a message, so when I heard his voice instead of a machine I was unprepared. "My son is dead. Shot himself. I have to cancel my appointment for today." I will never forget his response: "I understand. Thank you for calling, Mary."

In my closet was a black suit that had a shocking-pink silk blouse. I left the blouse on its hanger and as I folded the suit, I thought, "Why wasn't there some premonition when I bought it? Has this happened to my child?" I started hyperventilating. A rhythmic audible shallow breathing. It was an involuntary heaving of breath that never released itself into a cry. Throughout the next several days, it would come from nowhere, in mid-conversation, eating, in the bathroom. These spasms would last up to a minute and then just go away, leaving an unreleased, unbearable pain in their wake.

Grant met me at the airplane, trying to ward off the press, which by this time was calling it a suicide. A formal investigation by the Los Angeles Coroner's Office later confirmed that his death was accidental.

Richie collected guns and kept some on his bedroom wall. He had been toying with one of them, a gun called a Snake Charmer, when it went off. It was eventually taken off the market because of its "hair-trigger" instability.

It is important to me that Richie be remembered as he was—a defiant believer in life.

We held the service outdoors, the coffin resting under a vast oak tree. Ed Asner said Kadish, the Jewish prayer for the dead. Richie had always thought Ed was a "good guy." And it just seemed right and good.

My parents, Dick, many people, young and old, stood under that tree and spoke about the young man they knew—some since childhood. So many of the people who are a part of my life came with their strength and love, including Bill.

The next day, a funeral director brought Richie's ashes to me.

Dick Meeker, Grant, and I, holding the remains of my son close to my belly, boarded a private plane that took us north to Mammoth Airport, where a rental car was waiting. Dick got behind the wheel and drove us to a place near the Owens River. We walked to a small bridge where father and son had spent some very happy times. Grant and Dick stood together on the bank as I made my way to the bridge. It was a sunny day, as I remember; the water was clear and high as I knelt over it. I opened the container and emptied it into the rushing water.

What was meant to be a prayer became an outraged demand. "You take care of him," I screamed at the sky.

Missing you has become so much a part of me, so familiar in its shades of black and smoke, its tangible density or feathery tendrils of images that move always through the routines of my day, that I can't remember what it felt like to be Mom.

I'm looking at the now empty head of a dandelion's stem whose fragile spores have been blown away. Wasn't it here just a moment ago in its gossamer incarnation? Fragile, yes, but there in my hand? Let me see the proof of goneness. There is just empty space.

When I see myself on film, a scene captured from Dick Van Dyke, perhaps you were seven or nine or six, as the camera recorded my actions, you, too, are recorded somewhere just offstage. What were you doing then at just those moments? I want that time to be replayed. How frantically I would step through the film, breaking the rules of this rerun to catch you up in my arms. I'd take you to this today I live in and every "Mom, look at this!", "Would you tell me a story?", "What's six times eight?" would be ours again without a thought of tomorrow.

And There
Went Bill

❧

*B*ACK IN NEW YORK,
Bill had begun to pull himself toward the leaping-off point necessary for flight, and, of course, flight by definition, is untethered. He
had actually said to me, early on, that for all his bad reputation as a
lady-killer, he'd never walked out on a woman. They had all left
him. Well, he didn't walk out on me, either. He simply became very
busy with meetings, especially at night. Bill left for Paris one day
without warning, calling me dutifully once or twice a week and saying he would come back soon. So there I was, and there went Bill.

I stopped seeing my analyst, and taking a firm hold of the straps
of my boots, held my breath and pulled. Denial has always had a
pejorative cast to it. But, isn't the conscious denial of danger what
makes a hero?

My Affair with
Dick Cavett

I HAD ALWAYS AD-
mired the scope of Dick Cavett's knowledge and his ability on
camera to listen and change direction based on what he hears and,
of course, I love his superb wit. We've had an on-and-off phone
relationship through the years. My conversations with him stimu-
late my own sense of humor, and I find myself laughing not only
at him but at myself as well.

I decided to escape the miseries of summer in Manhattan and lease
a small beach house in the Hamptons. I'd heard that he had a house
in Montauk and asked his advice. He put me in touch with a company that specialized in the Montauk area only, but they, in turn, suggested a realtor who, after unsuccessfully trying to sell me a farm in
Connecticut, reluctantly found a Westhampton beach house for me.

I had envisioned long walks on the beach at dusk, coming away
with insight and renewed vigor. Instead, I very often curled up with
a novel and an insight-dulling martini.

The phone rang one night as I was sitting there ever closer to
emotional bankruptcy and the first thing I heard was "So you got
a place at the beach." Instant guilt. I recognized the voice I never
thanked—Dick Cavett.

He asked if I liked riding. "I'll give you my horse, she's the best, and you can see the best house in the world."

We decided, after analyzing the analyst situation, he to be in New York for a session on Tuesday morning, me to New York for my new one Wednesday afternoon, that the following Saturday we'd meet. My coupling instinct was still so strong, I couldn't resist. I fantasized that he might be currently separated from his wife, the beautiful, talented actress Carrie Nye. And that he would at some point put his arms around me and lead me to the best bed in the best house in the world and make inspired and inspiring love to me.

I drove to Montauk, and we met in front of the local drugstore since his house was too remote for a first-time visitor to find. The always dapper, perfectly groomed Dick Cavett of television sprang at me in baggy boxer shorts, sneakers of a shade of gray that evolves only after having been worn for five years minimum, a tee shirt that more closely resembled an undershirt, a cowboy scarf tied around his neck, and a baseball cap on his head.

He seemed glad to see me in the way a young boy on a first date might—nervous and eager to please. It melted any apprehensions I had about the man I thought would put me away with his polysyllabic self-confidence.

We decided to leave my car there and ride to the house in his van, the interior of which resembled the recently abandoned dwelling of a large family of Gypsies. Draped over the turn indicator was a damp bathing suit, its companion piece hanging from the radio knob. So much for music! The floor and front seat were strewn with newspaper, odd bits of rope, envelopes, and one sandal. On the backseat, nested amongst similar items, was a giant standard black poodle who was introduced to me as Louis, his best friend of sixteen years. Louis raised up as best he could on his arthritic legs, wagged his tail, and during the fifteen-minute ride to the house, proved his age by providing a kind of one-dog-band concert of tuneful expulsions.

The house, as promised, was the best house in the world, *potentially*. It stood untouched by latter-day carpenters or, for that matter, caretakers, painters, or plumbers. Resting on a bluff high above the ocean with trees of all sorts, it was beautifully but needlessly sheltered from the scrutiny of neighbors, the closest of whom was a good five acres away. The inside of this wedding-cake house was yet another reflection of the man: like the van and the dog, great possibilities but gone to seed. He had made an obvious and endearing attempt to clean, neaten, and straighten everything.

We went horseback riding on the beach, which wasn't as much fun as I thought it would be because the horse tended to get its hoofs stuck in the sand, and so we didn't cover much ground. But we looked good.

If ever I can eliminate the height factor from my list of requisites for a lover, I'll know I've grown up and left Daddy where he should be. But the thought of waking up in the "spoons" position with someone whose toes are pressed against my calves is even harder to contemplate than crouching down for that first passionate kiss. In spite of his wit, gentleness, and good looks, he was short and I couldn't get past that. It appears I'm a height bigot. But then again, Mr. Cavett had only invited me for a nice day in Montauk.

Growing up is hard to do.

The San Remo

◈

GIVEN MY FRUITLESS
search for a man with the potential for more than a few dates, and
certain, at last, that Grant and I wouldn't be writing a song about
"Love lost, yet found again," I decided to go it alone and commis-
sioned an apartment to be designed just for me.

It was to be the tiny jewel of the San Remo Apartments' North
Tower, right on Central Park West. There were views of Manhattan in every direction since it was the entire twenty-first floor. Just
1800 square feet, but each adorable foot would be all mine, with
the ability to welcome a guest for a short stay.

The demolition job before starting was enormous. There wasn't
a single wall that remained in its original position when we finished.
I took great delight in customizing every inch of it to suit my
singlehoodedness.

One of the first architectural features to be decided upon was the
building-in of a wet bar in the foyer. I amortized that appointment
without any effort in the time I lived there.

I'd been cruising the antique shops looking for furnishings and,
in particular, a bed that would be small enough to be cozy but large
enough to handle the occasional night visitor, as well. My decora-

tor, the famed Angelo Donghia, pointed to an original Art Deco, seven-foot-high, sunburst headboard and frame that was spectacular and at the same time bade me rest awhile. Several hues of mahogany had been finely cut into dartlike slivers, the effect creating an explosive sun from a central point on the headboard. I was infatuated with its elegance.

Then I asked its price. Eighty-five thousand dollars brought a speedy end to the love affair. Eighty-five thousand for a bed! While dabbing at my tears, Angelo pointed out that one of his craftsmen could, not easily mind you, but could, copy it. It might take a while. Well, it did. For nearly a year I slept on a frameless mattress. And when, at last, it arrived, the copy had cost me only $72,500. Except for some other horrendous mistakes, long delays, and a threatened lawsuit from the downstairs neighbors, the outcome was everything I'd dreamed it could be.

As always, from the outside, my life looked pretty good. Just as the devastating complications of my illness, diabetes, are not easily seen, so, too, were the grief, fear, and loneliness of those days.

I'd chosen to live on the West Side because of its charm and diversity—the essence of New York. The mom-and-pop stores on Columbus Avenue—the Italian shoe repair, the Greek diner, the Jewish delicatessen—are mostly gone now, but their simplicity beckoned to those of us who called ourselves artists. As someone back then said to me, "The nice thing about Central Park West is that you can live there and pretend you're not rich."

The Pope

⬿

A S A PRESENT TO MY
parents, I was having their house in Los Angeles remodeled and re-
decorated. During the four-week period of work the three of us
were going to visit England, France, Austria, and Rome.

I could hardly believe my good fortune to learn that at the same
time a small group of New Yorkers was going to be in Rome for
an audience with Pope John Paul II. I was told that one of the or-
ganizers of this event included a single businessman who wanted to
meet me, and who might be persuaded to include my family in the
golden circle at the Pontiff's feet. Why, this would be the most
meaningful experience of my father's life! It might even be the miracle my mother needed!

I met with this man (I'll call him Clark) at lunch. He was ingra-
tiating, and not bad-looking. Clark was a major contributor to a
charity close to the Pope's heart. Clark then said that he would be
delighted to add the three Moores to the group of six. When I
pointed out that I couldn't make a gigantic contribution, he quickly
assured me that perhaps at a future time I might be helpful in some
way. This was his gift to me for all the pleasure I'd given people.

He was very energetic, seemingly sincere and prone to mixing metaphors, "You've got to taste all the colors of the rainbow, Mary, to really see life's music." He asked me to have dinner with him in New York the following week, which I did and we sketched in the rough time and place that the audience might occur. The event would be a Mass celebrated by the Pope, followed by a reception.

Clark took me home and at the door, he and I kissed—just one, but a good one. He was leaving on a trip the next morning and by the time he'd return, I'd be on the first leg of my trip. So we said *arrivederci* until Roma.

I called my dressmaker to whip up something Pope appropriate— tradition dictated black, long sleeves, and high neck. Shortly before we were to leave, I received a call regarding a number of details pertaining to the audience. The woman on the other end of the phone said, "Don't bring anything special to wear for the occasion; this Holy Father is much more relaxed than any of his predecessors. He likes color." As there wasn't anywhere else I'd ever wear the drab dress I'd had designed, I had its maker add red silk piping around the neck, and down the front closing, and around the sleeves to breathe some life into it, and hoped the Pontiff wouldn't think me drab.

Upon our arrival at the Excelsior Hotel, an enormous arrangement of flowers was delivered to my room, along with a note from Clark saying he would like to take us all to dinner but wanted me alone for "dessert." Yes, dessert was in quotes. Under any other circumstance I would have had a cream pie ready for his face, but I didn't want to upset the enormously important plans that were being made for our salvation.

After dinner and before "dessert," Clark made a big point of asking my father's permission to take me for a walk. I saw the most important event in my father's life going up in smoke if I didn't handle this very carefully.

During the walk, I was treated to a most detailed description of a supposed dream he'd had about me which made me livid. I laid it out for myself—if I went to bed with this creep, my parents would meet the holiest leader of their faith. But I wasn't going to be a whore for Christ. It was very much like an O'Henry tale but I could control this ending. When we reached my door, I looked him square in the face and said, "Clark, I'm only going to say this once to you. Good night."

Two days later, the Holy Father said Mass with Cardinals serving as altar boys, in his private chapel at Castel Gandolfo outside Rome. You didn't have to be Catholic to feel the impact of that experience. There were only twenty or so people in attendance. My parents received communion from his hand.

Afterward, he greeted us in an anteroom. He clasped our hands and looked us each in the eyes, which had a very strong effect on me. I seriously considered returning to Catholicism, but I knew that this thought was in response to being in the presence of someone whose power is beyond comprehension, rather than being a true calling to the faith.

My mother and father wore expressions on their faces I had never seen before.

I couldn't help but notice, too, that in my specially adapted garb I looked just like one of the Cardinals.

Cardiology—The Study of the Heart

✥

$\mathcal{W}$HEN WE RETURNED
to New York we agreed that a night in my apartment might allow
for a gentler resetting of time zones for Mom and Dad before they
headed back to California.

My mother was still suffering from a bronchial infection she'd
developed during the last two weeks of our trek. When we arrived
in New York, she had a temperature of 101 degrees and was cough-
ing so badly she was nearly choking. It was frightening because of
a recent stroke and subsequent surgery she'd had just a few months
before.

I called an internist I'd seen once since my move East, but was
told by his answering service that because it was Yom Kippur he
was at Temple. However, a Dr. Levine, a cardiologist, was covering for him and would call back.

Moments later, Dr. Levine called, and after hearing about my
mother's symptoms and history, he said she should be examined.
He would meet us at Mt. Sinai Hospital.

As we walked into the emergency room we were met by an over-
worked admissions nurse who said, "Dr. Levine is waiting for you,"
and pointed to a figure at the end of the hall.

There was light from the room behind him, creating an aura around his white-coated, lanky frame as he slouched wearily against the door frame. His chiseled features revealed singular concentration as he wrote on a clipboard. He looked up, startled, as we neared him and smiled briefly, saying, "I'm Dr. Levine—Mrs. Moore?" He guided us into the examining room.

"Umm," I thought, "cue the violins. He's good-looking, a little like Jimmy Stewart . . . Ben Casey? He's young—too young for you, Mary. Stop it. Music out."

His manner was gentle as he explained every step of the examination to her. He then asked my father and me to leave for a few minutes while he listened to her chest and drew some blood.

When at last he opened the door, the doctor's face showed concern and he said to my father, "Your wife really should be admitted, given her history." He shook his head slowly from side to side in reaction to my mom, who jumped to her feet, saying, "No, no. I'm going to my daughter's. Just give me some antibiotics. I promise I'll take them." He looked at me, seeking my help. I did my best to convince her to stay, but after a month of my being the decision maker all through the trip, she was ready to reascend the throne.

He wrote a prescription and took down my address, saying he would like to look in on her the next day. I told him how much I appreciated his making the unheard-of house call. "It wouldn't be a good idea to have her leave the house," he said, and then as he wrote something on the chart, "You've got a lot of fans around here."

"And you're not one of them?" I pouted. "Well, no," he said, "I mean, I think I saw you on *The Dick Van Dyke Show* when I was a kid. I haven't had a chance to watch much TV, what with my residency and fellowship."

My little fantasy of a brief affair that would enrich us both for the experience did a slow fade as I realized I had no points—that, in his mind, I was simply an older woman.

The next afternoon, he arrived looking just as attractive in a sports jacket as he'd been in the medical garb and stethoscopic lei around his neck. He saw Mom in her room and said when he came out, "Well, that's better. I'm pleased. If she's without a temperature tomorrow she can travel home.

"And how are you holding up?" It was a courtesy question, but I had awakened that morning, I swear, with some tightness in my chest which I told him about. "Better have a listen," he automatically responded, and asked where my room was. "This way," I said, wanting to kick myself for having told him.

"What now?" I thought frantically. "Is he going to see my breasts?" I wore a dressing gown with a front zipper! "Oh, how stupid. Just stop it." I submitted to a professional and thorough bronchial examination. He said as long as my temperature was normal there was nothing to be done, and then wrote something on a piece of paper. He handed it to me, saying, "This is my home phone number. I'm off tomorrow, but if either of you has an emergency, I want you to call me." I couldn't help smiling at this sweetness and as I took the paper, I said, "Does extreme loneliness come under the heading of an emergency?" "I can't think of a better reason to be awakened," he said, and smiled at me as though he were dealing with a coy child. He was.

As he started to go, I said, "Your fee—your bill. What do I owe you?" He thought for a moment and then said, "Nothing." I opened my purse and extracted several twenties and a couple of fifties which I stuffed into his hand. But he refused them, shook his head, and as he backed out of my bedroom said, "Really, no. Thanks, anyway." I showed him to the door, and we made idle chatter while waiting for the elevator. Not once did I see that look in his eyes that says, "Mary Tyler Moore!" He was talking to a person that's all.

"What a guy," I thought. "He doesn't know who I am, nor does he care, and he won't take my money?"

The next afternoon I put my appreciative but homesick parents on a westward-bound flight. I called an old friend who, like me, was recently divorced. Pippa and I had dinner at the new restaurant on

Columbus, which was getting good reviews for its food as well as no small amount of attention for the number of people who entered singly but left in pairs. Well, you never know. As we left still single, I asked her to come back to the apartment for an after-dinner drink. We had several, during which we poured our tortured hearts out to one another over the illusive nature of contentment. When the anesthesia had worked so well that we were no longer finishing sentences, we said farewell with encouraging, hopeful wishes for each other in the search for "self" or a new man—whatever.

It was three a.m. and in my state, I figured that Dr. Levine had had enough sleep. He had probably been sleeping all day, so he wouldn't mind getting a call at this early hour.

When he answered I asked, "Do you cook?" "No," he said with confusion. "Well, neither do I, so I guess we'll have to go out to dinner," I said. I couldn't believe my brazenness. However, he replied, "I'd like that. I'll call you tomorrow." I floated, giggling down the hall to my bedroom so pleased with myself, but determined to cut down on the drinking.

He called the next day but not in the morning. Which put me through some hand-wringing as I reviewed my pretty bold and very thoughtless pre-dawn call. He said he'd make a reservation at Cafe des Artistes if I liked, and pick me up at eight. I liked his asking me first—before deciding where.

During our candlelit dinner, he admitted that he'd found me attractive but never would have acted on it. Had I not called him, it would have remained a mere comment in his libido. As we shared our lives with each other, the information that he was eighteen years younger than I came piercing through my dyscalculic brain, making it difficult for me to pay attention, much less carry my side of the conversation. There was disbelief that I could be attracted to someone only a year older than my son would have been. That drove me to recalculate again and again, trying to make the answer come out differently. Maybe—eight minus the ten, not eight plus ten. I was always adding phantom zeros.

"*CATS*? No, I haven't seen it. What did you think of it?"—let's try again—1954 minus 1936. "No, very little opera." Oh my God. We were going to have to keep this very quiet. Maybe it would just be a friendship and nothing more.

All hope of the latter solution was shattered as soon as I turned the key in the lock. There was no question of friendship or age difference. This was going to be a romance.

He was allowed about eight hours off for sleep every three days. In addition, he was "covering" another doctor for the extra money. Consequently, his favorite kind of date turned out to be sleeping. We fell into what might be described as a domestic pattern early on, one of a show or dinner and sleeping—not a show *and* dinner— a show *or* dinner and then sleep.

During our awake times, I came to know a man who was committed to helping beyond the health of the body, to facilitating the healthy outcome of his and others' constructs and goals. There was no guile about him. He was an advocate by nature, a logical idealist—religious in his acknowledgment of heritage and traditions. This sense of responsibility to one's fellow man was an ethos that was new to me—not the concept of altruism, but of its being driven by faith. I'd either had a very defined sense of religion—dogma carving every action and thought—or none at all, as with Bertie and Grandma.

I was falling under the spell that the handsome doctor cast. His being a doctor gave our couplehood an equality that the age difference and my success might otherwise have denied us. And so we began to take ourselves seriously.

There was a Christmas party at Mt. Sinai for the Cardiology Department that Robert asked me to attend. After discussing the ramifications of going public with our relationship, he decided that seeing the looks on the faces of his colleagues as he walked in with this most unexpected date would be too good to pass up. And so we went to the party and danced and talked with his superiors about Dick Van Dyke and the rest of the cast, about Ted and Ed and Betty and Gavin. They hardly touched their food, they were so busy try-ing to be close to, and chat with, me. Even as I could see they were eyeing young Dr. Levine with newfound admiration, I was in awe of them, every one of them. I was surrounded by seventy or eighty doctors, and their power was impressive.

There were two patients Robert wanted to visit briefly, and each of them was obviously touched that he would stop by. I was the stocking stuffer, and happy to be so.

Back at the party, we joined in relaxed conversation with a few of Robert's colleagues (Fellows who were honing their specialty skills). I heard how draining this period of doctoring can be, even for their wives, one of whom complained that she rarely saw her husband. She had laughingly introduced herself earlier as being a shiksa, like me. This Yiddish word is taken, almost always, as an af-fectionate term for a non-Jewish woman. However, her husband was quick to admonish her and said, smiling warmly at me, "It's re-ally not very nice. The real definition of the word is abomination." A bit of cold water on America's Sweetheart.

More cold water rained down after columnist Liz Smith men-tioned that I was going out with Dr. Robert Levine of Mt. Sinai Hospital. Whereupon she got an irate phone call from the father of another Dr. Robert Levine, an Orthodox Jew. The father de-manded that she exonerate (his words) his son by making it clear that it was Dr. S. Robert Levine who was the betrayer of all that is holy, not his Dr. Robert Levine.

*R*obert had been driving out to his mother and father's house in Port Washington, Long Island, on Saturdays or Sundays to spend some time with them, and do his laundry while he was there nap-ping, anyway. One Sunday afternoon he asked if I'd like to meet them. "Well, sure," I offered, thinking of it in terms of "This is my new pal," certainly not a "Mom, Dad, this is the girl I'm seri-ous about" situation. I guess in an effort to make clear to them that this was merely a super-casual kind of thing, he brought his laundry with him.

Irving Levine, his father, was the founder and director of the Institute on American Pluralism at the American Jewish Committee. His work centered on intergroup relations, reducing ethnic and racial conflicts. Robert's mother, Marion, is still the executive director of the North Shore Child and Family Guidance Center, a mental-health agency serving families in Nassau County and training professionals in the field.

Despite our mutual circumspection, I sensed a wariness from his mother that I seldom feel in people I've just met. My persona from television is so warmly thought of that I win most people over . . . for a time. But she hadn't been in my company long enough for her to see the evil lurking just below my surface that the snakes would surely call attention to in time. It must have been in my head, I thought, because neither Robert nor I had any intention of getting serious. But I guess mothers of sons are protective and maybe a little more tuned in than others to possibilities. Following her lead, the family was cautiously pleased to meet me.

In an effort to make the most of the time not dedicated to Mt. Sinai, Robert moved into my apartment on Central Park West, and in so doing added a couple of French horns and a cello to the violins.

He brought with him his clothes and books—lots of medical books and journals, both bound and unbound and tied them all together in stacks. The clothes, toiletries, shoes, etc., made it in one car trip. The books took several. Space was made to accommodate them in my library/guest room, which took on a decidedly scientific, leathery look. I liked it. I also liked listening to him talk to other doctors on the phone, while I tried to make sense of conversations that included more unknown nouns than I had ever heard in a foreign country.

At three o'clock one morning during a rare insomnia bout I had, he asked if there was anything he could do. I said, "Boy, a tuna fish sandwich would be great," laughed, and turned to the other side, scrunching into yet another position, once more searching for sleep. I must have been successful on that try because I was awakened by the smell of tuna fish—a wonderful salad containing chopped apples, celery, onions, with just the right amount of mayonnaise on toasted rye bread. I couldn't believe that he had taken me seriously, but more important, that he'd acted on it. I think it was at that moment that I knew I loved him.

Not two weeks after he had moved in, a terrible fight erupted from my side of the room one night. All I needed in those days was a drink for me to get cross about nothing, and a second one to be convinced that the issue of the moment was monumental.

This one started on the way home from having had a very pleasant dinner with his family. In the car, I recalled for him a comment his father had made in response to something I had said about my father. We had been talking about prejudice and the early age at which it can be fostered.

To illustrate my point, I had told the Levines of my father's response upon learning that at age fourteen I had gone on a date with a boy who was Jewish. "But why did you go?" he asked. "There's no possibility of marriage to a Jew."

I laughed and shook my head, fully expecting Robert's father, Irving, to see the ridiculousness, but he said with a serious expression, "We teach our children the same thing," as though sanctioning it.

"I felt like a fool," I said, "and you did nothing to help me on this." "You mean I didn't take your side?" Robert answered. "Well, fine," I snarled, and entered the "cone of silence" which, when unable to walk out of the room, or in this case leap out of the moving car and slam the door behind me, seemed the next best option.

The subject came to life again over more drinks back at my apartment, during which other imagined slights and disloyalties were recalled and deftly used to pierce his heart. I don't think my mother in her alcoholism ever treated me as badly as I treated this man. The final righteous thing to do was to cast him out of my life. Which I did. I told him to pack his things and be gone by the next afternoon.

I called Frank Adamo, my longtime friend from *The Van Dyke Show* and now my assistant, begging shelter, and then the limo service. And off I went, sobbing all the way to New Jersey. At Frank's, I refused several phone calls from Robert, who, having guessed where I was, wanted to put things right. Although I was now sober, I was too proud to back away from (as best I could remember it) a position of outrage over his disloyalty to me.

When I returned to my apartment the next evening, I found Robert sitting on the library floor surrounded by stacks of his books, all retied and ready to go. He looked so pathetic, and apologized for taking so long to vacate, citing a double shift at the hospital. There was something so metaphoric about those books, his only valuable possessions, which he had brought to the union representing his own richness of mind and spirit.

It took several hours to untie and, once again, replace the books on shelves. We talked about the prejudice I felt (real or imagined) at being older, not Jewish, and a celebrity. For the first time in my adult life, I was out of step with everyone around me. Most of the people in our lives, his friends and mine, were open to the newcomer, but I was very sensitive to the differences between us—not essential differences, but the perceived adjustments others had to make on my behalf. I didn't much like having to worry about whether or not I'd made the grade. And he loved me, never doubting his own achievements, in the glare of celebrity that surrounded me. Nor was he competitive or uncomfortable about our financial differences.

In the spring of that year we planned a trip, one that would offer a rest for Robert, escape for me, and a validation of our goodness as a couple for all to see. We chose Israel.

What a beautiful experience it was. We traveled to Jerusalem, Tel Aviv, and Balfouria, a small village in and around which a hundred or so of Robert's family lived, descendants of nine sisters who emigrated there from Philadelphia in 1923. We were welcomed by them and made to feel at home.

Only once as we walked hand in hand through the marketplace in the Old City of Jerusalem was I reminded that we did not fit the mold. A basket seller in a stall who was calling people over to see his wares exclaimed as Robert and I came closer, "Ah, what a lovely mother and son."

In Jerusalem we stayed at the King David Hotel. On that Friday night we decided to go to the main dining room to enjoy a Shabbos meal. We were weary and dusty from a very full day, but after showering and dressing, we entered the dining room, collapsing into our chairs, sure that the special meal we were about to have would revitalize us.

There were no ashtrays on the table, and when I asked for one we were told by the waiter that there is no smoking on Shabbos. Although we both smoked, I am sure Robert could have endured the deprivation, but I felt that my addiction was too strong to deny and still enjoy the lovely evening we were anticipating. More important, I was pleased to be incensed that a religion could dictate to a paying guest that smoking is forbidden. Clearly, I was acting out my frustration at being outside the norm—too old, and not Jewish.

We left the dining room and asked the front desk to recommend a restaurant that might be open. Jewish law says a hotel must serve its guests on that night, but important restaurants would be closed from sundown on Friday to sundown on Saturday. We were given directions to a place called Marakesh. (Not too kosher-sounding, but it was open!) After being seated and with mounting anxiety at seeing no ashtrays, I again asked for one and again was told that it was Shabbos—NO SMOKING. We trudged back to the King David all dressed up with nowhere to go, thanks to my unwillingness to bend a little, and had a room-service meal and several cigarettes.

We visited many sites that touched responsive chords in my memory, having learned their significance as a prisoner in parochial school—Bethlehem, Via Dolorosa, Gethsemane, and the Church of the Holy Sepulchre. Nothing compared to the effect I felt at visiting The Wall, with its millions of prayers and wishes written on small pieces of paper that were tucked into crevices and cracks by all who have come there throughout the ages. It is an Orthodox tradition that men and women visit separately, so I was alone and without a prayer, but I did put my forehead against The Wall and embraced with outstretched arms all the pleas hidden there. When Robert and I were reunited some distance from it, we both had tears in our eyes. We clasped hands and silently walked back to the hotel.

Standing with our arms around each other at the window of our suite, we looked down at the Old City bathed in light and talked about rituals and traditions, including the ritual of marriage we were denying ourselves. We agreed we'd each had too strong an upbringing, interwoven with expected rites and ceremonies of society, to live together for much longer without formalizing our commitment to each other.

And so it was that we pledged to a future together, as conventional husband and wife.

The Wedding

❧

MY FAMILY WAS MORE accepting of the impending marriage than Robert's was at first. It would be my third and there would most likely be no children. It was difficult for the Levine family to have faith that this older actress, who seemed to drink a bit, would give their son the stability needed to make a marriage work.

Marion, who was about to be my mother-in-law, was only five years older than I. She confided to Robert that as the director of a family mental-health agency, it might appear that she had failed personally as parental counselor.

Irving was obliged to be a little more receptive because of his long involvement with and knowledge of cultural pluralism.

To their credit, they buried their doubts and embraced me as a member of their family. Our relationship today, though far from traditional, is one of rich friendships and mutual love of Robert.

Our wedding grew from "just a few people" to an extravaganza of two hundred and fifty in the grand ballroom of the Pierre Hotel in New York.

We were given counsel by a progressive Rabbi Richard Chapin

from Temple Emanu-El. Although I didn't convert, I wanted to familiarize myself with Jewish law regarding the concepts of marriage.

We were married under a *chuppa* and said our vows in Hebrew. Our parents stood by us with our attendants, Beverly Sanders Newmark for me and for Robert, his brother Michael.

Even at my own wedding Cloris Leachman had the best lines, as she always had on *The Mary Tyler Moore Show*. A great-aunt of Robert's, ninety-seven years old, was late in arriving. Everyone was in place awaiting Robert's and my entrance through double doors that remained closed as we nervously awaited the aunt's arrival. Finally, she appeared, and as the doors were opened, Cloris said to the group sitting around her, "Oh, here comes Mary now," at which point the aunt shuffled down the aisle. Cloris, noting her, said to the others, "Of course, it's been a while since I've seen Mary."

It was a glorious musical celebration that included all kinds of dancing—males only, horas, women only, boogie, traditional, and the hoisting of the bride and groom on chairs. Not to be excluded from the festivities was that spirited folk dance of WASPS—the foxtrot.

The guests included my friends from television, my very reserved family, Robert's medical friends from Mt. Sinai, and his very exuberant family. My friends and relatives filled the tables on one side of the room, and Robert's family and friends, the other. There was a noticeable difference between the two at the start. My side was all smiles and nodding at each other, while Robert's was leaping and singing. Within a half hour the Levine squad, of which I was now one, invaded the Moores' and had them dancing on the tables.

7

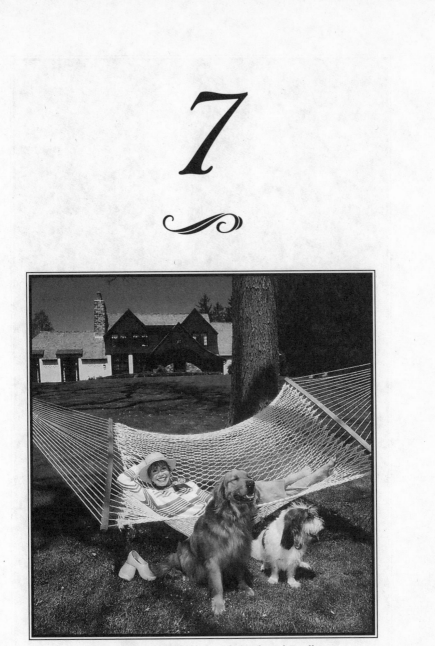

Former Mair takes a break with Dash and Dudley.

Anyone's dream come true—to dance with Gene Kelley.
Variety Show series, 1976.

"Whistle While You . . ."

⚬

THERE HAVE BEEN several projects to keep me off the streets as I wend my way inevitably toward low-heel shoes and flower-print smocks. They don't come into my life as frequently as I'd like, and I'm still not comfortable "making things happen," so, instead, I proudly wear my broken nails from gardening, and ignore the calluses on my calves caused by riding boots, hurling myself into the activities of nature that nourish me almost as much as performing.

HEARTSOUNDS

Heartsounds, a television movie in which I played opposite James Garner, was an exhausting (for both of us) piece about a man dying of heart failure over a five-year period.

This was filmed while I was still unsure that eight ounces of vodka a night was too much. During rehearsals on location in Toronto we discussed what to cut because the script was reading very long. The cuts suggested served the focus of dying Hal Lear and his real suffering and deterioration, but in so doing they carved away some of the facets belonging to Martha (his wife)—nuances that had drawn me to the role from the beginning.

That night, as I poured myself into bed, I was nearly paranoid. I was sure it was a plot: "Entice her with a good role and then cut." I had from eleven p.m. until two a.m. to work myself into a vise-like grip of resentment before I called Glenn Jordan, the director, to tell him I would be withdrawing from the project and why. He must have been directed by God himself in the way he reacted. He said he could certainly understand my concerns and promised to work with the screenplay writer Fay Kanin on it in the morning— *later that* morning. "No," I said, "I don't want you to go against what you've decided is right for the script. I quit."

The next morning, as I was packing my bags, stunned by the turn of events I'd wrought, a large contingent of creative and executive people entered my suite as though they were entering the den of a hungry cheetah. "We've solved it," I heard. "We've put back most of the cuts. And now that we've added an extra scene for you, it's even better." "Thank you, Mary," said one. "Well, how did you do it?" I asked. "We cut some of Jim's stuff."

I don't feel quite as guilty as I might, had we not each, Garner and I, been nominated for Emmy Awards, as well as the movie itself.

MARY

In 1985 CBS and MTM had decided on another series return for me called *Mary*. It was a situation comedy set in a Chicago newspaper office. Everything was done to ensure a minimal amount of comparison to *The Mary Tyler Moore Show* of the recent past.

The first rule should have excluded anything even remotely connected to news. How did that escape everyone? In the new series, all the characters were hard-edged—envy, anger, and despair being the foundation for laughter. The logic of this "innovation" on the part of the producer/writers was that since Mary Richards's friends were nice, this would be a nifty contrast.

The only way to make magic happen with this premise was through creative writing, an element noticeably absent. The show was about a bunch of mean-spirited people topping each other with one-liners. It was an unattractive setup, which was reflected in its low ratings.

I was resentful of my self-made predicament. I had assumed the two producer/writers would be knowledgeable on the basics of putting a show together, but they weren't. They were without the ability to create and then expand new characters, or to learn and then build on what works.

I wasn't making things easy for these two, either. I was so angry with myself for not having the ability to fix the scripts when they couldn't, or wouldn't, that I often snapped back at them when they lost patience with me.

One afternoon, following a particularly bickersome run-through, they came to my dressing room to see me. I asked them to sit, but they preferred standing. So, I sat and listened to a nonstop list of every grievance they could conjure up: from a lack of respect for them, to their declaration of unethical discussions I had had with fellow cast members behind their backs. I said nothing, despite my welling fury. Finally, as I sensed they were running down, I stood and directed them to leave.

Apparently, as they left the stage, they ran into the story editor, who knew about their mission. "Well," one of my tormentors said, "at least we got our balls back." "Yeah," said the editor, "but Mary's got your dick on the hood of her car."

The next week, I asked CBS to take the show off the air, which they did.

FINNEGAN BEGIN AGAIN

Finnegan Begin Again, a love story for Home Box Office with Robert Preston, was a terrific work experience. Pres, as he was called, contributed masterfully to the production as well as to our amusement in between setups. If ever the term "pro" was appropriate for a performer, it was he. Steady, smooth, sure, patient, and generous are all words he "owned" as far as I'm concerned.

One afternoon as we sat in our chairs on the sidelines waiting (as always, waiting), he began talking about *The Music Man*. I innocently asked if he still remembered the impossibly difficult lyrics to "Trouble," with which he stood up, adjusted an imaginary tie, shot his cuffs, and for an audience of about six people (most of whom were too young to have seen it) he did the entire song with choreography.

During the filming, my parents visited the set. Unfortunately, they missed meeting Pres, which would have thrilled them. Instead, they were treated to some minor scenes that involved supporting players with me. When the last take was finished, my father, shaking his head from side to side, said, "Well, it's a fascinating business you're in." Never having impressed him before, I said, "Gee, Dad, do you really think so?" To which he replied, "No, but it seems to amuse you and for that I'm grateful."

JUST BETWEEN FRIENDS

Just Between Friends, written by Allan Burns, was a nice little slice o'life starring Christine Lahti, Ted Danson, Sam Waterston (who would later play Abe to my Mary Todd), and me. It was the story of a very comfortable marriage (Ted and me) that ends when he dies in a plane crash. It is then discovered that he was not only having an affair with his wife's best friend (Christine Lahti) but that ole Chris is pregnant.

The character I played, as written and very carefully orchestrated, was that of a "vine"—a housewife and mother who wrapped herself around everyone in her family in order to avoid independence. It was a character, a certifiable wife type (they do exist), but I was reviewed as though I had chosen her because I admired her characteristics. Probably, because it was co-produced by MTM, they expected a "star vehicle," when in fact, it was an ensemble effort.

Must a leading lady always be admirable? I'm still not past Vincent Canby's review—Ah, go look it up yourself.

SWEET SUE

A. R. Gurney, the author of *The Dining Room, The Cocktail Hour, Perfect Party, Love Letters,* and recently, *Sylvia,* has been praised for his brilliance in sharing the very real feelings of the Protestant upper middle class—its repressive relationships, the tortured souls who seem to have everything. I recognize many of his people and their ritualistic behavior. This territory is often thought of as infertile, without the depth of other cultures. Only a few have managed to capture the wit, pomposity, and charm of this endangered species. F. Scott Fitzgerald and John Cheever come to mind, but Pete (as Gurney is known) is my favorite.

In 1987, I was pleased to be asked to be one of two people who would play the title role in *Sweet Sue.* His play is a would-be love story of an older woman and young man in which the two leads are each played by two people. Just as we often have conversations with ourselves, argue within our heads, two actors conversed with each other (as the same character) and the other character was also represented by two actors.

Sweet Sue was to be produced at the Williamstown Playhouse in Massachusetts for three weeks that summer, presumably to find backers for a Broadway run in the fall.

After my last experience on Broadway, I felt about theater as you might childbirth. It has its rewards and when it's over, you're glad you did it but as you're doing it you can't imagine that you allowed it to happen. However, I couldn't turn down the opportunity to say Gurney's words, and, anyway, I might get lucky. It could fail, giving me those always exciting first weeks to play with, without having to go the distance.

John Tillinger, a strong director of classics as well as mirthful romps, had directed most of Pete's plays, and we were guided by his most able experience and sense of humor in this one.

It was rousing good fun (John's English influence) for me to be hearing people laugh again, and when, lo, it *was* to have a Broadway run, I was delighted.

Even though the two sides of Sue were written to be equal in impact, when it was done in Williamstown, my character took the comedic edge. It happened because Maria Tucci, the gifted actress who played Sue's other half, chose to let me go for the laughs. My Sue became the funny one and, in my mind, the other Sue was my straight man. It worked really well.

However, when the backers decided that another "name" actress would draw twice the ticket buyers, Maria, fine as she was, didn't make the cut. Lynn Redgrave became everyone's choice. Why, she might even add a laugh or two, I thought.

Well, she was great—sounding very American, and finding stuff that hadn't been there before. As the rehearsals continued, she brought a new tempo to the piece. Her comedy was getting broader, and I found myself sometimes looking into the face of an actress from another play. She was mugging and sometimes getting laughs at the expense of my moments. Moments that had already been established in Williamstown!

She was fine and so was I, but our divergent styles did not make magic happen. We got decent reviews and ran for one hundred sixty-four performances, which was just long enough to sustain my enjoyment of it; and to relearn what had obviously escaped me for the moment—to "play well with others."

GORE VIDAL'S LINCOLN

Gore Vidal's Lincoln was a tremendous experience. Playing Mary Todd Lincoln was as unexpected a bit of casting as can be imagined until you calculate the commercial success my audience would bring to a rather intellectual miniseries. I felt a kinship with the woman, her distortion. The drive for which she was so criticized was focused on her husband and her children, despite the stories of her vanity and acquisitiveness. There was a purposeful single-mindedness about her that was very appealing to me.

Anyway, if it weren't altruism and insight that cast me in the part, I'm fine with the results which were big success for the show and for me, garnering this actress an Emmy nomination—no win, but still!

ANNIE MCGUIRE

Just as *Mary,* the variety show, developed more in reaction to the "mother of all sitcoms"—shaped to be "different from" rather than of itself—so too, the good-natured *Annie McGuire* of 1988 was determined to be loving, supportive, and so damned warm it didn't need a studio audience. People would be *kvelling,* not so much laughing.

This was the season for the "warmedy," shows about interpersonal relationships—funny in a sweet sort of no-pressure-to-laugh way.

The setup was: Annie (right away a big departure from the old, in not using the star's name in the title) McGuire, a divorced mother, meets and marries a construction contractor played sweetly and believably by Denis Arndt.

Some of the plots were unique. In one, Annie, on her way home from work one night, is mugged by a man in a wheelchair. She is guilt-ridden because she struck at what she now perceives to be a defenseless invalid, rather than mugger, and must wrestle with the issue.

Another dealt with the guilt Annie's new father-in-law, a right-wing Republican (John Randolph), felt over some fish he served Thomas E. Dewey in his restaurant the night before an important speech during the last crucial days of his campaign for the Presidency. Dewey became ill and couldn't appear the next day at the rally. (This is historical fact.) The episode was filmed à la *Citizen Kane,* Annie interviewing people who were involved with Dewey who might exonerate her still self-blaming father-in-law. Through a shadowy, intricate, black-and-white trip to the past, the truth is revealed—it wasn't his fish, it was someone else's potato salad that did him in.

It wasn't for lack of imagination that this one went down.

MARY TYLER MOORE'S EVERYWOMAN'S WORKOUT

In my mid-forties, I finally let go of the impossible promise of ballet class, and came to terms with the masochistic need I, and probably most dancers, have. I was ready to see that, since ballet wasn't going to play a part in my increasingly shrinking future, it was time to let go and move on to some more beneficial form of exercise, one that might even be fun.

A diabetic must make exercise a part of daily life. It helps control blood-sugar levels. There are other diabetes-related motivations for keeping fit, as well. Because of poor circulation, the feet are vulnerable to infection. A podiatrist once told me "They can just go." So exercise is not a bad way to avoid what must be a terribly depressing moment—to look down and find that your feet have turned into pies.

From the time ballet training starts at the barre, there is a race with everyone else for the position of "best one." "Best one" represents the dancer who will get the job, win the audition, succeed at what it is we are all there for. This is particularly destructive during the early teen years, that brief moment in which a ballerina's body type predicts her future. Winners and losers are based on the shape of the thigh, the length and straightness of the leg, heartlessly ignoring all the blood and sweat the youngster has invested up to that judgment time.

Even after ballet was no longer a career goal, I was advanced enough to be in a professional class. And this invited criticism and

comparisons. The attitude of the teacher, no matter how smiling
and warm, was that I was holding back. I could lift that arabesque
a bit more, if I wanted. "Yes, Natalia," she would coo, and then
turn a modified scowl to me. I'm a mature adult but was nevertheless
convinced there was something wrong with my attitude since Natalia effortlessly could leave her leg, unsupported, by the side of her
ear for twenty seconds.

And so I decided to abandon ballet and to try a few aerobics
classes.

The first class was an insult to my sense of the aesthetic. Everyone counted the beat in tens and twenties, instead of the musical
eight. No one bothered to point their feet when they were in the
air. They had a different approach to breathing, inhaling on the relaxation and exhaling when strength was needed. They went for ex-
traordinarily long counts on exercises, sometimes as much as thirty
to fifty repetitions. So, I had a little stamina building to do.

One positive difference that I felt right away was the easy, supportive instruction and lack of competitiveness in these classes. It
didn't matter to anyone, including the teacher, that I was able to
go all the way down in a split, or that I was having difficulty achiev-
ing the number of repetitions, but that my arm work was superior
to everyone else's, and that when I jumped, by God, my sneakers
were pointed! And no one is cooing, "Yes, Natalia."

One of my favorite teachers, from the beginning, was a young
woman named Laure Redmond, who taught a low impact class at
a neighborhood studio. I liked her choreography, as well as her calm,
but energy-filled sessions.

Even though no one pays any attention to their fellow exercis-
ers, everyone is going to check out a celebrity. One day, before class,
Laure said to me, "I'm always so glad to have you in class. When
you're here, everybody works harder." As we marched and lunged
and grapevined our way through the hour, I watched the others
watching me. It was fun.

One day Laure asked why I hadn't done an exercise video like everyone else. "Well, that's why, Laure. Everyone else has done one. I want to go to my grave the only actress never to have done a video."

After noting, during the next several classes, just how good I still looked in the mirror, I thought, "That's the thing—I'm healthy, I'm muscled and lean, and if it is true that my fellow jumpers and marchers get some extra boost from watching me, maybe I should do a video that speaks to my age group. Most of the videos on the market are for nineteen-year-old maniacs."

I asked Laure if she wanted to undertake the project and find the producer and distributor and evaluate the responsibility of the candidates. Within a few weeks, she had tied together most of the necessary elements.

I gave my share of the royalties to the Juvenile Diabetes Foundation, which made going on television to plug the tape more tolerable.

I went into boxerlike training with Laure in preparation for the filming of three videos. One is low-impact aerobics (one foot almost always on the floor); one is a muscle development video (done without hand weights); and one is for walking and working outdoors. It was pretty demanding since we filmed ten to twelve hours a day for six straight days. The result is well done, and looks terrific.

THE LAST BEST YEAR

In 1990 I worked with Bernadette Peters in an ABC movie called *The Last Best Year*. She played a lonely creature coming to terms with her life as she dies of cancer. My role was that of the also troubled psychologist who walks the journey with her to its inevitable but finally peaceful conclusion. It was a heavyweight project, and we went at it with more than a little investment of selves as we rehearsed and then filmed this true story in too few days.

Neither of us thought much of the production in its on-air form, but we liked each other immediately and shared a common respect for the other's dark places that give life to the people we play and are. She's also one of the funniest people I know—her humor coming at you from around unexpected corners and hidden turns.

Rhett Butler

❧

*D*URING THE LAST couple of weeks of *Finnegan,* Robert and I did something that seemed harmless. We answered an ad for golden retriever puppies in a local Virginia newspaper. We visited the house (a backyard breeding between neighborhood dogs had taken place) and, of course, fell in love with the pups. We had no knowledge of the personalities and history of the parentage, nor how the pups were being cared for. So, we did the next best thing: we selected the cutest one.

We named him Rhett Butler. He spent his days on the set where I was filming, being fussed over by too many people, and his nights chewing the fabric that lined the underside of my hotel bed (I was to find out). Robert gave me lots of encouragement by phone when I complained of too little sleep, the result of unproductive outings at midnight and four a.m. Somehow, I was able to finish the picture and bring the unhousebroken Rhett home.

We tried everything in an attempt to strike a compromise relationship with our adorable puppy. He was starting to chase me from room to room, biting and clawing at me, most untypical for golden retrievers. We got in touch with a dog trainer who came over and put Rhett through some evaluation routines. He spent about an hour with him, and then gave us the bad news: "Frankly, my dear, the dog doesn't give a damn."

It was his opinion that Rhett had not learned the difference between people and dogs at an early enough age, and would probably continue his attempts at dominating me much as he would a littermate. He further believed that the dog needed to be kept outside for a while to interact with another dog. We were truly saddened by Rhett's dreary prognosis in our care, but we knew that we had no alternative but to try and find a home for him that would suit his needs.

With mixed sadness and gratitude, we located a woman in New Jersey who had a big backyard and a big black dog that needed a companion.

The day Rhett's new owner came for him, I couldn't stop crying—sometimes quietly, sometimes with loud, racking sobs. For the next forty-eight hours I had a drink in my hand from morning to night. Rhett was Elizabeth and Richie and every other love that I had ever had in my care and lost.

Sobriety

ITH ALL THE LOSSES that poor Rhett symbolized, coming to my mind one by one, with my drinking out of control, with thoughts of my mother and her drinking, a memory from childhood came to mind—I had finally "stepped on the crack." This was a childhood rhyme that was said to you just as you were about to take a stride down the sidewalk— "Step on a crack, break your mother's back." And oh, did I take that superstition seriously. I would stretch my leg out so far, or back-step so quickly, to avoid doing this thing that was going to permanently disable my mother, that I became a target. The word got out that you could make Mary "go all stupid" every time.

Looking back at those days after Rhett, I know today it was a line that is crossed at some point during the progression of alcoholism. Sometimes it is called "hitting bottom." I think that was it for me. Drinking during the day had been my mother's trait. It was the source of greatest fear and shame for me—so when I looked at myself, I could no longer pretend that I wasn't really an alcoholic. I was my mother.

Robert, who had wisely and patiently waited for the right moment, said, with care in his voice, that he thought I should get help with my problem. In the past six months I had tried to "cut down" my drinking without success. I was at that time also taking Valium, which I had started a year before in an effort to reduce the hand tremor I had developed. In no time, I'd gone from ten milligrams at night to about fifty milligrams daily, as needed (this being at my discretion).

I nearly killed myself stopping that habit, simply going "cold turkey." For most of the day, every day, during the next three weeks I was in a continual state of panic. There was no focus for this feeling, just the adrenaline rush you might imagine from suddenly encountering a full-grown lion in your living room. I had been reading shocking stories about how easy it is to become addicted to Valium, and I took the evidence of my own addiction as a personal affront. I just clenched my fists and got through it because I was more afraid of what might happen to me were I to continue taking it. After the first week without the drug, I confessed the reason for my strange behavior to Robert, who had known nothing about my addiction. He said that since the withdrawal symptoms were beginning to lessen a bit it would be all right to continue the process, but that I could have gone into convulsions the way I had handled it.

Now here I was, again, trying but failing to stop self-anesthetizing with alcohol. Robert pointed out that if I needed help with a physical problem, I sought professional help. Why was this any different?

Sometimes invasion of privacy has a good payoff. I read about Elizabeth Taylor and Liza Minnelli having sought help for dependency at the Betty Ford Center.

I also remembered the starting point of the remarkable journey of Mrs. Ford. Eight years before, in the final season of *The Mary Tyler Moore Show,* Mrs. Ford made an appearance as herself. It was a phone conversation between us, my half of which was filmed at MTM Studios—her on-camera work at a hotel in Washington, DC.

First she had welcomed the crew and me to the White House with a shy smile and slurred speech. She glided from room to room with the occasional help of a doorway or chair back, or a promptly offered arm for balance, as she described the functions of the various chambers. She had to sit after a time to gather herself, citing the back problems that afflicted her as the cause. Her aides discussed with Ed. Weinberger, one of our producers, what color dress she should wear for the scene, while Grant and I looked at each other in disbelief and Mrs. Ford, still smiling, stared straight ahead at nothing.

We gathered at the hotel because it was policy not to distract those who would govern on Pennsylvania Avenue with a film crew. By the time Mrs. Ford was placed on the couch and given the phone for a quick rehearsal, we were now an hour and a half behind schedule for something that was supposed to take only fifteen minutes. Rehearsing was out of the question because she couldn't remember her lines. We tried several times to go through the scene, but inevitably she'd lose track, lose confidence, and be even less able the next time. We were scared, so was Mrs. Ford.

Having watched Julie Andrews in *Thoroughly Modern Millie* work with Bea Lillie, who had Alzheimer's, I suggested a similar approach. I stood next to the camera and said each line for her and she repeated it. Me—"Hello, Mary? This is Betty Ford." She—"Hello, Mary? This is Betty Ford." And so on, until the few minutes' work was completed. It was shocking and sad to see firsthand what had been whispered about.

But she found sobriety for herself not long after that at the Long Beach Naval Hospital, and determined that it would be her life's work to share the success she found there with others. She was particularly interested in women like herself, women who were thought to be above it all, immune to the disease.

And so, back in my bedroom, grappling with the present and the future, I wondered, "Who would think, looking at the four of us:

Liza, Elizabeth, Betty, and me, that we had anything in common?" We shared a problem. More important, we sought a solution.

While Robert refilled my glass (no point in making the gorilla angry) I called the Betty Ford Center in Palm Springs and spoke to a counselor. I told him my name and my story, and without seeming at all surprised, he said, "I'm glad you called." He had to call me back about room availability, which, of course, with my compulsiveness, I wanted tomorrow.

The twenty minutes I waited were nerve-racking. This was a big commitment. I wanted my life back. I was sick and tired of being sick and tired. I was pretty sure the cure meant I could never drink again. Well, I hoped that part wasn't true, because how could I ever go to a cocktail party, for example? What would I do New Year's Eve?

The counselor called back and said, "Come tomorrow—let us know when, and we'll meet you." I told him that if word of my being there got out, my professional life would suffer badly. I had the nerve to say, "People aren't really surprised to know that Liza and Liz drink. They're thought of as sophisticated. But if they knew that I did, it would shatter an image." I was reassured to learn that security had been increased since Liza's and Liz's stories had been revealed.

But, in fact, my stay there would inevitably be trumpeted by the press, and though I certainly couldn't be convinced of it then, it turned out to have a positive impact at an important moment.

Robert and I concocted the most complicated series of lies to cover my whereabouts for the next several weeks, perhaps as many as six. My family was told something about a local play I'd be doing—a very small, very local play. The Levines were told I'd be in LA working on that same low-profile piece. That night I slept fitfully—the way I used to before Saturday-morning confession.

As we headed to the airport, Robert's face was such a naked blend of expressions. And I could read them clearly—pride, concern, anxiety, uncertainty, and absolute, rock-solid love. Going in, I knew this had to be for myself, but if ever there was a person who deserved my success, it was Robert.

I could feel his eyes on my back as I walked the length of the jetway to the plane's door. As I took my seat by the window I thought I saw him in the clump of people through the glass. I waved, hoping it was Robert and that he could see me still. The flight attendant came by and asked if I'd like something to drink after takeoff. "Yes," I answered, "a double Bloody Mary."

The volunteer who met me at the airport was very solicitous. When I confessed that I'd had a drink en route, he replied, "You're in great shape. Some of them have to be poured into the car."

Checking in was a study in progressive demoralization. Oh, it started out nicely enough—"Welcome, Mrs. Levine." Then, "That's the name you're using, is it?" "Yes, my married name," I reply. "Are you ashamed of being here?" "No." I smile and say, "This is great!" "Well, now," he says, as my bags arrive, "we'll just have a look here," with which everything in my bags was taken out, turned inside out, shaken, squeezed, and sniffed. All the zippered pockets were gone through. They confiscated my medicines—thyroid pills, and, of course, all my insulin syringes, saying that after they had been analyzed by the lab, medications would be given out at seven a.m. in the nurse's office each morning.

"But," I said, "I need my insulin with me at all times. I have to inject it several times a day." I was their first diabetic/alcoholic, and policy had not yet been established on that. Next they asked for my purse, which I really resented. To search my purse while looking straight at me was insulting. I was beginning to think they were incapable of making value judgments about the people who came there.

After I was shown to my room, a cheery cell with built-in cabinets and two beds, I was driven to Eisenhower Hospital about a mile away for my physical and blood test. I don't think if I added up all the physicals I've had since adulthood, that the aggregate would cover any more territory than that one did. There was no discussion about it, either.

In 1984, the Center consisted of a cluster of large, one-story buildings, each containing a living room and kitchenette, attendant/counselor's station, and a long hallway, off which about fourteen bedrooms were located along with a group-therapy room. That was our dorm.

They were strict about male/female co-mingling, allowing no more than a nod in passing between the sexes. There were three dorms. Ours—female—one for the males, and one mixed. I don't know what was going on in the mixed dorm except they were an older bunch and maybe they were considered not worth worrying about from a sexual standpoint. Other buildings contained large meeting halls, dining room and kitchen, an ecumenical chapel, and a gymnasium. There was also a swimming pool on the grounds.

It was pretty quickly decided that rather than run the risk of inducing a coma, I would be allowed to keep with me, and administer, my own insulin. There was also juice in the kitchenette in case my blood sugar dropped.

Since people check in almost every day and about an equal number are discharged, there was a turnover in roommates. I had three very different, quite likable women to bunk with during what turned out to be, for me, a five-week stay. The patients are as diverse as can be imagined—a sixty-five-year-old Texas farm woman, a nineteen-year-old cocaine addicted/alcoholic student, housewives, teachers, executives, all touched by the same problem—chemical dependency.

During the first week of our stay, we were allowed no contact with the outside world, no phone calls or letters, so that the Center, our goals, became the "all" and "only" in our lives.

The Center's tenets for the recovering alcoholic are based on the principles of Alcoholics Anonymous, and AA meetings are a part of the daily schedule. Also included are one-on-one counseling, group therapy, grief therapy (for those who are conflicted over a loss that was never resolved), lectures on the etiology of addiction, films, literature to read, and a diary to keep for your counselor's edification.

Despite my pain and confusion at not having reached any conclusions about myself, at being in a state affectionately called "mokus" by AA members ("She's new, still 'mokus,'" "I can't think, I'm 'mokus' "), the irony of Mrs. Ford delivering, with such insight, confidence, and warmth, lectures on the triumph and joy of sobriety to us miserable unfortunates was not lost on me. It was a great lesson in humility and hope for me, personally. She spoke several times during my stay, and became the beacon I sometimes needed to navigate this most surprising turn in my life.

There is a rigorous stripping away of self-delusion and denial at BFC that is the foundation for rebuilding the ability to face life. It sometimes includes the stripping away of long-held medallions which one (I) might have called respect—the kind that is earned. But the truth, which was eventually revealed, is that all of us were suffering from the same disease and no one was above it all. It was a painful and exhausting process to endure, until we were deemed ready to return to the real world outside that nursery for broken children.

About a week into all this relentless self-probing, a situation arose that caused me to have a particularly strong reaction. I don't remember the specifics—something to do with our dorm being scolded for keeping a messy kitchen, and having our personal possessions (tea, crackers, candy) confiscated as punishment. Sounds pretty unimportant, but at the time it enraged me, and I was driven to assert myself on the subject of the staff's dominance. I stepped forward from the group who had been assembled for the castigation, planted my feet, and said something like, "You have no right to take away what is ours." It was a living, breathing metaphor, the whole thing.

The counselor's reaction was swift and emotionless. "If you don't like it here, Mary, leave." Well, that was an option I hadn't considered. I slunk to a corner of the sitting room, where I wrestled with the distorted enormity of the insult. An hour or so into my self-piteous rage, one of the maintenance staff shuffled in, dragging a plastic garbage can behind him. Despite my protests, he methodically cleansed all the cabinets of the ethnic treats our family and friends had sent us—things to put in our faces instead of alcohol while we endured the deliverance of our new souls.

Fuming with the indignation of a plucked hen, I flew to the pay phone in the hall and then lost a few more feathers on the way to my room to collect coins to use. I returned to find the phone in use! While I waited, my fury mounting, I recounted all the faults I'd found with the Center. I'd fix my alcoholism on my own! I wasn't going to spend one minute more in this insensitive, rude atmosphere. I'd have given anything for a drink.

When the airline reservationist answered I gave her my name and asked what flights to New York City were available. She was gone for a few seconds and then came back on the line to say, "Miss Moore, I read about your being at Betty Ford, and I want to say what an inspiration it is to know that even you can have this problem and be unafraid to deal with it. Thank you." It took a while for the importance of what had happened to replace the anger I'd become so fond of. I said something about calling her back and hung up the phone. My knees had gone all soft and as I stood there, my forehead cooling against the instrument's metal, I allowed myself the first cleansing, tearful surrender to wash over my still rigid self.

Despite the odd moments of angry child triumphing over unfamiliar truth, I began to let go of the defensive layers of fabric I'd pulled around myself against an unpredictable world. I allowed myself to face it tentatively, feeling pain when it was appropriate, and through the guidance of new friends, I began to accept the fact of life that it was all right to do so.

Days sometimes flew by unfocused eyes as my subconscious fingered all the nuances of the shape I was becoming. And all the while, I consciously placed myself in a state of vulnerability—absolutely trusting that I'd emerge from this darkness reborn.

The transformation was not without its moments of susceptibility, one of which nearly did me in.

An eighty-one-year-old woman had just joined our ranks as desperate for help as the rest of us, but too fragile for the emotional buffeting necessary for change (at least that's how I saw her). One day during a group therapy session, I watched in horror as she became the focus of criticism, backed up against a wall for her relentless denial of the alcoholism that brought her there. I lashed out at the psychologist when I could bear it no more, pleading for some deference to her years. There was undoubtedly some sort of identification issue with this woman—maybe once removed and circuitously through my mother. I argued against her treatment as though she weren't even in the room. I think she was as baffled by having become the center of this harangue as I was determined to save the day. When it became obvious that the counselor and I were in a no-win yelling match that was taking time from the others and really upsetting the old lady, I chose the familiar coda of room leaving and slamming of door to end this cantata.

That night, after everyone had gone to bed, I began the strangely compulsive process of leaving. I didn't want to, but I couldn't stop myself. There remained two more crucial weeks of treatment, and I needed that time to strengthen the values that I was just developing. I pushed those thoughts aside now, unable to stop myself, and phoned for a cab. All the while, I couldn't believe I was walking out on the best hope I had for a healthy life.

While I packed my bags, I did the best I could to comfort my confused roommate and, after swearing her to silence, allowed her to help me carry my possessions across the lawn, where a cab was coming to fetch me. It was the oddest feeling to duck behind a tree and freeze as someone from another dorm walked past us. "Shhhsh! Don't make a sound!" I was Burt Lancaster making his escape from

Alcatraz. Hell, I was free to leave any time I wanted, and yet I was consumed with guilt and fear.

After being shown to my room at the local Marriott, I sat frozen, staring at my unpacked suitcase, wondering what I would tell Robert, my family, his family, the world (they all knew now). I did the only thing that might relieve this sick feeling of disappointment with myself. I picked up the phone and dialed room service. And now, the Hallelujah Chorus is heard because, folks, I didn't order a vodka, I ordered a cheeseburger with fries. It never tasted so good before. Not much question about it, I'd done the right thing in leaving.

I felt responsible for the shock our night nurse would feel when she found my empty bed, and so I called to let them know that I was safe. Oh, and also, most important, that after an hour and fifteen minutes on my own—"I'm not drunk."

I told the nurse in a most condescending voice that it was too bad that there weren't more like her at the Center; that, yes, there were only a few insensitive counselors who'd treated me badly, but that was enough. I asked her to let the admissions office know that I'd be calling in the morning to give them my assessment of where the program was failing, and what they could do to change the situation. I hung up feeling quite righteous and walked to my bag. Near the top of my things lay the journal I'd written in every night since my arrival. It was too soon to glance through it. Those words weren't memories, they were fresh wounds. Staring at that journal, my ambivalence about leaving the Center heightened as I realized I would not have been able to mine so much of my hidden emotions, nor discard so many of my rationalizations, had it not been for the grueling treatment I'd been experiencing.

The next morning I was awakened by a call from Mrs. Ford herself, asking me to come back for a talk. That phone call saved my life.

I returned on my knees, pleading for reentry. Mercifully, they recognized my sincerity, and welcomed me back to the fold.

I remained there for the next two weeks, and did the most valu-able, productive work of the entire five-week stay.

It had been many years since I'd taken a plane trip without a drink to celebrate the Wright brothers' miracle of flight. The trip home from Palm Springs to New York would be the first temptation I'd face, solo. Of course, that was the obvious peril most everyone thought of as we discussed that mythic day in the inconceivable fu-ture when we'd be pronounced "ready" to be sent home. But an inner resolve robbed the trip of its expected horrors, and the time flew faster than I did. Soon I was in Robert's protective embrace, having survived my first Pavlovian cue to drink.

As I unpacked my bag, babbling away to Robert about the send-off and well-wishes of my fellow recoverers, I was riding a wave of gratitude to Betty Ford and self-congratulatory bliss. Out of nowhere, I felt the awareness that something was off-kilter, not quite right. Of course! It was five-thirty and I was putting my things away, gliding from closet to suitcase and now to the dresser, where, in the world as I'd known it, there should be a drink and a bowl of nuts to make this occasion special. I went back to my chore.

Waiting for dinner to arrive after ordering, getting through a business-cocktail party, waiting for Robert to come home at the end of the day, are but a few moments that required real work to get through those first few weeks. The first Christmas, the first birth-day, Robert's first birthday with me, Easter, the Fourth of July bar-becue, and, of course, the daddy of them all, New Year's Eve, all lay in wait. I couldn't have made my way through the maze of booby traps I had set up for myself through years of drinking had it not been for daily AA meetings, Robert, and the support of my brother, John.

My wayward kid brother held a well-earned role of leader for me. I'd talk to him several times a week—New York to LA, asking his opinion and advice when things got confusing for me.

It was through sober, accepting eyes that I learned to allow John his still unpredictable, sometimes brash, daredevil behavior without trying to "talk some sense into him." Indeed, his behavior had been incubated in a tough life at home, while I was in Aunt Bertie's and Grandma's home. He loved Harley-Davidson motorcycles (had hocked everything to buy one) and traveled with a bunch who dressed, as he did, in a lot of black leather. His apartment was open to anyone who needed a place to sleep. I loved him and admired him for his impropriety, and he gave my needs for perfection the same wide berth. We laughed warmly at each other's peculiarities.

Ten years prior to my dealing with alcoholism with the help of the Betty Ford Center, he had done it all on his own, through AA meetings. He truly pulled himself out of the snakepit. John had tenure in one AA meeting place in particular, and was treated with respect in the way that the tough defer to acknowledged power amongst themselves. He was called Big John, towering over his domain at six feet, eight inches. The women loved him. Whenever we'd go to a meeting together, they were all over him.

His tack with newcomers to AA was playing the role of bad cop. He'd watch them attend their first few meetings, listening to their stories of how they got there, and when he felt the timing was right, would introduce himself. He'd face him or her with a fixed stare, and say that he'd been watching and felt he had to say—"I don't think you're going to stay sober." He got all kinds of responses from tears to a threatened loss of teeth, but one thing was constant—they determined to prove him wrong.

He was a good teacher.

I sometimes think I'm lucky to have been an alcoholic.

It is not an irresponsible thing to say. Had I not been forced to confront myself, I might never have come to know and admire that person I am.

Smoking

❧

$\mathcal{A}$ VERY IMPORTANT caveat to newcomers in AA is to make no big changes in the first year of sobriety. Marriage as well as divorce are discouraged, as is giving up anything but drugs and alcohol. Until there is some distance between the novice in sobriety and the watering hole, it is wise to choose the less bumpy trail. Lower the brim of your hat against the sun, keep your horse on the same feed, sit both cheeks easy in the saddle. Stop me!

I groped my way through that initial year of "firsts"—first cocktail party attended sober, first argument successfully negotiated, first rejection, loss, pain, and the big killer, Christmas, all without alcohol. I watched with fascination as Robert, the initiator of my adventure, began to deal with his own inappropriate behavior. He was a cardiologist and he smoked.

Robert is a natural caregiver and I, an excellent taker. I took advantage of his help, but I spent so much time taking my emotional temperature that there was very little time to empathize with his own course correction—giving up smoking. I was so consumed with my fragility as a recovering alcoholic that I wouldn't or couldn't step two inches out of my way to help him. I continued to smoke throughout meals, in bed, even in the car with the windows rolled up. It must have been like sleeping with his executioner. In those days, I was smoking three packs of cigarettes a day.

There's a reel of Dick Van Dyke and me smoking in character as Rob and Laura in a few Kent commercials that were used on the show. It's awful to watch. We might just as well have been holding a couple of AKC's and extolling their virtues. But after having begun this most sophisticated accompaniment to drinking in my late teens, I could honestly say, thirty-odd years later, that I never smoked a cigarette I didn't thoroughly enjoy in all that time.

I mentioned the extent of my habit to Eric Stoltz, a smoker and whose mother I recently played in a movie. He took it in and then said, "So, basically you smoked, and in between cigarettes, you did two series." Well, yes, that is pretty much right.

Smoking is every bit the personal assistant that drinking is. It makes life easier. Its presence is a literal and figurative buffer between you and the face you're talking to, easily morphing into another person when you're lonely.

Today, I think most smokers experience the same denial as alcoholics regarding the impact of this abuse. But at the time, I saw Robert as dedicated to things medical, and because he was a doctor, would of course feel that he had to be perfectly healthy. But *his* decision to quit was a big intrusion into my life, and I was damned if I was going to stop. I had just given up alcohol! Wasn't that enough?

But he slugged through withdrawal, and by my twelve-month anniversary of sobriety, I was so intrigued with meeting life on my own power, taking its knocks and bumps in stride, that I was ready to join Robert in this feat. It wasn't that I thought being totally "clean" makes one a more noble person. But such a life gives a return and the jolt to the senses stimulates creativity.

The fact that I'd begun to have retinal bleeding was a tiny motivator, too. "You know, Mary," the ophthalmologist said, "the laser will stop the course of your current hemorrhaging, but it won't prevent it from happening in the future. Smoking constricts the blood vessels, causing their death—that death promoting new growth or neo-vascularization, which can outrun the treatment."

It was time to do it. I was also annoyed at being treated like a second-class citizen wherever I went. "Would you mind putting out your cigarette, Miss?" "Mary Tyler Moore, you smoke?" (And let's not forget Israel.)

I picked a target date three weeks ahead. During the intervening days, I reminded myself exactly what I was doing, and when I was doing it. I kept a journal, a record of each cigarette smoked, the time, where I was, and how I felt. In the second week I changed from my favorite brand to a less satisfying one. Then I only smoked standing up. Then only standing up outdoors. All these wrinkles and crimps created an awareness and a gradual acceptance of what the patterns had been, and what I was committed to changing.

I quit with the help of Nicorette gum. I was supposed to use it for three months but I continued well into eight months, having to withdraw from it, as well, later.

I found the first couple of weeks without cigarettes to be far more stressful than giving up alcohol.

The advice given to keep you on track is to walk and exercise steadily, and then diet. Even if one is careful about substituting, there's a phenomenon of chemical interaction that dictates a weight gain almost always.

Being thin is, for the most part, genetic with me (my parents, even in later life, resembling gray-haired Ken and Barbie). But there have been times when, after having leafed through too many issues of *Vogue* and *Bazaar,* I have felt downright chubby, and done my best to emaciate myself.

In fact, the first season of *The Mary Tyler Moore Show* reflects that absurdity. I was very thin and, funnily enough, when I looked in the mirror, I didn't see what everyone else did.

Dave Davis, one of the writers on the show, became seriously ill with hepatitis that year. He wasted away at home for six weeks before he was strong enough to walk onto our stage and return to work. At seeing his shrunken form shuffle toward us, Jim Brooks rose to his feet in disbelief and said, "My God, Dave, you look like one of Mary's arms."

But even always-slim Mary gained enough non-smoker poundage to warrant some re-evaluation of food intake and gym output after a year of not smoking. Once I admitted that a little more exercise than before was a good thing, it ceased to be a problem.

Anyway, everyone gets something, and nobody gets everything, and that's the way it is.

Good-Bye, MTM

❧

SEVEN YEARS AFTER Grant's departure, Arthur Price, the new president of MTM, Mel Blumenthal (who had risen to partner status from the legal department, which he headed), and I discussed the company's future. As is the case with most privately owned corporations, much of MTM's profits went back into the company, financing more shows and further growth with *future* returns. Consequently, it's always a guessing game as to when to "take the money and run." What's the value now? Will it increase? How's it going? The answers seemed to point to a sale.

It was a relatively easy choice for me since I hadn't been involved in the running of our little empire, and therefore wouldn't miss the power seat it provided. What I saw was the opportunity to cash in the chips and hit the gift shops. Fine art was half-off, while it lasted, horses, houses, and, lest I seem completely hollow, charity, the arts, and animal issues all beckoned me. And so when a British company called TVS made us an offer, we all agreed it had been a good run and said farewell to a Camelot whose flags were now a bit frayed.

It is said that I'm one of the truly wealthy women in my field. Well, based on the figures of the sale I might have been. Alas, one-third of my share from the sale was in the form of TVS stock, which hit bottom before it could pay a dividend, and stayed there. So, instead of being real, real rich, I'm merely very well-off.

MTM was eventually sold to IFE (International Family Entertainment). I am at this writing working on a film for the Family Channel, which is owned by IFE, which owns MTM. At the start of production, I received a lovely arrangement of flowers from myself. The well-wishing card was signed "MTM."

John

❧

$\mathcal{I}$T HAD BEEN FIVE YEARS
since the doctor told us that my brother had developed kidney cancer—a particularly pernicious sort called hypernephroma, which his-
torically responded poorly to treatment. Since then John had bravely
reached for every weapon appropriate for the battle: chemo, radia-
tion, and toward the end, a blood treatment only available at a center in Boston. It required him to haul his six-foot-eight, muscularly
deteriorating body onto a plane every six weeks for a two-day rein-
fusion of his blood, leaving him without the strength to even walk
for the next two weeks.

His ties to the people at "Radford" (the AA meeting in Studio
City) were his life's breath. He could not be away from them for
long without feeling the gnawing at his core (the desire for alcohol) that was even meaner than the cancer. He vowed to his doctor at the start, in a voice that threatened more than promised, "I
don't care how bad it gets, I won't take a drink."

And he didn't. He took a great deal of pain medication and was
selected (based on the degree of pain) to wear a morphine attach-
ment at home that he could adjust as needed. A friend from AA
stayed with him at home, bringing him food and helping him to

❧

the bathroom. He could no longer walk unaided. He lost his voice as a result of tumor growth around a nerve that serves the vocal cords, and could speak only in a whisper.

But there was no mistaking the words when he called me one day to say good-bye. He had stashed hundreds of painkillers, and had tried to end his life by taking (I can't say overdose, because he'd been overdosing on prescription drugs daily for a year or more) enough to kill himself. He fell asleep before he could ingest enough to finally end his pain. He felt he could do it again, this time with some improvements in the technique.

I asked, "Will you wait for me to be with you? I don't want you to be alone." "How long will it take you to get here?" "I'll be there tomorrow afternoon," I said, and then I called Robert.

When we arrived at John's house and entered his bedroom, he was sitting in the only piece of furniture that didn't hurt him—a recliner chair covered with pillows. His face was beyond white. His skin was almost misty.

It was impossible to hug him—he hurt too much in so many places. He whispered, "Hello," and said he was glad we'd come. Robert asked to see what pills he had collected. There were Dilaudid, Valium, Percocet, Halcion, enough to fell the giant that he was—and, of course, the morphine pump.

There wasn't much to say, and when he extended his hand, I silently gave him the first batch of pills and water, which he took until he couldn't stand the taste anymore. He asked me to mash them into ice cream, the only food his stomach could tolerate.

Robert called the company that held a code for the pump that would increase the dosage of morphine. He programmed the added infusion, while I spoon-fed the potion. Even as he approached stupor, my brother was crying out from the pain.

We called Mom and Dad to come. We sat, all of us, including John's caring helper, Michael; a mixture of sadness, anticipated relief, and fury.

After a half hour, the pump's dosage was increased again and

Robert took my hand, saying, "Here he goes, Mary." We watched him so intensely that he must have felt it because his head rolled to one side, but still he kept breathing.

A half hour later, my father got up from his chair and said, "I'm going home." After he left, John's eyes opened for a moment and he said, "This isn't the way I thought it would be." I gave him some more of the mash, spiked even further, and Robert pressed the button, again.

Five hours later he was still alive and still in pain. I could not believe that he was living through it, nor could Robert. It had taken a lot for Robert to overcome his instinct to cure but added to his guilt, now, was sorrow at having let John down.

As John slowly came around, I called his oncologist to confess our deed and beg for advice. He was not surprised at the attempt we'd made, nor its failure. John had been given so much medication over the last five years that his body was now impervious to drugs. The doctor made me feel better when he said, "If I were ever in the same situation as John, I'd be grateful to have a sister with your courage." I felt even better when he said, "There's a pain specialist I'm going to put you together with." I just wished to God he'd done it earlier.

John went into the hospital, and a brilliant doctor named Jason Hymes began custom-tailoring John's pain management. It went so far as to surgically sever the sensory nerves in his arm on one occasion, and a portion of his spinal nerve toward the end.

He was able to come home for two months in relative comfort until shortly before Christmas, when breathing became difficult. He was readmitted.

We were told he could be placed in the ICU where his life might be extended for a few weeks by machines, or we could make him comfortable in a private room and let him go at his own pace. We chose the latter for him at his request.

Christmas Day, usually the source of so much anxiety in our family—a tradition of drinking, arguments, and disappointment with one another—was spent in John's room at the hospital. Mom and Dad brought a turkey, mashed potatoes, peas and onions, plates, forks, a carving knife, and cranberry sauce in a cardboard carton. Aunt Bertie was there, as was John's daughter, Carole Ann, with her fiancé. We sang carols, exchanged presents, and shared our dinner with some of the nurses who let us use their kitchen. John had had me buy presents from him for everyone.

As Robert and I sat holding John's hand, at one point, he told us he had seen God that morning, that he appeared before him and said, "John, you're going to a place where you'll feel normal." He was so happy there was a place, at last, called home. He had no more fear.

Later that night, after a long silence with just Robert and me in the room, John said out of nowhere, "Mary, let me go."

He died the next morning at three a.m.. He simply stopped breathing.

It is a blessing that he was finally able to face death with serenity, to go so willingly. Had we been successful in our earlier attempt to help put an end to his suffering, he would have run blindly into death, instead. There's no question that John's moving into his Creator's arms was the better death to experience. But, if I could have forced the end of his pain, were I asked to do it today, again, I would.

My Mother

❧

$\mathcal{A}$ FEW YEARS EAR-
lier, soon after I had "graduated" from the Betty Ford Center, and
John was recovering from his initial surgery, my mother almost died
from another severe bout with alcohol and its secondary effects. As
I sat at the bottom of my brother's bed, we talked about how desperately she needed help.

We called the Betty Ford Center and spoke with a staff psychologist whose specialty was intervention—a carefully prepared,
but unexpected, meeting of family and friends with the alcoholic.
She came up to Los Angeles and spoke to John and me about the
fundamentals of putting it all together, how to help everyone understand the process. My dad was the toughest sell. Despite his
agony of having lived the years of her destructive drinking, I think
he felt he was pulling the rug out from under Mom. But the truth,
and basic kindness of his role in this planned event, helped him overcome his reticence.

As John and I made arrangements with the counselor and coor-
dinated the first secret session with those who would be involved
(Bertie, Dad, Mom's best friend, a now deceased aunt and uncle,
and, of course, John, Robert, and me), we felt like scheming six-

year-olds who were planning the prank of all time, and on their own mother! This was serious, though, and as we talked late into the nights, sometimes we were giggling with anticipation over the miracle we were hoping to pull off. (Even at life's crucial moments, humor begs entry.)

The intervention was a tearful, flat-out success. She went like a lamb, did her time, and remained sober for the rest of her life: seven years of getting to know each other.

They still remember her at Betty Ford. She, as always, won 'em over. It's hard for a therapist to keep a straight face when, after asking a patient if there has been any alcoholism in her family, she says, "Yes, my kids—I got it from them." My mother gave me a tremendous appreciation for humor, and I wouldn't have missed that for anything. Maybe in order for her to have been so funny, she had to be not quite the mother I may have needed.

Three months after John's death, Mom suffered a brain hemorrhage in her sleep. She died twenty-four hours after I arrived at the hospital.

She was so vulnerable lying there. So tiny, it seemed—fragile. She did not respond to anyone, but she shivered once. I wondered if she felt cold.

She was almost always cold.

That night before she left us, I bent close to her and whispered, "I forgive you, Mom." And then I thought, if she can hear me, she's probably thinking, "The little brat—get her!"

When she died, she took with her her own personal experiences of me. I mourn for us both our never-to-be-completed images.

My Father

❧

 $\mathcal{W}$ HOEVER IT IS THAT calls himself my father, the truth is that I love him. I find him charming and responsible, and someone whose respect I still seek. I see him as a victim himself of not enough love. He never talks about *his* father except to allude occasionally to a lack of understanding between them. Coming from him, that says volumes. Whatever went wrong in his young life, it created an undeserved deficit for him.

There is something very touching about this man who is so strong and so threatening, and so capable of fury. As he lay ill, close to death earlier this year, I felt I was looking at a pitiable creature who was likely in more pain than another more loving person would be.

I think because of his Catholicism, he felt that as long as he kept his love and respect for God and Jesus Christ primary in his life, he was fulfilling his obligations. People didn't matter as much as the fervor with which he went to church every Sunday, made his confession, and received communion. But, dear God, what did he confess?

My father has said the purpose of life is to prove oneself worthy of heaven.

Square Things

&

I'M NOT SURE WHAT this says about me, but I've spent countless hours working on square things. During the time that Blue Chip stamp collecting was at its peak in the seventies, I became completely caught up in it, like every other housewife on the block.

These stamps were given to consumers as incentives on food and other products purchased, and could be exchanged for prizes when enough had been collected. The idea was to find the most competitive stores that gave the most for the money spent.

I became trancelike, gluing them into the little square books. It gave me such pleasure. I wasn't always making the purchases in person, but I made sure that whoever did forked over the booty.

There I was, the flagship of MTM, a company that was investing and earning millions of dollars, a star in my own right, happily whiling away my leisure hours licking stamps and pasting them into books in return for a two-slice toaster.

Some people saved up for the big prizes like a washing machine or a television set, but I preferred the short-term return and looked forward to starting those little books all over again. I usually gave the prizes away to the people who did the shopping for me to begin with.

&

ℐ liked filling in the squares of crossword puzzles, but was no match for my mother, nor would I have wanted to be. She was an obsessed crossword-puzzle solver—doing the *New York Times* Sunday crossword puzzle in ink and in about one hour's time.

I'll never forget our arrival in Venice (on the trip she met the Pope), where we were shown to the largest, most gloriously appointed corner suite in the Gritti Palace Hotel overlooking the Grand Canal. The painted ceiling and carved gilt moldings, the Aubusson rug, serving as a backdrop for the splendid seventeenth-century furniture, had me gasping. Dad was slowly shaking his head in stunned disbelief at the opulence that was to be our home for the next few days.

"Wow, look at this! Did you see this view?" I called to Mom from the window. Below lay the visual essence of Venice—gondoliers poling their laughing tourists and lovers back and forth. I turned and found her sitting at the writing table completely engrossed in a puzzle that she'd found in the lobby. "Hmmm?" she responded, lifting her eyes. "Look," I cried, "look at all this!" "Ummm, I will," she said, "just a minute," and returned to her raison d'être.

I also liked Scrabble, but again not with my mother. Since our relationship was competitive (at least from my point of view), I didn't want to bring that element into game-playing, as well.

She played a game with her best friend, Maxine, every day of the over thirty years they knew each other. The Scrabble my mother played was championship caliber. When she died, I put the tiles "Q" and "U" into her casket to take with her.

Needlepoint is a hobby I took up in the early 1960s. A character actress named Kathleen Freeman, who'd made a few appearances on the *Van Dyke Show,* introduced me to it and taught me the rudiments of the craft. It was supposed to help me quit smoking. Well, it didn't work, but it kept my mind from wandering into areas I wasn't ready to look at. Over the next twenty-five years, I made twenty-six floral-designed two-by-two pillows to line the backs of three couches, six handbags of various sizes, four or five belts, four foot-stools, one rug eight-by-five, one rug five-by-three, and individualized pillows showing the familiar MTM hat as it would look, had it been thrown in the air and then landed on the initials of about eighteen or twenty of the cast members and creative people who were a part of *The Mary Tyler Moore Show*.

After having "in and outed" the needle through all those canvas squares with the single-mindedness of the demented, I am no longer interested in much of anything square. Am I all squared away?

I don't want to imply that my life (the puzzle) is solved, but I have definitely figured out the upper left-hand corner.

On the Perks of Celebrity

❧

$\mathcal{S}$OMETIMES FAME CAN be embarrassing.

It was about eleven p.m. on a Saturday evening. Robert and I were to leave at seven in the morning for a vacation on St. Bart's in the Caribbean. Bernadette Peters was with us enjoying the final delicious course at Bouley Restaurant, when I realized that the increasingly burning sensation I felt was, in fact, a return of the dreaded cystitis, a bladder infection I had experienced before. If not treated immediately with an antibiotic, and just as important, an anesthetic in pill form, it can become extremely painful and difficult to treat. On the way home from the restaurant I asked Robert for the two prescriptions. He gave them to me, albeit reluctantly. (It's the ethical issue. I think he visualizes a banner headline: DOC KILLS KIN— HIDDEN ALLERGY CAUSE.)

In the interest of time, while Robert stayed home and packed, I was going to take the limo and fetch the medications at the pharmacy. Bernadette refused to let me go alone (an all-night pharmacy often looks like the emergency room of an inner-city hospital). Bless this dear friend, who has given me support on a number of occasions.

❧

The pharmacy counter had a long line of variously needy people in front of it. Behind it, the pharmacist was carrying on a rather
loud argument with someone, while the woman ahead of me
moaned aloud over a burned hand she held close to her chest.

We'd been standing there for several minutes watching a very
cranky woman take prescriptions and pass them to the pharmacist,
when the phone rang. Answering it, the exasperated pharmacist then
announced to the assemblage that "if Mary Tyler Moore is here,
she has a phone call." I cringed.

The tiny sea of people parted, and all conversation seemed to stop
as I made my way to the phone. It seemed to me that the house-
lights dimmed at that moment, and a tiny spotlight shone on my
face as I answered. I heard Robert's voice expressing his concern as
to whether I'd brought money with me. Of course I had! I felt like
the kid whose parent asks her in front of everyone if she remembered to go to the bathroom before leaving the house.

Bernadette joined me again as I took my place in line, to suggest
several obnoxious fuchsia-hued lipsticks for me. I was laughing—
she was doing a good job of keeping my mind off the increasing
urge to pee and the interminable waiting. After what seemed like
a month, the woman behind the counter, now looking like a prison
matron, motioned for me to give her the prescription, which I did.
As I started to back away to wait for it to be filled, she said in a voice
that I could swear was amplified, "I have some questions for you.
If you're Mary Tyler Moore, why does this say Mary Levine? And
who's the doctor—another Levine?"

I did my best to explain to her the complications of a two-name
marriage *sotto voce,* so as not to include any more of the very interested group around me than was necessary. I was commanded to
speak louder. She "don't hear so good."

"Address?" I blurted out my correct address, certain afterward that
in our midst was a serial killer making note of it. "Phone?" I was
able to fake one digit. "Age?" Now this was something to consider.
I have never lied about my age except to make myself a year older

for the *Van Dyke Show*. (I was supposed to be the mother of a five-year-old then when I was, in fact, only twenty-two.) Later as I approached the age when one might consider taking off a few, I couldn't because Richie was born when I was nineteen. I was supposed to be well-bred, sophisticated, not a child bride from the hill country.

"Age?" she repeated. "Fifty-three," I said. "What?" "Fifty-six!" I screamed back.

As I looked away several people, including Bernadette, quickly turned their backs to me, revealing in the rapid rise and fall of their shoulders, their reactions. When, at last, the woman beckoned me to her she patted my hand and said, "You were my least whacko one tonight. That'll be eighty-nine fifty." I borrowed twenty-one dollars from Bernadette, and we left.

8

John the horse and his mother, Fanny, a palomino quarter horse.

The family Levine.

Hide the Blue-Eyed Horse

❧

The animal shall not be measured by man. In a world older and more complete than ours they move finished and complete, gifted with extensions of the senses we have lost or never attained, living by voices we shall never hear. They are not brethren, they are not underlings; they are other nations, caught with ourselves in the net of life and time, fellow prisoners of the splendor and travail of the earth.

HENRY BESTON (1888–1968)
FROM *THE OUTERMOST HOUSE*

*R*OBERT AND I WERE living in my "forever single" apartment that I'd so painstakingly designed for myself. We were tripping over each other and the dogs, who were now members of our household: a golden retriever named Dash, looking very much like Jon Voight, and a companion, Dudley, a long-haired basset, the image of Dustin Hoffman. Closet space was scarce, since I still owned most of the dresses Mary Richards wore only once on the series. So we began to look for a larger place.

At some point in the apartment search, the real-estate agent suggested that finding the right place would be a lot easier if we got rid of the dogs. It was at this point that we got rid of the agent, and decided to look for something in the country, where we could all do some sniffing, scratching, and digging.

I never expected the house we found up the Hudson to become a part of my life, I just thought it would make life easier. But, Greenawn, already named for the cool shade provided by the thousands of trees on its hundred and twenty-two acres, has gently nudged me into caring for its soil and all that it produces—flowers, reeds, water lilies, and a vegetable garden.

There are ponds connected by a running stream that invites company as it makes its way around gardens, under a small bridge, becoming a waterfall for a minute, and on to its next stop, a pond on our neighbor's farm.

During our first year of experiencing nature, we spent some time at the local equestrian center, and horses overtook what was to have been a simple country hobby. After seeing how beautiful the trails were from atop rental horses, we bought two of our own. Then, realizing how much it cost to board and groom them, we spent a few hundred thousand dollars building a stable, groom's apartment, and a paddock with run-in shed. Of course we had to set aside a yearly salary for the horse manager who would take care of them.

We soon agreed an extra horse for weekend guests would make our lives complete. Never mind that I didn't have anyone to cook for these weekend guests, at least we'd be able to ride together.

The three horses were so exciting to watch romping in their paddocks, or lazily grazing. They seemed to know how much pleasure their beauty gave to us. From time to time, lifting their heads at some new information on the wind, they'd look to us to make sure we were watching them. They knew their value.

It was the ongoing dream of a child who wanted to be a ballet dancer when she grew up. Well, now I was grown and not a ballet dancer. So, I borrowed another child's dream: to own my own horse from its birth. It fit in nicely as the obvious next step of our countryfied evolution. True, it would mean adding stalls to the barn, and, of course, we'd need a sandy training area.

Fanny, my seven-year-old, double-registered palomino quarter horse, was bathed, brushed, had a bothersome tooth removed, and was driven to a breeding farm not far away. There, during her ten-day sojourn, she was pleasured nineteen times by an equally magnificent palomino stallion looking for a relationship. When she returned her nostrils seemed to have permanently dilated. That was the only sign of change.

Eleven months later, though, one night in May, her labor began, and a very beautiful, very wet colt was born a few hours later. I don't remember ever being transfixed before, but I then understood what the word meant. I remained in this state as the wobbly-legged, confused beauty tried to stand and then find milk. I wanted to pick him up and help, but nature has its own course. Man seldom does better. Mother and son: she, nuzzling and licking; he, having tasted, at last, the source of life, lay exhausted at her feet.

What is this power of instinct? How did the mare know what was happening to her as she stoically endured the pain? Has she talked to her own mother or friends about birth? If anything, why wouldn't she resent the cause of the pain, and when it finally emerged give it a good whack?

In the morning, I threw on the clothes of the night before and ran to the stable. John (I named him for my brother) had dried off since his arrival, and he looked pale, almost ivory in the daylight. I watched how attentive Fanny was with him. She allowed me to slowly approach her foal, keeping her very large eyes on me, while she snorted and stomped in place as warning. It was magnificent, her maternal vigilance—the power of it.

I bent down and stroked John's neck and flank, noting at how young an age instinct made him wary of all but his mother. Small twitches, a quick turn of his head to be sure, and then I was accepted—for a time. While my face was touching his, I saw, for the first time, the color of his eyes.

John, it was confirmed, was an albino—ivory coat, white mane, pink skin, and blue eyes. I thought he was the most mystically beautiful animal I had ever seen. And like his namesake, he was devilish, too, charging toward our dogs on the other side of the fence, and then twisting in mid-air to kick his hind legs at their intrusion.

Some reading on the subject of albino horses pointed out that their pink skin is sun-sensitive and can lead to cancer, and that their blue eyes make them sometimes intolerant of bright light. So they're not generally welcomed by those who breed.

We invited everyone to come see our colt, and everyone who knows horses agreed that he was remarkable, not just because of his coloring, but because of his proportions and head structure.

One of the local gentry who seriously indulged in breeding as well as showing horses and eventing, with ribbons and cups to attest to this expertise, stopped by for a look one day. He had never seen our horses or the new stable, and seemed to be impressed by both.

I showed him John with pride in his beauty and full of proprietary amazement at having been a party to his creation. I watched my guest arch an eyebrow, arrange his mouth in a not-so-well-hidden sneer, and shake his head. "You have some fine animals," he said, as he gave the stalls a last look.

"But if you ever have anyone over to buy one of them, hide the blue-eyed horse."

A moment of keen awareness accompanied the reaction I felt to what he said. I was making conversation with him, so I didn't have a chance to roll it around in my head until he left, but I knew something was about to splash over me and bring some sort of epiphany with it.

It was a metaphor for the way I had lived a good lot of my life:

Be wary, be perfect, and if you can't, then do not enter life's contest.

But I loved this imperfect animal. And as I felt the warmth between John and me, and my brother and me—how different we were, yet how connected, I could feel the ease with which I loved my mother and father and Bertie for all their colors. No matter if they were bright or muddied or without pigment at all. Me, too.

Now, as I am writing this book, I am no longer hiding my faults or theirs, and I forgive us, all. The blue-eyed horse has given me the ability to celebrate us for the odd and beautiful collection that we are.

After All

TEXT PHOTO CREDITS

Index

Academy of Television Arts and
    Sciences awards. *See*
    Emmy Awards and
    Nominations
Adamo, Frank, 102, 104, 258
*Adventures of Ozzie and Harriet,
    The,* Hotpoint commer-
    cials for, 61–62, 63
Albee, Edward, 124
alcohol drinking/alcoholism
    brother John and, 34, 289
    diabetes and, 282
    Betty Ford and, 279–80
    "hitting bottom," 278
    Moore and, 34, 200, 204–5,
        231–33, 257–58, 277,
        278–89, 290
    mother and, 7–8, 32, 33, 46,
        63, 180, 300–301
    treatment at Betty Ford
        Center, 281–89,
        301–2
Alcoholics Anonymous, 283,
    284, 288, 290, 296

Amsterdam, Morey, 85, 106
Andrews, Julie, 117, 120, 280
animals
    aversion to cruelty to, 27–29,
        72
    backyard breeding, puppy
        from, 276–77
    Beston on, 313
    experimentation on, Moore's
        feelings about, 138
    horses, *311,* 314, 315–17
    Moore's dogs, 121–22, 132,
        137, *263,* 276–77,
        313–14
    Richie's rescued pigeon,
        166–167
Annie McGuire ("warmedy"),
    271–72
Archer, Gordon, 12–13
Arnaz, Desi, 145
Arndt, Denis, 271
Asner, Ed, *140, 239*
    casting as Lou Grant, 146–51
Assassination threats, 217–18

Azenberg, Emanuel, 203, 204, 213

Ball, Lucille, 88, 145
Benti, Joseph, 180
Benton & Bowles, 94
Beston, Henry, on animals, 313
Betty Ford Center, 289
  buildings, 283
  Moore at, 281–88
  mother treated at, 300–301
  patients, 283
  treatment for alcoholics, 283–85
Betty White Show, The, 4
Bill (lover), 234–36, 241
Blue Chip stamp collecting, 304
Blumenthal, Mel, 294
Bob Crane Show, The, 164
Bob Hope show, 71
Bob Newhart Show, The, 142, 164, 175
Booth, Shirley, 113
Bourbon Street Beat, 79
Brando, Marlon, 53–55
Breakfast at Tiffany's (Broadway musical), 118–19, 141, 157, 214
  cast, 122
  Philadelphia tryouts, 122–23
  problems, 122–25
  rehearsals, 122, 124
Brooks, James, 142, 146, 152, 171, 293
Burnett, Carol, 194–96
Burns, Allan, 142, 146, 268

Ted Knight and, 170–71
Burrows, Abe, 122, 124, 125
Busey, Gary, 164

Calvada Productions, 83
Capri pants, *58,* 86, 101
casting offices, making rounds of, 75, 77–78
Catholicism
  and childhood squabbles, 23
  father and, 8, 97, 179, 180, 247–48, 302–3
  Moore and, 64–65
  mother and, 59
Cavett, Dick, 242–44
CBS, 85, 141–42, 161–62, 169, 267
Chamberlain, Richard, 122, 124, 125
Change of Habit, 126–127
Channing, Carol, 117
Chapin, Richard, 261–62
chorus dancing, 72–75
Christmas festivities, 44–45
cigarette smoking, 104–5, 106, 259–60, 290–92
  withdrawal from, 291–92
comedian(s)
  Moore as, 87–88
  timing of, 87, 89, 196
commercials, 78
  for Hotpoint Appliances, 61–62, 63, 65
  for Kent cigarettes, 106
Cronkite, Walter, 107
crossword puzzles, 305

dancing
ballet, giving up, 272–73,
314–15
as lone pursuit, 50, 193
nun's counseling on, 63
Ward Sisters Studio of Dance
Arts and, 36–40, 49–50
Danson, Ted, 268
Darling, Joan, 174
Dash (dog), *263,* 313
Davis, Dave, 146, 293
Dean Martin and Jerry Lewis
show, 71
Denoff, Sam, 141
Desilu Studios, 82, 83, 88
commissary, 103
diabetes, Type I
and alcohol drinking, 136,
282
diagnosis of, 133–34
and exercise, 272–73
insulin injections for, 134
laser treatment for retinal de-
tachment and, 134,
291–92
life adjustment required by,
135–37
monitoring, 135, 136
pregnancy and, 135
reaction to diagnosis, 133–34,
136
retinal bleeding and, 134,
291–92
revealing to public, 137–38
*Dick Van Dyke and the Other
Woman,* 141

Dick Van Dyke Show, The, 154,
155. *See also* Van Dyke,
Dick
alien invasion episode, walnuts
in, 109–11
audition for, 82–83
blond-haired brunette
episode, 87–88
Emmy Awards and Nomina-
tions, 112, 113–14
five-year run of, 116
focus of, 86–87, 89
house purchased with money
from, 90
innovations of, 86
Moore's impact on, 87–88
Moore's salary for, 112–13
Moore's status on, 88
multiple-camera technique,
215
needlepoint learned while
working on, 305–6
pilot, 94
prop room, 105
rehearsals, 106–7
role of Laura Petrie on, 87–88
screen test for, 84
as television phenomenon,
112
toe-in-drain episode, 87–88
writers, 141
dogs, Moore's, 121–22, 132,
137, *263,* 276–77,
313–14
Donghia, Angelo, 246
drug problems

Moore's Valium addiction,
 199–200
Richie and, 199–200
Dudley (dog), *263,* 313
Durante, Jimmy, 71, 72–74

Eddie Fisher Show, The, 71
Emmy Awards and Nomina-
 tions, *1,* 113
 for *The Dick Van Dyke Show,*
  112, 113–114
 for *The Mary Tyler Moore*
  Show, 4, 174
 for *Stolen Babes,* 3–4
Engel, Georgia, 170
Equal Rights Amendment support, 224–26
Esparza, Tony, 219
exercise, 272–74
 aerobic, 273–74
eye problems, and diabetes, 134,
 291–92

fame, and embarrassment, 307–9
Family Channel, 295
Fanny (horse), *311,* 315
Fiedler, Arthur, 190
Finnegan Begin Again (television
 movie), 267–68, 276
Ford, Betty, 279–80, 281, 287,
 288. *See also* Betty Ford
 Center
Frankenheimer, John, 164
Freeman, Kathleen, 305–6
Friends and Lovers, 164
furs, aversion to wearing, 28–29

Gaines, John, 203–4, 205
Garner, James, 265–66
George Gobel Show, The, 71
Gish, Lillian, 118
Gomer Pyle, 89
Good, Jack, 190
Gore Vidal's Lincoln, 270–71
Gould, Wilbur, 216–17
Grant, Cary, 202
guns
 Meeker and, 60
 Richie's accidental death by,
  237–39
Gurney, A. R., 269

Hackett, Bertie (aunt), 6–7
 dancing lessons paid for by,
  36–7
 at KNXT, 6–7
 and Meeker, 75
 as nurturing mother-figure,
  10, 12, 21
 on trip West, 25–26
Hackett, Gail (cousin), 20–21,
 30–31
Hackett, Harold (uncle), 20,
 23, 30–31
 Hollywood home of,
  30–31
Hanson, Jack, 113
Harper, Valerie, *139,* 154
 casting as Rhoda, 153
 and *Rhoda,* 169–70
Heartsounds (television movie),
 265–66
Hepburn, Audrey, 118

Hepburn, Katharine, 88–89, 114
Hill, George Roy, 117
Hill Street Blues, 175
Hope, Bob, 71
Horseback riding, as hobby, 314, 315
Horses, *311,* 314, 315–17
Hotpoint Appliances commercials, 61–62, 63, 65
Hudson, Rock, 78
hunting, Meeker's interest in, 60
Hymes, Jason, 298

I Love Lucy, 145
Immaculate Heart High School, 48–49, 62
International Family Entertainment (IFE), 295
Israel, Joel, 209
Israel trip, 258–260

Jax (store), 113
Jews, 85, 255, 257, 261, 262
Jimmy Durante show, 71, 72–74
John (horse), *311,* 315–17
John Paul II, Pope, 247, 249
Jordan, Glenn, 266
Just Between Friends, 268–69
Juvenile Diabetes Foundation (JDF), 137–38, 274
   Moore as International Chairman of, 137–38

Kanin, Fay, 266
Keaton, Michael, 195, 196

Kellerman, Sally, 122, 123
Kelly, Gene, 185, *264*
Kennedy, John F., assassination of, 107–8
Kent cigarettes/commercials, 105, 106, 291
Kershaw, Doug, 191
Knight, Ted, *139,* 170
   casting as Ted Baxter, 152
   and fear of character takeover, 170–71
KNX Radio, high school mail room job at, 51–52
KNXT, 179
Kurtz, Swoosie, 195

Lahti, Christine, 268
Lange, Hope, 234–35
Last Best Year, The (television movie), 274–75
Last Picture Show, The, 152
Leachman, Cloris, *139,* 154, 262
   casting as Phyllis, 152–53
Leonard, Sheldon, 80, 83, 112–13
Letterman, David, 195
Levine, Irving, 256, 257, 261
Levine, Marion, 256, 261
Levine, Robert (husband), *312*
   age difference, 253–54, 259
   cigarette smoking and, 291
   first date with, 253
   and Juvenile Diabetes Foundation, 137–38
   marriage to Moore, 260, 261–62

meeting at hospital, 250–52
and Moore's alcoholism,
    278–79
Moore's attraction to, 251,
    252, 253, 254
personality characteristics,
    254, 278, 290
religious differences, 255, 256,
    257–58, 261–62
wedding, 261–62
Lewis, Jerry, 71
Lillie, Bea, 117, 280
Lindsay-Hogg, Michael, 214–15
Lorillard, P., 106
Lou Grant, 175
Lund, Art, 122

MacLeod, Gavin, 139
casting as Murray, 151
Manhattan Transfer, 190–91
Martin, Dean, 71
Mary (situation comedy),
    266–67
Mary (variety show), 194–96
Mary Poppins, 116
Mary's Incredible Dream, 190–92
Mary Tyler Moore's Everywoman's
    Workout, 274
Mary Tyler Moore Show, The,
    140, 292
  "A Boy's Best Friend"
    episode, 188–89
  casting, 145–53
  "Chuckles Bites the Dust"
    episode, 172–74
  closing of, 4–5, 193, 224

director, 145–46
early days, 142–44, 145–62
Emmy Awards and Nomina-
    tions, 4, 174
filming of, 155, 156
first episode evaluators,
    161–62
first episode filming, 161–62
first episode rehearsal, 156–57,
    158–59, 160
Betty Ford on, 279–80
multiple-camera technique,
    155, 156, 215
rehearsals, 154–57
script supervisor, 161
writers, 141, 142–43, 146,
    161
Mathews, Larry, 57
Meeker, Richard Carleton, Jr.
    (son), 57, 129
and acting as possible career,
    219
birth, 66–68
death, 237–40
and deep-sea fishing, 167–68
and diet, 135, 137
drug problems, 197–98, 199
drums as hobby of, 125
and father, in Fresno, 198–99
high school graduation, 200
image of mother, 116
love of beach and ocean,
    166–68
and mother, 68–70, 79–80,
    116, 119, 135, 137, 200,
    219

in New York City, 121
and parents' separation, 92
personality characteristics, 70
at private school, 113
and rescued pigeon, 166–67
school problems, 92, 197–98,
    199
sharing of feelings with
    Moore, 135, 137
Tinker and, 96
tonsillectomy, 119
Meeker, Richard (husband),
    59–63
    divorce from, 94–95
    education, 60–61
    as father, 70, 90
    as husband, 79, 90
    marital problems, 77–78,
        90–93
    marriage in Catholic Church,
        64
    Moore's disappointment in,
        75–76
    Moore's engagement to, 61,
        62
    as older man, 59
    separation from, 90–92
    as sportsman, 60
Merrick, David, 123, 124, 125
Minnelli, Liza, 279, 281
Moore, Carole (niece), 19, 299
Moore, Elizabeth "Liz" (sister),
    79–80
    birth, 66
    death, 179–81
    humor of, 180

Moore, George Tyler (father), 3,
    6–9, *15,* 17–18, 89
    audience with Pope, 247–49
    and Christmas tree decorating,
        44–45
    dating rules of, 62–63
    and daughter Elizabeth,
        179–80
    illness of, 302
    lack of nurturing by, 6, 7,
        8–9
    Meeker and, 61
    personality characteristics, 6,
        7, 12, 31, 32–33
    religiosity of, 8, 97, 179, 180,
        247–48, 302–3
    on second marriage, 97
    and son, 18, 23
    storytelling abilities of, 8–9
    and success of Moore, 119,
        268
Moore, John (brother), *15,* 31,
    46, 47, 288–89, 300, 301
    alcohol problems of, 34
    birth, 23
    Catholic school experiences,
        47–48
    illness and death, 296–99
    and parents, 18, 23, 33–35
Moore, Louis Tilghman (pater-
    nal great-grandfather), 18
Moore, Marjorie Hackett
    (mother), 10–13, *15,*
    41–42, 66, 221
    addiction to pinball machines,
        10–11

alcohol problems of, 7–8, 32, 33, 46, 63, 180, 278, 300–301
at Betty Ford Center, 300–301
brothers and sisters, 11
conversion to Catholicism, 59
and crossword puzzles, 305
death, 301
denial of sexual abuse experience, 13
friendships of, 11
lack of nurturing by, 10, 12, 21
personality traits, 7–8, 11–12, 33
treated at Betty Ford Center, 300–301
Moore, Mary Tyler, *1, 2, 15, 16, 57, 58, 139, 140, 177, 264, 312*
acting technique, 117–18
alcohol problems, 34, 200, 204–5, 231–33, 257–58, 277, 278–89, 290
and Aunt Bertie (*see* Hackett, Bertie)
and Bill (lover), 234–36, 241
birth, 6
and birth of son, 66–68
and Capri pants, *58,* 86, 101
Central Park West apartment, 245–46, 256
Chicago experiences, 207–10
childhood move to California, 23–24, 25–33
childhood sexual abuse experience, 12–13

as chorus dancer, 72–75
Christmas decorating by, 45
cigarette smoking, 104–5, 106, 259–60
as comedian, 87–88
and conclusion of *The Mary Tyler Moore Show,* 4–5
cosmetic surgery, 221–23
and dancing, 21, 36–40, 72–75, 183, 193, 213–14
as diabetic, 133–38
as director, 188–89
early childhood years, 6–13, 17–43
education of, 47–50
engagement to Meeker, 61, 62
and father (*see* Moore, George Tyler)
first affair, 210, 211
first young love, 42–43
on friendships, 169
friendships of, 169, 170, 183, 307–8
good-girl image of, 123–24, 281
and Valerie Harper, 169
Katharine Hepburn mode, 88–89, 114
hobbies, 304–6, 314, 315
as homemaker, 68, 93
home in Malibu, 163, 183
home on Hudson, 314
Immaculate Heart High School years, 48–55

immaturity of, for first marriage, 61

as independent for first time, 220–21, 228, 229, 230–31

as inept liar, 224–26

lack of parental nurturing, 7–8, 10, 12, 13, 21

living accommodations at parents' home, 46–47

living accommodations during school days, 46–47

as loner, 50

and loss, 194, 276

marriages of (*see* Levine, Robert; Meeker, Richard; Tinker, Grant A.)

martyrdom feelings, 24

maternal grandmother, 6, 7, 21, 25–26, 38, 39–40, 228

   death of, 123

maternal grandparents, 48–49

memorizing abilities, 22

miscarriage, 131–32, 133

moral upbringing, 21–22, 60, 62–63, 64–65

and mother (*see* Moore, Marjorie Hackett)

as mother, 68–70, 79–80, 116, 119, 135, 200, 219

motivation for autobiography, 5

paternal grandparents, 17–18

perfectionism of, 45, 137, 155, 316–17

personality characteristics, 5, 32, 38–39, 45, 50, 67, 72, 114, 137, 155, 174–75, 184, 185, 186, 189, 194, 196, 208–9, 224–25, 309, 316–17

physical characteristics, 49, 51

pregnancies, 65, 131–32

production company of (*see* MTM Enterprises, Incorporated)

reactions to reviews, 39

and religion, 22, 23, 60, 64–65

religion of parents, 7, 8, 18, 59

Rolls-Royce purchase, 163–64

in Russia, *178*

and school, 31–32, 33

self-image, 292–93

self-validation, 93

at St. Ambrose School, 32, 33

stage fright and, 38–39

as vegetarian, 27–28

volunteer work at UCLA, 193–94

MTM Enterprises, Incorporated (production company), 162, 164–65

buyout of Tinker's share, 230

creation of, 142–44

Moore as chairman of, 112

sale of, 230, 294–95

success of, 163–65, 175
symbol of, 143–44
Mullen, Marge, 155

National Broadcasting Company
(NBC), 71, 229–30
musical variety shows, 71
Tinker as head of West Coast
Programming at, 121
Tinker offered job at, 95
needlepoint as hobby, 305–6
Newhart, Bob. See *Bob Newhart
Show, The*
New York City
Moore's life in, 121–22,
213–37, 241–313
Tinker's hatred of, 121
Nixon, Richard, 122, 227–28
nuns, 31, 47–48
on Moore's goal of dancing, 62

O'Brien, Jack, 41–43
O'Neill, Tip, 225–26
Ordinary People, 177, 201–4,
205–6
as turning point, 206

Paramount Pictures, 201, 204
Paris, Jerry, 109
Parker, Penney, 80
People for the Ethical Treatment
of Animals (PETA),
28–29
Peppard, George, 167
Perfectionism, 45, 137, 155,
316–17

Persky, Bill, 141
Peters, Bernadette, 274–75,
307–8
Phyllis, 175
Presley, Elvis, 126–27
Preston, Robert, 267–68
Price, Arthur, 142, 165, 294
Procter & Gamble, 86, 94

Randolph, John, 271
RCA, 229–30
Redford, Robert, *177,* 202–3,
204, 205, 207–8, 210
Redgrave, Lynn, 270
Redmond, Laure, 273–74
Reiner, Carl, 124, 221
and *The Dick Van Dyke Show,*
80, 82, 83, 85, 104–5,
113
and son Rob, 114–15
Reiner, Rob, 114–15
Rhett Butler (dog), 276–77
losses symbolized by, 277, 278
Rhoda, 164, 169–170, 175
Rich, Bernie and Margie, 71
Rich, John, 105–6, 107, 112
Richard Diamond (detective
series), 78–79
Rose Marie, 85, 89
Ross, Glen, 105, 107
Russia, Moore in, *178*

St. Ambrose School, 32, 33
St. Elsewhere, 175
Sand, Paul, 164
Sandrich, Jay, 145–46, 174, 234

Sargent, Alvin, 201
school, 31–32, 33, 38
  dancing lessons and, 38
Schubert Organization, 213, 214
Screen Actors Guild, 112
77 Sunset Strip, 79
sexual abuse, childhood experi-
    ence of, 12–13
Shawn, Dick, 195
Shindler, Conrad, 18–19
The Sid Caesar Show, 85
Sinatra, Frank, 217
Something for Joey, 175
Steinem, Gloria, 224–26
Stolen Babes (miniseries), Emmy
    Award for, 3–4
Stoltz, Eric, 291
Stroub, Dr., 70–71
surgery, cosmetic, 221–23
Sutherland, Donald, *177, 205*
Sweet Sue (play), 269–70

Taylor, Elizabeth, 279, 281
television. *See also specific topics*
  Emmy Awards and Nomina-
      tions, (*see* Emmy Awards
      and Nominations)
  multiple-camera technique,
      155, 156, 215
Texas Wheelers, The, 164
Thomas, Danny, 80, 83, 103,
    113
  in *The Dick Van Dyke Show,*
      109
Thoroughly Modern Millie,
    117–20, 280

threats on life, 217–18
Three for the Road, 164
Tillinger, John, 270
Timing, comedic, 87, 89
Tinker, Grant A. (husband),
      94–100, 113, *129, 130,*
      146
  children of, 96
  as head of NBC West Coast
      Programming, 121
  marital problems, 95, 182–87,
      204–5, 211, 231
  marital separation, 186–87
  marriage, 98–100, 142, 162,
      220
  Moore falls in love with, 95
  Moore's family and, 97
  and MTM Enterprises, 162,
      165, 188, 229
  as older man, 94
  personality characteristics, 94,
      184
  and RCA, 229–30
  Richie and, 96
  at Twentieth Century-Fox
      Television, 142
Trainor, Jimmy, 105–6
Tucci, Maria, 270
Twentieth Century-Fox Televi-
    sion, 142

Universal Studios, 116, 167
  change in focus, 126
  multipicture contract, 116
  Thoroughly Modern Millie,
      117–20, 280

Valium addiction, 279
    withdrawal from, 279
Van Dyke, Dick, *58*, 80, 85,
    113, 291
    creative genius of, 102–3
    and *Mary Poppins,* 116
    personality characteristics, 84,
    102
Van Dyke, Marge, 101
Van Dyke Show. See *Dick Van
    Dyke Show, The*
vegetarianism, 27–28
    Donner Pass experience and,
    27
Vereen, Ben, 190
Virginia house, grandparents',
    17–18, 48

Ward Sisters Studio of Dance
    Arts, 36–40, 49
Warner Bros., 80–81

Wasserman, Lew, 117, 119
Waterston, Sam, 268
Weinberger, Ed., 280
*What's So Bad About Feeling
    Good?,* 167
White, Betty, 170
White Shadow, The, 175
Whose Life Is It Anyway? (play),
    213–18
    physical challenges of,
    213–14, 215–17
William Morris Agency,
    112–13
Winant, Ethel, 146, 153
WKRP in Cincinnati, 175
women, 101. *See also* Equal
    Rights Amendment
    support
    on television, dress of, 86
    working mothers, 69–70
Wood, Robert, 162